# THE CONCEPT OF IDEALS IN LEGAL THEORY

# Law and Philosophy Library

VOLUME 63



*The titles published in this series are listed at the end of this volume.*

# THE CONCEPT OF IDEALS IN LEGAL THEORY

by

SANNE TAEKEMA

*Katholieke Universiteit Brabant/Faculty of Law/*
*Department of Jurisprudence and Legal History*

KLUWER LAW INTERNATIONAL
THE HAGUE / LONDON / NEW YORK

A C.I.P. Catalogue record for this book is available from the Library of Congress.

ISBN 90-411-1971-X

Published by Kluwer Law International,
P.O. Box 85889, 2508 CN The Hague, The Netherlands.

Sold and distributed in North, Central and South America
by Kluwer Law International,
101 Philip Drive, Norwell, MA 02061, U.S.A.
kluwerlaw@wkap.com

In all other countries, sold and distributed
by Kluwer Law International, Distribution Centre,
P.O. Box 322, 3300 AH Dordrecht, The Netherlands.

*Printed on acid-free paper*



Printed in the Netherlands.

*For Jean-Pierre*

# CONTENTS

# ACKNOWLEDGEMENTS

This book is the result of a research project I did at Tilburg University, the Netherlands, which was funded by The Netherlands Organization for Scientific Research (NWO). The text is a revision of the Ph.D. thesis I defended in Tilburg in December 2000. Such projects do not take place in isolation; the completion of this one depended on the support of a number of research groups as well as individuals. I want to take this opportunity to thank them.

For five years, the Faculty of Law at Tilburg University hosted the Pionier programmc *The Importance of Ideals in Law, Morality and Politics*. I was fortunate to work within this programme and to be able to discuss ideas with colleagues in the group and visiting guest researchers. My colleagues in the department of Jurisprudence and Legal History, with whom I have been working since, have been equally supportive. I am especially grateful to Wouter de Been, Bert van den Brink, Anna Meijknecht, Timon Oudenaarden, and Geertje van Schaaijk for their intellectual and moral support.

For their comments on various parts of the manuscript of this book I would like to thank Bert van Roermund, Philip Selznick, Bärbel Dorbeck-Jung, Hans Gribnau, Willem Witteveen and Pauline Westerman. Brian Morgan was kind enough to check spelling and style for me.

This book could not have been written without the help of Wibren van der Burg and Paul van Seters, who supervised the research project and carefully commented on the text. I thank them for both their criticism and encouragement.

I dedicate this book to Jean-Pierre Simons, with love.

# CHAPTER 1

# IDEALS IN LEGAL THEORY: AN INTRODUCTION

## 1. COMMON SENSE UNDERSTANDINGS

In the nineteen-thirties there were two Dutch neighbours, Van Stolk and Van der Goes, who were involved in a dispute over a footpath. Relations deteriorated so much that Van Stolk decided to place a hideous construction, a wooden pole decorated with old cloth, on his land to spoil the view of Van der Goes. Van der Goes went to court. After the judicial decision that placement of the construction was illegal, Van Stolk decided to make the construction into a water tower, first without even bothering to connect it to water, but later making it into a workable tower. Again Van der Goes went to court, claiming that this constituted an abuse of ownership rights. Dutch law contains the rule that the use of a right, which is legitimate in the abstract, can be illegitimate in specific circumstances in relation to another person. Now that the construction had the appearance of a working tower, the Dutch Supreme Court had to decide what criteria had to be fulfilled to constitute an abuse of rights. Simply harming the interests of another is not enough, according to the Court; the owner must have the sole purpose of harming someone and must have no reasonable interest in the exercise of his right. Given the context and history of this case, these criteria were fulfilled in the case of the water tower: building a tower simply to spite one's neighbour constituted an abuse of ownership rights.[1]

This Supreme Court decision tells us much about the scope and nature of the right to private property. The right to property creates a sphere of freedom of movement and decision, in which a person can make his own autonomous choices. This freedom is not unlimited, but every limitation needs to be well-argued. As the Dutch jurist Paul Scholten said in his comment on this case: "Ownership is not a power given for a specific purpose, but the recognition of

1 There are two Supreme Court decisions in this case, HR 13-3-1936, NJ 1936, 415, and HR 2-4-1937, NJ 1937, 639; the first annotated by Paul Scholten.

a freedom not to be defined."[2]

Why, you may ask, this excursion into the law of property in a work which, according to its title, is devoted to ideals in legal theory? Because the personal freedom of which property is a guarantee can be understood as a legally recognized ideal. Ideals are not directly obvious aspects of the law, but this book is motivated by the idea that ideals are nevertheless important and irreducible features of legal systems. How we should conceive of ideals exactly and what place they have in law is the leading question of this book.

'Justice is blind'. A recurrent image of law in art is the figure of Justice: the figure of the blindfolded lady with scales and a sword. This figure represents an ideal: the perfect administration of justice. Blindfolded — without prejudice; carrying scales — in complete fairness; and carrying a sword — backed by power to enforce the decision. The three features of the image of justice all suggest omnipotence. The blindfold makes it seem as if a judge can close her eyes to shut out any preconceived judgments about the people involved in a case and decide it only on its merits. The scales suggest the competence to weigh arguments minutely. Once a decision is reached, the sword guarantees that it will also be effective.

The figure of Justice reflects some of the common sense understandings about the ideals of law. Less obviously, so does the case of the water tower. Justice represents unattainable characteristics of a perfect judge: an ideal appears, first, to imply perfection, and, second, to imply unrealizability. At the same time, ideals have appeal. Ask someone to give an example of an ideal and often he or she will come up with a political slogan: 'Liberté, Egalité, Fraternité' or 'Peace and Love'. These were the banners for political or social upheaval; they moved people to political action. The ideal in its perfection brings out flaws in the current situation and gives a direction for improvement. It is, however, so lofty that we can never quite reach it.

In the case of the water tower, the ideal of freedom only appears after a detour through a range of rights, relations, and responsibilities. The focus is on the limitations of the right to property, but when the question is put how far these limitations extend, we are suddenly confronted with the freedom of the owner as the core value to be protected. The perception of the ideal is different here, and so is the relationship between law and the ideal. Here we trace the meaning of freedom negatively, by examining its limitations. It is clear from the start that an owner's freedom cannot be exercised to the full. That would be the ideal of freedom, which in reality is constrained by other people and

[2] In Dutch: "Eigendom is niet een met een bepaald doel gegeven bevoegdheid, maar een erkenning van een niet te omschrijven vrijheid" (noot NJ 1936, 415).

other values. Here we see more clearly than in the case of justice that the realization of an ideal is hindered by all kinds of constraints and obstacles. There is another difference between the two examples. The figure of Justice is in a sense the impersonation of the aspirations of all legal agents; she is the guiding light for the whole of law. In the case of the water tower, however, the ideal of freedom remains in the background until we come to a difficult legal question. Personal freedom informs our understanding of the case, but it appears in a specific legal form here — as property rights. We might say that freedom is an ideal which law is designed to protect. It is a reason to have all kinds of legal rules, but it does not seem to be an integral part of our understanding of law in the way that justice is.

The two examples raise questions about the role and character of ideals in law: Is there a difference between an ideal like justice and an ideal like freedom with regard to the connection to law? Are these different kinds of ideals? The case of the water tower also draws attention to the limitations to which an ideal is subject and the connections the ideal has to different elements of the legal system. How should we conceive of limitations and conflicts? Are these caused by the relation to rules or principles, by factual circumstances, or maybe by other ideals? What to think of the relations of ideals and rules, of ideals and facts?

These are the kinds of questions that I aim to answer in this book. I will try to unravel the concept of ideals, and provide a sensible interpretation of the different features of ideals that came up in the two examples. Before I start the investigation, however, I want to bring some order to the questions that guide it, and reveal some of the theoretical background to these questions.

My main aim is to arrive at a defensible concept of ideals, which can be used in a theory of law. This makes it necessary to pursue two main sets of questions, the first set regarding the concept of ideals as such, the second set regarding the role of ideals in a theory of law. These will be guiding questions throughout the book, but a first impression of the issues concerned can be given here. An inquiry into the concept of ideals raises philosophical questions about the nature of ideals and their place in our world. In philosophy, ideals are traditionally connected with notions of the good or notions of value. When considering the nature of ideals the relation between ideals and values needs to be examined as well. Any interesting view on the nature of ideals presents ideals in a certain context and, most importantly, advances a view about ideals and reality. Thus, the first set of questions are questions about the nature of ideals and their relation to reality; this is the subject of the next section (1.2).

The second issue then is how to use such a concept of ideals in a theory of law. Again, we can distinguish between ideals as such and the place of ideals, now in the realm of law. In connection to theories of law, the question is whether ideals are to be seen as a general category or whether there is a specific category of legal ideals. If there are specific legal ideals, I also want to know what role these have to play in comparison to other ideals. The question of legal ideals as a category is further introduced in section 1.3. The second aspect of the place of ideals in legal theory is how the concept of ideals is connected to other aspects of the domain of law. More specifically, what interests me is how the concept of ideals is related to other concepts that are central to theories of law: rules and principles. To this issue I turn in section 1.4. Finally, section 1.5 gives an overview of the other chapters in this book.

## 2. IDEALS AND VALUES

The first set of questions concerns the nature of ideals in general. What type of entity are we thinking about? The first indication can be drawn from the observation that ideals function as guides for improvement. The unspoken premise here is that ideals are worth aspiring to, that they are something valuable. Of many things we are inclined to say both that they are an ideal and that they are a value. Both justice and freedom can be regarded as an ideal or as a value. So can world peace, love, solidarity, equality. Is there a difference between the ideal of justice and the value of justice?

Thus, the first question regarding the general nature of ideals is whether a meaningful distinction can be made between ideals and values. And if such a distinction can be made, what does the difference between ideal and value consist in? In order to get a first impression of the kinds of questions arising, it is helpful to look into the background of the two concepts.

As a philosophical term, ideal has a longer history than value. The adjective 'ideal' is derived from the Greek 'idea', which was already used in a philosophical sense in ancient Greece, most famously by Socrates and Plato. From this use as an adjective accompanying the Platonic idea, the substantive 'ideal' was first used in the eighteenth century.[3] The term 'value' arose in the context of the economy, at first simply meaning: the worth of a thing.[4] Only recently, near the end of the nineteenth century, did it acquire a broader,

[3] It was used primarily in aesthetics and ethics, see the entry "Ideal" in the Dictionary of the History of Ideas (Wiener 1973, 549-552).

[4] See the entry "Value and Valuation" in *The Encyclopedia of Philosophy* ( Edwards 1967, 229-232).

philosophical meaning. It has become the generally used term both to refer to the positive qualities of an object or state of affairs — speaking of something 'having value'; and to refer to people's basic commitments — speaking of something 'being a value'.

Since the concept of value has been introduced, it has become the subject of vigorous debate and it has given rise to a wealth of theories about the nature of values. The problems that form the subject of value theory are equally relevant in the context of a study of ideals: they concern the relation of ideal to reality, knowledge of ideals, the possibility of truth and criticism. Therefore I will give a sketch of the main topics related to the nature of values and give a brief typology of value theories.

In any inquiry into the nature of values, there are three theoretical components which are sometimes hard to disentangle, but can be distinguished. These are ontology, genealogy[5] and epistemology; i.e. an account of what values are, an account of their origin, and an account of our knowledge of them. On these issues a number of '-isms' have been developed: cognitivism and non-cognitivism, realism and anti-realism, naturalism, subjectivism, etc.[6] Most often, the focus is on a combination of ontological and epistemological questions: do values really exist and how do we know them?

The central question of value ontology is whether values exist mind-independently in the extra-human world (Bransen & Slors 1996, 1).Value realism answers this question positively, anti-realism answers it negatively. In value epistemology opinion is divided over the question whether value judgments can be true or false, that is, whether we can have knowledge of values. Cognitivism asserts that value judgments are truth claims, while non-cognitivism denies this.

Cognitivism and non-cognitivism are broad categories: each comprises a number of theories respectively asserting and denying that values are subject to judgments of truth and falsity. Two important varieties of cognitivism are rationalism and moral realism.[7] The first theory claims that value judgments

[5] I will not pay separate attention to the way values come into being; the issue is touched upon in passing throughout this book. For extensive treatment of the issue, see *Die Entstehung der Werte* (Joas 1997).

[6] These are different positions in meta-ethics, that is, theories about the status of moral judgments and moral values. For the time being, I will simply treat value as equivalent to moral value; the issue of different kinds of value, more specifically legal and moral value, will be treated in the next section.

[7] My account of the varieties of cognitivism and non-cognitivism is based on Arrington's book on moral epistemology (1989). References can be found there. Well-known proponents (continued...)

are true by virtue of their relation to a self-evident first principle. Justification is a process of rational deduction from that principle. Moral realism claims that value judgments are true by virtue of their correct appreciation of the moral quality of a situation. Emotivism and prescriptivism are influential non-cognitivist theories.[8] Emotivism claims that value judgments are expressions of feelings of approval or disapproval, while prescriptivism claims that value judgments are commendations for the choice of objects and actions. In both cases, value judgments are not assertions that something *is* in fact good or bad; they express a person's feeling or attitude towards it.

The connection between epistemology and ontology is found in the reasons why value judgments are or are not capable of being truth claims. Epistemological realism makes truth or falsity dependent upon the existence of a value in the extra-human world. It is backed by a realist theory of the ontological status of values. Value judgments can be true or false because values exist: they are correct or incorrect appreciations of those values. Other cognitivist theories, however, are supported by an anti-realist ontology. Rationalism does not claim mind-independent existence of values. Truth of a value judgment depends on a self-evident value, but that value only needs to be self-evident for human beings — there is no need to claim independent existence. Non-cognitivist theories are very clearly anti-realist: they make value judgments directly dependent on human, mind-dependent, feelings or attitudes. Thus, we see that the two pairs of opposed positions do not correspond: there is a large field of cognitivist anti-realism, in which we can locate theories such as rationalism.

The distinction between realism and anti-realism has the advantage of clarity, but it leaves open a number of questions, particularly regarding anti-realism. What positive theories are connected to the idea that values do not exist mind-independently in the extra-human world? Pondering this question leads to a host of other concepts which determine the shape of these theories. Two pairs of such concepts are especially relevant to my project: objective and subjective, absolute and relative. All of these figure in discussions on the ontological status of values, but not always with a clearly delineated meaning.[9]

[7](...continued)
of rationalism are Alan Gewirth and Bernard Gert; John McDowell and Mark Platts are leading moral realists.

[8] Emotivism was advocated by Ayer and Stevenson (see Stevenson 1963). Prescriptivism was developed by R. M. Hare (1952).

[9] Of course, and this makes it more complicated, they are not restricted to the question of ontology: they have epistemological relevance as well. Often, ontological and (continued...)

The issue of value objectivity and subjectivity is the most slippery. The claim that values are objective has been described as the ontological claim that values are "part of the fabric of the world" (Mackie 1977, 15). This can be interpreted as ontological realism, as saying that values are part of the fabric of the extra-human world, a position which one could also call objectivism.[10] Often, however, it is the more modest claim that values have a specific, verifiable, basis in social reality. This means that values can be objective, but still mind-dependent and part of the human world. Of subjectivity, we can give a similar account: strict subjectivism is the doctrine that values are no more than an individual's mental states.[11] Again, there is the more modest idea of subjectivity that values always need to be recognized by a subject to exist. Once the restricted versions are rejected, objectivity and subjectivity become combinable features. We can then say that values have objective and subjective components. It then remains to specify to what extent values are objective or subjective. I will reserve the terms objectivism (or ontological realism) and subjectivism for the strict views on value objectivity and subjectivity. There is, however, also an intermediate position in describing the ontological status of values: the idea that values are intersubjective. Values are then seen as the shared standards of a human group, which means they are not dependent on an individual's affirmation but neither do they need to have a basis in reality.[12] We can draw a parallel with the existence of a legal rule, which is not part of the non-human world either, but part of the shared norms of a group. Exactly in what sense a rule or value can be said to exist when it is intersubjective is a difficult question because of the ambiguity of the idea that it is shared. The claim that values are intersubjective needs to be backed

[9](...continued)
epistemological arguments for a position are mixed together. For example, relativism is usually a denial of the epistemological claim that cross-cultural assessment of beliefs about values is possible, backed by the ontological claim that values are never more than the intersubjective standards of a particular group.

[10] Objectivism is the term used by Mackie. I think the term ontological realism is clearer because it refers directly to the reality of which objective values are supposed to be part. See Bransen & Slors (1996) for a discussion of ontological realism.

[11] A good example of subjectivism is the theory of Gauthier, who claims that values are an individual's considered preferences (1986, 49).

[12] An intersubjective view on values is part of Rawlsian constructivism. In his recent work, Rawls relies on intersubjective agreement about certain political values by way of a reflective equilibrium strategy (1993, 95-97). See section 2.2 for further discussion of Rawlsian constructivism.

by an account of what the shared quality of values consists in.[13]

The contrast between values as absolute or relative is important because of the development of value relativism.[14] Value relativism is primarily a position on the validity of values; it denies the absolute validity of values — the idea that values can be valid on their own account without the need to base validity on something else. Value absolutism, as the view that some values are valid without further justification, combines well with the epistemological view of rationalism: the idea that ultimate values are self-evident can be the basis for the claim that they have absolute validity. It can also be combined with versions of epistemological and ontological realism. The common denominator of different kinds of relativism is the idea that the validity of values is always relative to a certain context. The most well-known type of relativism makes values dependent on culture: values are only valid for those people belonging to the culture of which those values are part (Harré & Krausz 1996, 11). Thus, cultural relativism and an intersubjective ontology are natural companions. Relativism can be more radical than that, however. It can shade into subjectivism when the validity of a value is seen as relative to one person's belief or feeling. It is important to realize that relativism can be combined with either cognitivist or non-cognitivist claims.[15] One can hold that value judgments can be true or false within a given culture, or that such judgments are a matter of shared sentiment.

All of these concepts play a role in this study. The theories I discuss, all use them with somewhat different meanings. I will use the conceptual distinctions made here as a framework to place them in. The focus on ideals makes for a specific perspective. My starting point is the relationship between ideal and reality, that is, I will try to answer the question: what is the ontological status of ideals? In Chapter 2, I will develop two distinct concepts of ideals,

[13] The issue of objectivity, subjectivity, and intersubjectivity is further complicated because objectivity and subjectivity are sometimes used as mutually exclusive terms. For instance, Mackie, who denies value objectivity, calls himself a subjectivist but defends the view that values have an intersubjective basis (1977, 26).

[14] For an overview of types of relativism, see Harré & Krausz 1996. Relativism is by no means limited to theories of value. Harré and Krausz distinguish two catalogues of relativisms: by subject (semantic, ontological, moral and aesthetic relativism) and by negation of types of absolutisms (23-24). It is the latter catalogue that is important here. Harré and Krausz distinguish between three absolutisms: universalism, objectivism, and foundationalism (4-5). Relativisms can be distinguished as to the kind of absolutism they deny. Objectivism corresponds to ontological realism, foundationalism to rationalism. Universalism is the view that values are valid for all human beings.

[15] Cognitivist relativism is defended by Gilbert Harman and David Wong, see Arrington (1989, 202-247) for a discussion. Non-cognitivist relativism quickly shades into subjectivism.

connected to philosophical traditions. The distinction, which is based on the relation between ideal and reality, cuts across the typology of value theories sketched here, but I will use the positions indicated here to clarify variations of the two concepts of ideals.

## 3. MORAL IDEALS, LEGAL IDEALS

My interest is not in ideals as such, but in ideals that arise in a legal context. I have said that my aim is to investigate the concept of ideals, but that investigation is qualified by the focus on law. This raises the question whether a general concept of ideals suffices to understand ideals of law. Such a question can be understood in two ways: first, as the question whether there are special features of legal ideals creating the need for a specific concept; second, as the question whether to distinguish different categories of ideals, falling under the general concept of ideals. Is there reason to distinguish a special category of legal ideals or are all ideals equally relevant to law? Here, I want to explore whether the concept of ideals used in moral theory can be applied to ideals in a legal context as well. My reason to focus on moral theory is that this is the field in which the concept of ideals is used most often.

The dominant view of moral ideals is as follows. Moral ideals are usually contrasted with moral rules; they are said to differ in that rules specify what is morally required, while ideals indicate what is encouraged (Gert 1988, 172). Thus, ideals are exceptional moral standards, which ask for actions going beyond obligation (Beauchamp 1991, 242). In some respects, such a characterization of ideals seems easily transportable to other contexts than morality. In a legal context, we can also think of ideals as exceptional standards, which ask for actions going beyond obligation. However, there are a number of connotations that come with this concept as developed in moral theory that are less apt for a legal context.

The most important of these connotations is the attachment of the ideal to a particular person. In the accepted view, an ideal as a standard of laudable, but non-obligatory conduct is usually accompanied by an important distinction between the meaning of the ideal for the person following it and its meaning for others (Urmson 1958, 204). For the person committed to it the ideal generates moral demands but not for others. Generally, it is not a standard used to criticize the person holding the ideal either. An example is the case of a doctor volunteering to practise medicine in a war-zone. Such a person feels that his ideal of being a good doctor requires him to do his job under any circumstances however hazardous: it feels like a duty. No other person, however, would be prepared to hold this doctor to a duty to risk his life. We applaud his behaviour but do not think it is a matter of obligation. It is especially this view of ideals as personal standards that is less applicable to ideals of law. This is clear when we consider the examples of justice and freedom with which I began this chapter. It is possible to regard justice and freedom as standards to which a particular person is committed, but this does not seem to be the central meaning of these ideals for law. One can also understand justice and freedom as ideals that are part of, or underlie, the legal order itself; or one can understand them as the shared ideals of the legal community. The connection between law and certain ideals appears to be more direct than via the personal commitment of individuals.

Its personalized character makes the dominant moral concept of ideals less apt as a concept applicable to ideals of law. It can also be criticized for being too restrictive to cover all moral standards that can be seen as ideals, because the distinction between the obligatory and the supererogatory is not as hard and fast as this view presents it. Therefore, this does not seem to be the right starting point in search of a general concept of ideals. There are, however, two other options to pursue: 1) a general, non-moral, concept of ideals that is equally applicable in all practical contexts, including both the moral and the legal,[16] and 2) a broader concept of moral ideals that is also applicable to law. In the first case, the idea is to identify the features of ideals in general, covering anything from the rational actor in economics to romantic love and world peace. Central to such a concept would be that ideals are normative standards specifying a state of affairs that is worth pursuing. In the second case, an alternative is suggested for the specific interpretation identified as the dominant view of ideals in moral philosophy. The moral character of ideals is seen as an integral part of the concept, but ideals are not seen as personal and by definition non-obligatory. Such a concept would resemble the general concept of ideals as normative standards except in the respect that ideals are to be pursued on moral grounds. Both options will appear in this book. Both concepts seem to fit my examples of justice and freedom, so that at first glance the first question of the need for a specific concept of legal ideals seems to receive a negative answer.

Thus, it is apparent that it depends on the restrictiveness of the general concept of ideals whether it is applicable to ideals of law. Both of the interesting options seem equally applicable. Neither of the two options decides

[16] E.g. along the lines of Von Wright in *The Varieties of Goodness*, a study of different forms of the notion of goodness (1963).

the second question whether there is a need for a specific category of legal ideals. The need for a category of legal ideals arises if there are other reasons than conceptual differences to conclude that some ideals have a specific and strong connection to the field of law. If a general, non-moral concept of ideals is advanced, it is a plausible next step to distinguish categories of ideals that have relevance to certain domains or contexts in order to give the concept of ideals explanatory power. The question remains how strong the connection between a certain context and the relevant ideal is; that question will be addressed. If a moral concept of ideals is defended, the need for a category of legal ideals may seem less obvious. To some, institutional characteristics define the realm of law, and the role of ideals is always extra-legal. In that case, a category of legal ideals is superfluous. To others, law is so directly connected with moral ideals that there is no need to single out a special group of legal ideals. Here, we can recognize well-known positions on the connection between law and morality.[17] The issue of law and morality is one that is closely linked to the question of the category of legal ideals. Although the recognition of specifically legal ideals is less obvious in the second option, both a general concept and a moral concept of ideals do leave room for a distinction between moral and legal ideals. In the first case, both moral and legal ideals can be seen as subcategories of one general concept of ideals; in the second case, legal ideals can be seen as a subcategory of moral ideals.

## 4. RULES, PRINCIPLES, IDEALS

In legal theory today, the concept of ideals is not commonly used. Law is usually described in terms of rules and, more recently, principles. Sometimes, values are also seen as a necessary category to understand law, but not ideals. Why introduce them?

Rules can be seen as the basic normative category. In their most common form, rules are prescriptive norms of conduct: they determine how one ought to behave. Do not hit your children; brush your teeth twice a day; pay your income tax. But rules are not always simply prescriptive as in these examples; they are to an important extent connected to institutions. This is already apparent when we consider the duty to pay income tax. We only have that duty because there is a system of tax law with rules that institute income tax. Tax, contract, marriage, these are all institutions that are created with rules and,

[17] These positions, legal positivism and natural law theory, will be discussed extensively in Chapter 8.

once they are instituted, produce other rules.[18] Institutional rules are an important part of law, and they can serve to ground the distinction between primary rules and secondary rules made by H.L.A. Hart (1994, 91-99). Primary rules are rules of obligation, while secondary rules are about the primary rules: they specify how to identify a rule as part of the system (rules of recognition), how to change a rule (rules of change) and how to apply a rule (rules of adjudication). Secondary rules are necessary for the existence of a legal system; they distinguish a legal system from other codes of social rules.

Thus, we see that law is and should be primarily understood as a system of rules. That, however, is not the whole story. Those who focus exclusively on rules have been rightly criticized for ignoring the role of other normative concepts in law, the role of principles. Dworkin's criticism on Hart's legal positivism is one of the most interesting defences of the importance of principles, and I will use it to introduce the differences between rules and principles. According to Dworkin, rules are applicable in an all-or-nothing fashion, while principles are not because they have a dimension of weight or importance (Dworkin 1978, 24-27). In the case of a conflict between rules, one rule takes priority in such a way that the other rule is not valid in that case. A principle, on the other hand, can yield to another principle while retaining its significance. For example, consider two rules, one specifying that ownership of an object is established by securing possession of that object, the other specifying that ownership of immovable property is established by being officially registered. These two rules conflict, but that conflict is solved by giving priority to the second, more specific rule, construing it as an exception to the more general rule. When principles are involved in a conflict, this leads to a determination of the relative importance of each principle with one taking precedence in the specific case. This does not fix their relative weight in cases to come. Consider two principles of judicial procedure: the judge's duty to decide a case within a reasonable period of time and the judge's duty to motivate his decision well. There will be cases when these duties conflict, but one cannot say beforehand that the relative importance of the two principles will always be the same.

These differences in kind between rules and principles have been explained

[18] I follow MacCormick (MacCormick & Weinberger 1986, 49-58). He distinguishes between institutive rules (determining when an instance of the institution comes into existence), consequential rules (determining what consequences follow when it is in existence), and terminative rules (determining how the instance ends). What MacCormick calls the 'philosophical' sense of institution (as a concept regulated by a set of institutive, consequential and terminative rules) used here is to be distinguished from the sociological sense of an institution, referring to an organized form of social activity (55-56).

by Robert Alexy as stemming from the character of principles as 'Optimierungsgebote' (1985, 19). This means that principles are norms which prescribe that something be realized to the highest degree possible considering the legal and factual possibilities. Thus, principles can be fulfilled to a certain degree, whereas rules can be either fulfilled or not. Rules are norms that are fixed within the realm of legal and factual possibilities (20). A rule about due care will specify to what extent care has to be taken, while a principle about due care will demand the best care possible, which makes it open-ended. Alexy shows how their character as *Optimierungsgebote* can explain differences between principles and rules, both those noted by Dworkin and those mentioned by others. It explains the different role in conflicts: the principle's demand for the highest degree of realization survives non-application while the fixed demand of a rule is either met or not. Often, principles are seen as different from rules because principles are more general norms than rules (e.g. Raz 1972, 838). This is a rather vague criterion on its own, because rules themselves can also be on different levels of generality or specificity. However, a higher level of generality is a likely result of the relation between rules and principles. An important reason why rules are fixed determinations is that they are the outcome of a weighing of principles. The more general nature of principles is then explained by the fact that only the rule takes into account the limits of law and facts. It is a principle of criminal law that a suspect taken into custody must be brought before a judge as soon as possible; it is a rule of Dutch criminal law that this must be within three days.

Alexy's account of principles is also illuminating because it provides a starting point for considering the role of ideals. He points out that principles are not straightforwardly deontological but also have an axiological dimension (1985, 24). A principle is not simply a prescriptive norm; it prescribes the highest degree of realization of an ideal or value. To put it in terms of Alexy's definition of *Optimierungsgebote*, we can say that the axiological dimension is found in the 'something' which is to be realized according to a principle. Or, following MacCormick: "Thus legal principles are the meeting point of rules and values" (MacCormick & Weinberger 1986, 73). Values or ideals are the desirable states of affairs that one aims to realize, and principles are the norms prescribing how to go about this realization under certain legal and factual conditions.

In this way we get a threefold system of normative categories relevant to law: rules, principles, and ideals or values. For descriptions of rules and principles, I follow Alexy, Dworkin, and MacCormick; in this book I will concern myself with ideals and values. As I have indicated above, this involves examining whether ideals are to be distinguished from values. I will also consider whether the relation between ideals and principles as sketched here remains plausible in the light of a thorough study of the concept of ideals.

## 5. THE AIMS AND STRUCTURE OF THIS BOOK

In this book I want to develop a concept of ideals that can be used in legal theory. To pursue this aim I follow the strategy of comparing and evaluating two existing theories that focus on ideals and law: the theories of Gustav Radbruch and Philip Selznick. The choice of these two theorists was motivated by two ideas. First, the idea that the most profitable study would be of theories that combine a view of ideals with an interesting theory of law. Second, the idea that it would be the most interesting to compare two theories with different philosophical backgrounds. Both Radbruch and Selznick make ideals or values the focus of their theory of law. Radbruch sees law as that part of cultural reality which aims to realize the idea of law consisting of the three values of justice, purposiveness, and legal security. Selznick sees law as a normative system oriented towards the master ideal of legality. The philosophical tradition to which Radbruch belongs is that of the neo-Kantianism developed by Windelband and Rickert. Selznick, on the other hand, is highly influenced by the American pragmatism of John Dewey. The two philosophies differ considerably in their account of the nature of values and ideals, of the relation between value and reality, and of the role values have in philosophy and science. Evaluation of the theories of Radbruch and Selznick on the nature of values and the role of ideals in law will lead to an improved conceptualization of ideals and their role in law, for which I use and extend the most convincing elements of their theories.

To finish this first chapter, I will give a short overview of the content of the remaining chapters of this book. In Chapter 2, I start by giving a general picture of the philosophical discussion about the ontology of ideals. I describe two philosophical traditions advancing different concepts of ideals: a transcendent and an immanent concept. The main point of disagreement concerns the relation between ideal and reality. I will go into the development of ontological and epistemological views within each tradition and consider the characteristics of ideals that follow from these views.

The next four chapters provide an examination of the theories of Radbruch and Selznick, each consisting of a chapter describing their theory and a chapter evaluating their views on ideals. Chapters 3 and 4 deal with Radbruch's theory. In Chapter 3, I will introduce his theory insofar as it is relevant for an understanding of his views on ideals and law. I will go into his main methodological theses and their neo-Kantian inspiration. I will give a brief sketch of his legal philosophy and the much-debated 'turn' in his post-war work. In Chapter 4, I will focus on values and law, and evaluate his ideas. I will discuss Radbruch's conception of values, the relation between value and reality, the different elements of the idea of law and the role these have in law.

In Chapters 5 and 6, Selznick's theory is the subject of discussion. Chapter 5 serves as an introduction, in which I go into his sociological perspective, pragmatist philosophy and the main aspects of his theory of law: legal naturalism, and his theory of legal development. In Chapter 6 I will evaluate his theory of ideals. I discuss his combination of pragmatism and naturalism, the latency of values, the concept of the master ideal, and the role of ideals in the relation between law and society.

Chapter 7 provides a comparison of Radbruch and Selznick and an assessment of their strengths and weaknesses. On the basis of that evaluation I then develop my own ideas about a theory of ideals in law. I use pragmatism as a basis supplementing it with other theoretical insights, including Radbruch's, to achieve a satisfactory theory of legal ideals. Finally, in Chapter 8, I discuss the present state of the debate between legal positivism and natural law and argue that the theories discussed in this book provide an intermediate position that does more justice to the value-oriented nature of law, promising a better account of law than the traditional theories.

# CHAPTER 2

# TWO CONCEPTS OF IDEALS

## 1. AN ONTOLOGICAL DISTINCTION

In the present chapter I propose a distinction between two concepts of ideals. In pursuit of the question what a defensible concept of ideals must look like I have focused on the relation between ideal and reality. There are two basic ways of viewing that relation: as opposition or unity. I refer to the concept of ideals that sees ideals as essentially opposed to reality as the transcendent concept of ideals; the concept that sees ideals as an integral part of reality I call the immanent concept of ideals.

The distinction between the two concepts thus has its starting point in the different answers to the ontological question what ideals are. In the course of this chapter it will become apparent that the two concepts also differ considerably in regard to both the question of gaining knowledge of ideals and that of justifying adherence to ideals. Epistemological difficulties can provide reasons for a revised account of the ontology of ideals. The epistemological positions depend on the ontological status of ideals, because the kind of entity ideals are is to a large extent determinative of the way in which we have access to ideals and of the reasons admissible for the justification of the belief in certain ideals. The development of the different concepts of ideals can be seen as a search for the most plausible account of both their ontology and epistemology.

The distinction between a transcendent and an immanent view on ideal and reality is the starting point for discussion of two traditions of thinking about ideals. Both traditions originate in a clear and strong assertion of, respectively, the transcendence and the immanence of ideals. The development of the traditions is explained by the reaction to problems generated by these strong core positions. Thus, I sketch a move towards less extreme accounts of the two concepts, in which opposition and unity are interpreted more modestly.

My aim with this chapter is twofold. First, I want to give a description of the two concepts of ideals that will shed light on the features of ideals. In the first chapter, I have already raised a number of questions and issues regarding the nature of ideals. For example, from the discussion of justice, it became apparent that, at first sight, ideals seem to be unrealizable standards. In the discussion of freedom underlying property law, the ideal appeared as implicit in the legal rules. Features such as unrealizability and implicitness will be subject of discussion here. I have also raised the question whether ideals and values are different or identical. In this chapter, I will examine which of these characteristics are included in the different concepts of ideals and I will pay attention to the other characteristics following from the concepts. Secondly, I want to use this discussion to formulate hypotheses that can guide my study of Radbruch and Selznick. These hypotheses will concern both the characteristics of the concept of ideals and the problems generated by each concept. My perspective in judging the promises and problems of the concepts is on the role that ideals should be able to perform. There are two functions of ideals of which a concept should give a satisfactory account: ideals need to serve as standards of evaluation and ideals need to give guidance to practical concerns.

## 2. IDEALS AS TRANSCENDENT

Ideals appear as transcendent if one starts from a dualistic view of the world. Dualism in the context of this discussion means the dualism of fact and value. There is more than one way to understand the fact-value distinction: most commonly it is understood as a logical distinction between types of reasoning. First advanced by Hume and Kant, it is the idea that one cannot derive a statement of value, of what ought to be, from a statement of fact, of what is the case.[1] The fact-value distinction I am concerned with here is more fundamental: it is not a distinction between types of statements but an ontological distinction between kinds of existence. Facts, as parts of perceivable reality, are of a different nature than values. The question then is: what are values? How are they different from facts, and in what way are they related? I will start with a discussion of the Platonic view, as the clearest account of a transcendent concept of ideals, and go on to discuss Kantianism, constructivism, and subjectivism as reactions.

1 As Stuart Hampshire points out, Kant defended the stronger thesis that there is an unbridgeable separation between moral and factual judgments, while Hume was only concerned that derivations of 'ought' from 'is' are not logically conclusive (Hampshire 1949, 162). Hume's is-ought problem has been the subject of vigorous debate in ethical theory (e.g. Searle 1964), non-observance of the distinction is known as the naturalistic fallacy (see Frankena 1939).

Fact and value can be seen as forming two different realms, the natural world in which we live and a world of perfection, of how things ought to be. This is the structure of a Platonic world of ideas.[2] Such a view has three central features: the ontological status of the world of ideas, its relation to the realm of fact, and our knowledge of it. In Plato's theory the realm of ideas was primary: the world as it should be was also seen as the real world. The perfection of the realm of ideas entailed that it was eternal: there is no reason why something perfect should perish. Similarly, being perfect, that is completely good, also meant that it was true — falsity implies imperfection, a lack or incongruity. If one identifies Platonic ideas with ideals, which I think is defensible,[3] ideals in this view are perfect, eternal and true. These are large claims, which need to be substantiated. That, however, is problematic because of their separate realm of existence: how can these features of ideals be proven when ideals form their own distinct realm? Some connection is needed, first of all, so that we can know something about ideals, and, secondly, so that the significance of ideals for the world which we inhabit is made clear.

This connection brings in a second dualism: that of mind and matter. The link between the world of ideals and the natural world is established via the human mind (Reale 1990, 48). By way of his rational capacities a person gains insight in the character of ideals. We obtain information about ideals because we have special rational capacities that allow us access to them. This does not do much to clarify the rather mysterious picture that has arisen: a world of perfect ideals to which we have a direct link because of our rational capacities. But there is another, more indirect connection in Plato's view that should not be overlooked. Ideals form the patterns on which the world of which we are part is based. A beautiful thing, for instance a flower, is a reflection of the idea of beauty; however imperfect a reflection that flower is, it shows something of the idea of beauty. For Plato this means that ideals are the source of the valuable aspects of our world.[4] This gives ideals an important role in the

2 See Reale (1990, 47-63) on Plato's theory of ideas. Reale distinguishes six basic characteristics of ideas: being intelligible, being incorporeal, being in the fullest sense, being unchangeable, being self-identical, being a unity (49). In my discussion I focus on the first four. On the separation between ideas and reality, see also Devereux (1994, 193).

3 As noted in Chapter 1, the use of the term 'ideal' as a substantive is relatively recent, the use of the adjective 'ideal' was already used as referring to ideas by the Greeks. I use ideals in the context of Platonic philosophy as well, because many of the features attributed to ideas by Plato are later seen as features of ideals.

4 It is precisely because the ideas are of another (metaphysical) realm, that they can be causes of our (physical) reality, according to Plato. Something could only be a cause of something (continued...)

constitution of the world.

For our knowledge of ideals, this means that there is a direct and an indirect way to gain it: direct revelation to the mind, and indirect proof in the world as we see it. This second route cannot stand on its own, however, because we do not know to what extent the ideal has influenced the make-up of our world unless we have some idea of the ideal in its pure form. We need some understanding of perfection to recognize how imperfect the things are that we perceive. How do we know the world of ideals? The Platonic view was that humanity has special capacities that enable it to understand the ideal world. Human beings have been gifted (perhaps by a divine creator) with intelligence that gives them a grasp of another realm. This is in part a highly problematic and in part an attractive argument. What is attractive, is the idea that the human mind has traits that give it a special relation to ideals. What is problematic is how the link is established between mind and the external realm of ideals.

The problem of the exact relation between ideals and the mind that knows them can be solved simply and radically by doing away with the external ideal altogether. Why should we suppose that there is a perfect world of ideals simply because we have a notion in our heads of a realm of perfect value? There is no reason to assume that there is something out there that causes these notions of ideals to appear in one's mind: people are capable of thinking of ideals without impulses from outside. This line of reasoning is strengthened when it is combined with the Cartesian separation between mind and matter. Descartes in his theory of the *Cogito* raised doubts about the possibility of any certain knowledge except concerning one's own thought (Descartes 1637, 32). On the one hand, there is the mind or thought of the subject, on the other the matter of the outside world. If one accepts this account of the fundamental difference between mind and matter, it becomes plausible to regard such notions as ideals as internal to the mind that thinks of them, that is, as notions that are generated by mental processes themselves instead of notions reflecting a pre-existing world. In such a view, two dualisms are joined: the fact-value distinction combined with the mind-matter distinction leads to the view that ideals are generated by mental processes.

This shift from an interpretation of transcendence as a separate realm to transcendence as part of intelligent thought is developed most forcefully in

[4](...continued)
else if it was external to it, thus ideas could be causes because they were transcendent (Reale 1990, 58).

Kantian philosophy.[5] The Kantian version of transcendent ideals sees abstract ideal notions as necessary elements of human thinking.[6] This means that ideals are acknowledgeable for every rational being; they are abstract notions that regulate our pursuits because they formulate ideas of what things should be like that all rational beings must accept as valid.[7] There is a rational necessity to the most abstract ideals that nobody who fully employs his rational capacities can deny. The argument is that we need to accept such notions in order to understand ourselves as willing and acting creatures. More broadly, we need to accept the validity of certain ideals in order to construct coherent theories of what we are and what the social world is. Kant himself employed such an a priori argument to show that freedom is presupposed by our understanding of ourselves as moral beings.[8] His notion of freedom was a formal notion; it did not specify a certain content. In the same way, one could argue for abstract notions of justice, equality, truth, etc. as necessary presuppositions of understanding ourselves and the world we inhabit.[9] In what sense should one understand this necessity of abstract ideals? Here the old Platonic argument resurfaces — at least to a certain extent. In the discussion of the Platonic world of ideas, I discussed the need for an idea of perfection in order to understand the source of value in our world and to see to what extent ours is a world of imperfection. Similarly, in a Kantian argumentation, abstract ideals of goodness, of justice, of truth, of beauty are necessary presuppositions of our thought or cultural world. In contrast with the Platonic ideas, these abstract ideals are not seen as having an independent existence, but are notions that persons necessarily think of, that is, they are 'present' in people's minds without any claim to separate existence. The most rigorous version of the rational necessity of ideals is that in which the specific content of certain ideals is taken as necessarily true and universally acknowledgeable.

5 My account cannot do justice to the complete system of Kant's own philosophy. The arguments here are inspired by Kant's ideas, and can be found in various neo-Kantian theories. Of these, I have primarily used Heidelberg neo-Kantianism of the late 19th century, and the 20th-century work of Emmet and Rescher.

6 A Kantian theory of ideals argues for transcendent ideals (as not part of reality) by way of transcendental arguments, that is, arguing from the preconditions necessary to make knowledge or experience possible (see Walker 1978,14-23). Thus, I use 'transcendent' to refer to the ontological status of ideals, and 'transcendental' to refer to a Kantian type of argument.

7 The regulative function of ideals is stressed by Emmet (1994), who studies the role of various Kantian ideals in practical philosophy.

8 This argument can be found in the *Grundlegung zur Metaphysik der Sitten* (1785, 454-455).

9 Kant himself did not extend the line of argumentation to the cultural world as such. It is used by certain neo-Kantian theorists such as Rickert (1928, 269-70) and Radbruch (see Ch. 4).

That, however, raises problems for the theory. How can we argue for substantive notions of e.g. justice or freedom on the basis of the a priori argument that such a notion is necessary to understand ourselves or the world we live in? The argument depends on a rational procedure, which can in principle be reproduced by any rational being, by which one can establish that a certain ideal must be presupposed to understand oneself. The extent to which certain ideals follow from such an argument is limited, however. This line of argumentation, based on a priori necessity, only works for formal value notions: we may need to have some idea of, for instance, goodness but it is not possible to argue for a specific content as an inescapable presupposition of our life. If a formal, abstract, ideal notion is all we can establish, then the regulatory, guiding role of ideals is severely limited.

To deal with the limited guidance of abstract ideals, the constructivist version of a transcendent concept weakens the claims of rational necessity. In this weaker form of argument, ideals can perform important theoretical and practical functions. Ideals are then seen as necessary elements in the construction of theories.[10] Claims regarding the necessity of ideals are more modest: the ideal is regarded as necessary for the construction of a coherent theory, but only in the context of that theory. The ideal is the object of rational argument, but not necessarily valid for all rational beings. When discussing constructivist views, the term 'ideal' can seem ambiguous because there are often two kinds of elements involved in such theories that have an ideal dimension. For instance, in Rawlsian normative theory the person in the original position represents, among other things, idealized impartiality and rationality (Rawls 1971, 142-150). The ideal dimension of those aspects of the theory differs from the ideality of, for instance, views of the good life, another ideal element in Rawls' theory (e.g. 1971, 472-473). The first type of ideal element is rightly regarded as an idealization, a methodological tool to clarify argumentation. It should be distinguished from an ideal because an ideal demands to be pursued. Unlike an ideal, an idealization lacks the appeal that stems from being worthy of aspiring to.[11] Ideals are one kind of element in

[10] See for instance Van der Burg (1997, 27) and Daniels (1980, 55-56) on ideals in wide reflective equilibrium.

[11] A good example of idealization in a theoretical context is the rational actor in economic theory. Economists use the ideal of a completely rational actor in their models to get a clearer view of economic processes, although they know very well that real life economic actors also act, and sometimes should act, on other impulses or motives than are covered by the ideal of rationality. The ideal of rationality serves as an element in a model of pure economic reasoning; it is a tool to isolate such reasoning in the expectation that this will (continued...)

theory construction: they are abstract notions regarded as appealing because they present something valuable. They can thus be seen as part of existing views and as normative standards.

In this picture of ideals, their validity has either a subjective or an intersubjective basis, depending on whether the coherence sought in theory construction is viewed as coherence of one person's views or as coherence of the views of more people. Constructivism with an intersubjective basis is the more interesting kind because it gives ideals a more solid justification. Ideals are justified by their acceptability to those who work with them, in conjunction with their fit in the theories of which they are part. Because they are constructed, their validity depends on their coherence with the rest of the theory, which is something assessed by those who use that theory. In this view, the idea of rational acceptability has been relativized somewhat to allow a more substantive vision of ideals than the Kantian theory of a priori necessity proposes.

A more radical criticism of the Kantian view is advanced by the fourth, and last, version of the transcendent concept that I will discuss: the subjectivist form of the transcendent concept. This version moves much further away from the Platonic view of ideals than both the Kantian and the constructivist views, because it also jettisons the rational component of the Platonic view and the intersubjective basis of ideals. In this subjectivist view of ideals, they are no more than personal desires or preferences.[12] One person's ideal might be to own the latest BMW sports car, while another might desire a truly democratic society. The ontological status of these ideals is the same: they are both no more than personal preferences. On this view, ideals escape the domain of argumentation. Because they are essentially personal, there is no way of convincing another person of the validity of your own ideal except by appealing to that person's own desires and preferences. The importance of ideals in such a view is found in one function only: because ideals are personal and unknowable, they should be kept beyond the limits of debate and theory. Nothing can be said of them that can generate shared knowledge. This is an extreme view, of course, radicalizing the mind-related character of ideals by locating them in the thought and imagination of a particular person. There are other, less radical, relativized forms of the concept of ideals, but they usually depart from the more immanent, practice-related view of ideals, which is the

[11](...continued)
illuminate the functioning of economic processes.

[12] E.g. Gauthier: value seen as a measure of individual preference (1986, 59); or Russell: value seen as expressed emotion (1935, 40).

subject of section 2.3.

The radical character of the subjectivist form of ideals ensues from the combination of the transcendent with the personal. These two characteristics both lead to the idea that ideals are in no way determined by the world of fact: the transcendent character of ideals because it makes them otherworldly, their personal character because it makes them the result of an individual's whim or desire. In the other direction, there is a connection between ideal and fact. Because people act on the basis of their ideals, ideals play an important role in determining the parts of reality to which people belong and with which they interact. Such relations are seen as one-directional influence of ideals on reality: ideals play an important role in the constitution of reality, but facts do not have a direct influence on ideals.

In the other modes of the transcendent concept of ideals, the relations between ideal and reality are developed along similar lines, but in a more subtle way. In the Platonic view, we saw that physical reality is one of the two ways in which we know ideas, because the ideas are at work in reality as causes. In the Kantian view, reality as we perceive it is the starting point for reasoning: the ideal is necessary to understand certain aspects of reality. We need to presuppose an ideal as ordering force to give a rationally satisfactory account of things. In the constructivist view, factual considerations are important for the development of theories because theories — at least insofar as they are descriptive — are developed to explain puzzling facts. Ideals are also thought of in reaction to certain factual phenomena, but in the context of a theory. The exact construction of the ideal, however, depends on the way it hangs together with the rest of the theory, as does its justification. Ideals are justified by their coherence with a theory and by their acceptability in the context of that theory. Facts, of course, play a part in this process of justification but only in their capacity of providing reasons for theorists. By this I mean that coherence and intersubjective agreement between the users of the theory justify the ideal, not the facts themselves, which only provide reasons why some version of the ideal counts as acceptable for such people. In the construction of ideals, facts are reckoned with but they are not an independently decisive factor for the determination of ideals. Here too, ideals are in the end confined to the realm of the subjective.

Subjectivity is a key notion to understand the latter three versions of the transcendent concept. There are two senses of subjectivity that play a role here. In one sense of the word subjective, these views are in agreement that ideals are subjective, namely when subjective is understood as pertaining to the subject, that is to a thinking, self-reflective being by virtue of these qualities of thought and self-reflection. There are a number of different ways in which the idea of value as part of the human mind can be developed, ranging from the idea that abstract value notions are necessary presuppositions of human life, to the idea that values are identical to unreflected preferences. Secondly, subjectivity can refer to a specific epistemological quality of a belief: it then means that there are no criteria for establishing the truth of a certain belief, and that truth is a matter of personal conviction. That ideals are subjective can thus mean, first, that ideals are part of the thought of intelligent beings, and, second, that ideals are no more than one person's unverifiable beliefs. In the first sense, it is accepted by all three transcendent theories that ideals are subjective, while the subjectivist view is the only one defending that ideals are subjective in the second sense. The weakest point of seeing ideals as subjective in the second, epistemological, sense is that it entails that there is no way of really knowing another person's ideals and no way of criticizing them. This goes against our way of reasoning in most practical pursuits.

*Features of the Transcendent Concept*

After this discussion of the dualistic origin of the transcendent concept of ideals and of the different forms of this concept, I can now identify what general features are distinctive of the transcendent concept. The transcendent concept of ideals has four features of ideals as its core: ideals are perfect, they are abstract, they escape complete formulation, and they are inherently unrealizable. Perfection is the most important characteristic deriving from the Platonic view of ideals. Whether the ideal is regarded as the underlying, true reality or as a mental construct, is of no consequence for the form the ideal takes: in both cases, the ideal appears as a flawless entity.[13] And although their perfection derives from different sources in these theories, it is by virtue of their perfection that transcendent ideals can have their specific role in argumentation. They function as standards that can explain certain concerns or directions of deliberation and action. There are ways of organizing things of which one can only make sense by seeing them as under the direction of an ideal. Similarly, ideals are needed to recognize and designate the flaws in a situation or argument. The perfection of ideals makes them into standards against which one can compare real-life situations and thereby isolate certain

[13] According to Nicholas Rescher, perfection is one of the three features of a Kantian view of ideals, combined with being archetypal, or paradigmatic, and imaginary (Rescher 1987, 115). I think the quality of being imaginary can be identified with being subjective (in the broad sense) in my account. I disagree with Rescher about ideals being archetypal: this is still too much a Platonic notion of an ideal.

features of that situation. Theoretically, working with perfect instances makes it possible to gain more precise insight into the exact mechanisms of processes and to break down a phenomenon into its composing factors. Practically too, it is helpful to know in which respects a situation does or does not answer to a perfect ideal, because that points out directions for improvement.

The other features, abstraction, impossibility to formulate, and unrealizability, are very closely linked to the perfect character of ideals, and to each other. To a certain extent, abstraction is needed to reach perfection: it is in concrete situations that imperfections abound, which need to be stripped away to generate a perfect ideal; but the abstract character of transcendent ideals amounts to more than ignoring imperfect details. A perfect instance of something can still be relatively concrete: it is fairly easy to create the image of a perfect car on a computer, which is still a concrete object, in an imagined form. The difference with a transcendent ideal is that the ideal cannot in itself be presented as a concrete object: the ideal is always at a distance from particular instantiations of it. This is why an ideal always appears to escape complete formulations of it: the abstract qualities that belong to it are never quite captured in a concrete example.[14] The ideal of truth can be expressed in a true theory or statement, but this does not exhaust the meaning of the ideal. True theory A and true statement B are examples of what truth might mean, but as soon as one considers how the truth of theory A relates to the ideal of truth, one notices that there are a lot of provisos involved in the truth of theory A. The theory is true 'considering what we know now', 'based on the evidence gathered so far', etc. The ideal of truth, in contrast, implies complete knowledge, or full evidence. In comparing the abstract ideal to different concrete instances of it, different dimensions become apparent against which the ideal promises more than can be found in such particular instances. Any specific formulation of the ideal, trying to give a definitive definition, fails because formulations are given with certain contexts in mind, while the ideal transcends such contexts. The dimensions of perfection and abstraction make ideals reach beyond any specified expression.

The combined features of being perfect and abstract also lead up to the fourth main feature of the transcendent concept of ideals: ideals can never be completely realized. The impossibility of formulating the meaning of an ideal completely might appear to be similar to the impossibility of realizing an ideal completely, but these are different matters. That ideals are inherently unrealizable does not necessarily imply that they cannot be formulated. Human

[14] Amongst those stressing the impossibility of complete formulation of an ideal: Van der Burg (1997, 25) and Emmet (1994, 61).

beings cannot fly without props, but that does not mean that one cannot formulate exactly what a flying human being would be like. The inherent unrealizability of ideals means that they are necessarily of such a nature that they are incapable of being completely fulfilled: there is always a residue of the ideal that escapes realization. To a large extent, unrealizability is based on the perfection of ideals: the flawlessness in every aspect that characterizes ideals is unattainable in the real world. The world has many features that bar perfect arrangements, features ranging from scarcity of resources to the development of new illnesses. Combinations of such features make it impossible to realize one's ideals: on the way to perfection, one always encounters obstacles that force one to settle for less than perfection. The impossibility of formulating ideals completely contributes to their unrealizability indirectly: because every formulation focuses on only some aspects of the ideal, attempts at realization on the basis of such a formulation are bound to fall short. Defining justice as every person having an equal share of resources may make justice seem realizable, but once attempts are made to divide equally, even only as a thought experiment, it becomes clear that the ideal of justice also encompasses considerations of need and merit. So it may be possible to realize justice as equality in some manner, but that is a far cry from complete realization of the ideal of justice. The inability to formulate ideals thus reinforces their unrealizability.

In my discussion of the features of ideals, as advanced by the transcendent concept, I have not distinguished between the different versions of the transcendent concept. For most of these, it is indeed unnecessary: the Platonic, Kantian and constructivist versions of the concept of ideals may have different ontological bases, but the four features of ideals that were discussed can be recognized in all of these theories. However, a slightly different story needs to be told about the radically subjectivist account of ideals. As we saw, the ideal element is subdued in subjectivist theories: ideals are no more than personal values or preferences. As such, all the features mentioned are significantly revised in a subjectivist theory of ideals. They all become relative to a particular person. It means that ideals are not inherently unrealizable, but unrealizable for the person who holds them, and that they are perfect only in the eyes of the beholder. The feature of abstraction seems to lose relevance altogether: one of the main characteristics of a subjectivized view of ideals is that abstract values such as justice or freedom acquire the same status as personal ideals such as becoming a great athlete. The latter category is pre-eminently concrete, in the sense that such a personal ideal is always a vision of oneself in an ideal position. Thus, abstraction is no longer a defining feature of ideals in the subjectivist view. Similarly in this view, the inability to formulate the meaning of an ideal is not a defining feature of ideals as such. There are ideals that are hard to formulate, the more abstract ones, but others can be given precise content. The ideal of being a great athlete can be defined in terms of winning world championships and breaking world records, while a commitment to the ideal of justice does not entail the possibility of a precise definition. The ideal of justice as a subjective value may be rephrased as a preference for living in an environment of just relations, but that still does not give a formulation of what justice is about. The general argument about impossibility to formulate ideals applies to this subgroup of subjective ideals as well. In a subjectivist view, however, the points about abstraction and formulation do not create category differences: ideals are on a sliding scale from highly abstract to concrete and personal. The shared characteristic is that they are personal preferences, which can take all kinds of different forms.

## 3. IDEALS AS IMMANENT

The immanent concept of ideals is connected to world views with a monistic basis. A monistic theory sees the world as essentially a whole, in which different aspects can be distinguished, but these aspects always remain inseparable parts of the whole. With regard to the nature of ideal and reality, a monistic view of the world entails that the ideal is simply an aspect of reality. In itself, this statement is still obscure: what does it mean that the ideal is part of reality? What should we understand as the ideal? How should we conceive of reality? In this section I will discuss four versions of an immanent concept of ideals, starting with the most explicitly immanent view, the Aristotelian version. Modern naturalism is then presented as a more modest account, to whose problems pragmatism and reductionism, in turn, are reactions.

As with the transcendent concept, the origin of the immanent concept of ideals is found in Greek philosophy: in the work of Aristotle. In Aristotle's teleological view, the end or good of every being is entailed by its specific nature. For human beings, the good is *eudaimonia*, happiness or the good life.[15] The idea that the good for man is given with his biological nature indicates that for Aristotle the good is immanent in the natural world (Reale 1990, 319). This can be illustrated with the well-known example of the acorn

[15] For discussion of the place of the notion of *eudaimonia* in Aristotle's philosophy, see the essays of Nagel, Ackrill, Wilkes and McDowell in A.O. Rorty (1980).

and the oak. The acorn already contains the essence of the full-grown oak. The idea is that it lies in the natural course of development that the ideal comes to realization. Of course, this does not mean that this necessarily happens. The acorn can be eaten by a wild boar and never grow into a tree, and similarly, a situation can arise that prevents the realization of the ideal. However, that is not the normal run of things: the good is what a being naturally aims to be and will normally succeed in becoming. In the Aristotelian view, the ideal is inherent in the natural phenomenon, it is realizable, and it has a biological basis. Thus, Aristotelian philosophy has a rich view of reality: it contains purposes and ideals because these originate simultaneously with the phenomena themselves.

This Aristotelian view generates two serious problems. First of all, the biological explanation for the ideal of each species leads to an unduly unitary view of ideals.[16] Because we humans share a common human nature, there is one best way to live, which we are even by nature inclined to pursue. Such a view cannot make room for a plurality of ideals and genuine conflicts between them. All values are perceived and evaluated as either conducive to or detracting from the supreme good for man. This way conflict can always be resolved in the light of the human good. It means that, ultimately, there is no room for incommensurability of ideals: all ideals are explicable in terms of the supreme human good. This is highly problematic if one wants to recognize the equal validity of competing ideals in situations of conflict. In addition to this problem generated by teleological biology, there is the more general difficulty of the inherence of an ideal. Even without the biological basis, the view that an ideal is completely determined by the character and functions of a phenomenon is problematic. This would mean that the precise character of the ideal is generated and fixed by the shape of the existing phenomenon. This raises a question regarding the development of an ideal: can the ideal only change when the phenomenon to which it is connected does? Seeing ideals as inherent in phenomena implies that they can only change together. Especially in connection with human activities, it seems more plausible to allow that ideals can develop and change in different directions in the course of performing these activities. Seeing ideals as inherent aspects restricts the source of development of the ideal too much.

The modern form of value naturalism addresses these two points of criticism: it tries to make room for plurality of ideals and for the possibility of

[16] On the point of the unity of the good, there is disagreement among interpreters whether Aristotle did indeed see the good as one; I follow Larmore (1992), who defends that Aristotle held such a monistic view.

development.[17] Instead of the complete inherence of ideals in reality, it defends the more modest proposition that ideals have roots in natural phenomena, out of which they can develop in different ways. For example, the ideal of love has roots in the biological phenomena of sex[18] and parenthood. If one sees the function of sex as reproduction and the function of parenting as guiding the young to adulthood, one can see that these are possible without love, but also that they function better when love is involved. Raising children is perhaps the clearest example: a child's development is distorted if it grows up in a loveless environment. The precise contours of the ideal of parental love can vary: being either a strict or a liberal educator can follow from the idea of a loving parent. The value of giving a child a secure and warm relationship can take different forms.

Thus, modern naturalism retains the biological basis of ideals, but interprets it as providing the roots and general contours of ideals which can be developed in different ways. Human nature remains important because it explains the general structure of human life, with social interaction as a central component. People are constituted in such a way that they naturally incline towards life in a setting with other people. It means that the reasons for the claim that the social aspects of human life are important are based on biological inclination. Once the social character of mankind is seen as an integral part of what is natural, it is a small step to extend the argument about the natural basis of ideals to social practices. If people have certain natural characteristics, and having a need for social interaction is one of them, one can argue that organizing life in social practices is natural as well and consequently these practices are a natural phenomenon. I should note that this does not entail that specific social practices are thereby also justified by the naturalist argument. It needs an additional argument to be able to say that a certain social practice has a natural basis, if this is to mean more than being a *possible* expression of man's social nature.

Precisely on this point, modern naturalists introduce relativity into their theories.[19] The idea is that, although certain forms of organization and certain basic natural values are universal because related to the nature of man,

[17] Modern value naturalism or ethical naturalism is defended by the neo-Aristotelian Martha Nussbaum and by Philip Selznick. It is to be distinguished from empirical naturalism, "the general metaphysical doctrine that nothing exists beyond what is open to empirical investigation" (Darwall 1998, 27). The metaphysical view underlying modern value naturalism is still teleological.

[18] An example given by Santayana (1905, 9) and by Selznick (1961, 90)

[19] See, for instance, the combination of universality and local variation in Nussbaum (1992, 224).

concrete practices and their accompanying values are relative to the culture of which they are part. The argument in naturalistic terms is that it is one of the universal characteristics of human beings that they need to be part of particular and local cultures and practices (Selznick 1992, 103). There is a general human tendency to laugh and play (Nussbaum 1992, 219) but there are immense variations in games and jokes among different groups and subgroups. One might even argue that an important way of creating and enhancing group identity is by developing specific forms of humour and play. The commitment to certain universal values, which follows from an argument based on human nature, therefore does not preclude appreciation of the values of local practices.

In the context of social interaction, ideals are closely linked to the practices of which they are part. In relation to natural phenomena, we saw that the argument was that ideals have their roots in those phenomena. In a similar fashion, one can argue that ideals find their roots in social practices. Ideals have an inherent connection to social arrangements meaning that social arrangements have their specific accompanying ideals. The practice of friendship is guided by the ideal of friendship; the practice of education is guided by the ideal of good teaching. This view of ideals as connected to social arrangements is part of a view of the social world as consisting of more or less integrated practices. Ideals and practices are seen as mutually dependent: an ideal develops because there is a social practice, which in turn is kept viable by being guided by integrating values. The orientation towards values serves as a shared focal point of the participants in a practice: by understanding the directions given by the ideals of the practice, its participants can develop it further. When ideals are this closely linked to practices, we also need to know how to understand practices. Practices can be defined as coherent and complex forms of socially established cooperative human activity.[20] Practices range from family life and friendship to politics and medicine. Particular instances of each practice may differ, but they are seen as instances of one practice because they are similar in the core activities, the role of participants, the guiding norms, and, of course, the ideals of the practice.

20 The idea of practices is to a certain extent inspired by the theory of Alasdair MacIntyre (1984, 187-196). However, for my purposes MacIntyre's distinction between internal goods and external goods and its connection to practices which involve internal and institutions which involve external goods is unhelpful. Both practices and institutions seem to involve both internal and external goods; and both are directed by ideals or values. Therefore, I use the term 'practice' in a broader sense, without special reference to internal goods.

Because of this view of integrated practices, modern naturalism does not completely escape the criticism made of the Aristotelian view. It still leaves little room for variation in the different instances of a practice: the same ideal, the same norms, the same roles are seen in every instance of it. This implies a problematic unitary vision of ideal and practice: wherever the practice is found, the accompanying ideal of that practice is at work as well. In naturalistic theories, ideals are important aspects of a practice because they set the direction for full development of the practice. Modern naturalism, in its more modest interpretation of the natural basis of ideals, leaves room for development and change of the ideal. Although ideals are rooted in natural or social phenomena, they are not completely determined by the factual situation. The ideal reaches beyond the situation because it formulates ways in which the situation can and should evolve. However, by seeing ideal and practice as a mutually dependent unity, naturalistic theories still fall prey to the first objection to Aristotelian naturalism: how to account for the variety of ideals. The modern naturalist is no longer committed to a unitary view of the human good per se, but does apply the same logic to specific practices. There is always a core meaning to the ideal of a practice that follows from the nature and function of the practice. Thus, the good for a certain practice is one overarching ideal. Variety only has a place within these parameters. Thus, there is no place for radical reinterpretations of the meaning of ideals.

This is a point taken up by the pragmatist account of ideals.[21] Here, the natural ontology of ideals is dropped: ideals are no longer seen as following from (human) nature. Instead, the provisionality of ideals is stressed by making the link between an ideal and its factual basis more temporary and contextual. This is mainly the result of a different interpretation of the ideal's basis in reality. In a pragmatist theory, the focus is not so much on enduring and universal natural and social activities, but on the problem-solving experience of people. Ideals or values are seen as part of concrete experience in the sense that they are seen as the proposed solutions to problematic situations. Similarly to the naturalistic view, ideals are rooted in factual phenomena, but here the point of departure is the experience of a problem, not the inherent leaning of a phenomenon towards a certain value.

The focus of the pragmatist view on problematic situations makes ideals concrete, contextual, and provisional. They are concrete because they are connected to experienced practical problems. For instance, an ideal of friendship is invoked when two friends have an argument because one of them

[21] As found in the theories of William James and John Dewey. I mainly use Dewey (1920; 1929) in my description of pragmatism.

feels cheated. Recognizing that they both have an ideal of friendship as a special form of loyalty can restore the bond between the two.[22] What the ideal means is determined in relation to the problem they have. The ideal is therefore a concrete proposition for this situation. By the same token, it is contextual: the meaning of the ideal is limited to the specific situations in which it works. The factual circumstances of the situation determine the character of the ideal because the ideal is the answer to this specific problem; it is only possibly relevant in other situations with similar features. The ideal has a hypothetical character: its validity depends on its problem-solving potential because it is only valid insofar as it contributes to a better situation. If it turns out that the ideal does not or does no longer help to improve situations, it needs to be replaced or adapted. Of course, it also follows that, as long as the ideal does lead to more satisfactory experiences, it remains valid. Its provisional character means that the ideal is always subject to critical scrutiny.

Seeing ideals as connected to concrete factual situations gives the impression that one can gain knowledge of ideals by simply attending to the facts. This would be a straightforward way to solve the problems of plurality and change posed to Aristotelianism: gaining factual knowledge would suffice to understand ideals. Although this is not the pragmatist view, such a solution is part of the fourth influential theory with a monistic basis: the reductionist version of moral realism. Reductionism defines reality as the objective world whose existence we can ascertain by way of sensory perception. The main difference with the other theories discussed here is that reductionism replaces the teleological view of reality with a narrower empiricist view.[23] In such a strict view of what is real, the ideal can only be said to exist if it is reducible to what can be perceived with our senses. Such a reductionist view has been defended by ethical theorists who have argued that value is reducible to interest, or to perceivable manifestations of like or dislike.[24] Reductionism is a rather typical form of an immanent value theory, because by saying that value is identical to some other quality it denies that value is in any

22 It is important to recognize that in such a situation reference to an ideal can only solve the problem if the ideal is something they share. If it is the ideal of only one of the friends, it cannot restore their friendship and may even be more divisive. It seems that pragmatism has little eye for this negative side of values (compare Selznick 1992, 174).

23 In terms of the distinction in metaphysical views of note 17: reductionism is a form of empirical naturalism, while Aristotelianism and modern value naturalism are forms of teleological naturalism.

24 E.g. Perry: interest as the source of value (1926), or Railton: values as objective interests reducible to natural and social facts (1986, 685).

meaningful way a distinct aspect of reality. Aristotelianism, modern value naturalism and pragmatism have a different view of the scope of reality. Their view of reality is broader than that of reductionism, because they include value as a distinct dimension of what is real. For my purposes, the reductionist view is not the most convincing version of the thesis that fact and value are one: it raises the question why we would want a concept of value and fails to give convincing reasons in its answer.[25]

Considering reductionism does point out the distinctiveness of the pragmatist view of reality and knowledge. We saw that the pragmatist way to understanding an ideal is by examining the practice or situation to which it is connected: by studying how things work and how people act, one also gets to know the ideal that is part of this. Two things should be noted in connection to the epistemology implied by these ideas. First, that pragmatism holds an inclusive theory of knowledge;[26] and, second, that it implies the interdependent understanding of fact and value. What I mean by an inclusive theory of knowledge, is based on the importance of experience in these theories and the continuity seen between all aspects of that experience. Our access to both the facts and the values of our life is through our experience of them: "knowledge deals with the world in which we live" (Dewey 1929, 82). Thus knowledge has a broad scope: everything that we encounter can be the subject of knowledge. It is this view of knowledge as based on our experience which can plausibly tie the understanding of the ideal to its factual basis: experience not only shows what is happening but also what works well and what is problematic. Here the second point comes to the fore, because occurrences and their worth cannot be grasped independently. The way we experience things is mediated by our values and the values that drive us are a product of what happens to us. The clearest case for this line of argument is the interplay between negative experiences and ideals.[27] A painful experience, e.g. being denied a certain benefit you were expecting, is directly related to an ideal, in this case of fairness. Your experience cannot be understood without reference to this ideal, but neither can you grasp the ideal without having such experiences.

This idea of mutual understanding of ideal and experience also points out what is problematic about the pragmatist view. Ideals lack an independent

[25] Therefore, I will not include reductionism in my further discussion of the immanent concept.

[26] Pragmatism in general can be described as the application of the scientific method to any human activity: everything can in principle be the subject of knowledge, and every problem can be tackled by applying the method of intelligent inquiry (Dewey 1929, 200-201).

[27] More elaborate on this point: Van den Brink 1998, who sees moral emotional reactions as the main direct link to ideals (202-205).

source of validity: they are justified by their contribution to a satisfactory experience. However, our understanding of what is satisfactory is determined by reference to ideals as well. Thus, the ideal is required to function both as standard of evaluation of experiences and as justified by these experiences. A solution to this problem, a problem of circularity, could be found in a strict distinction between the end or goal of an activity and the ideals that are helpful in reaching that end. Thus, what is satisfactory is understood in terms of that end, while ideals are justified by their contribution to it. However, there are two reasons why this solution is itself problematic. First, this only relocates the problem, because now the end or goal is indeterminate: how do we determine what that end should be? Secondly, this is discontinuous with pragmatism's doctrine about means and ends. One of the central concerns of pragmatist theory is arguing against the separation of means and ends (Dewey 1929, 223). The means used to pursue an end must be evaluated in terms of their consequences for that end, but the reverse is true as well. Ends or goals can also be criticized if they require the use of unacceptable means. Therefore, means and ends should not be regarded in isolation, but evaluated together and in a larger context. This does entail that there is no easy way to solve the problem of circularity.

*Features of the Immanent Concept*

The discussion of different versions of the immanent concept of ideals has paved the way for a consideration of the cardinal characteristics of the immanent concept of ideals. So far, I have focused on the interpretation given to the ontological character of ideals: in what sense and to what extent does immanence imply that the ideal is an integral part of a being or a practice. Thus, the first important characteristic of the immanent concept of ideals is their inherence in a natural or social phenomenon. We saw that there was a move away from the complete inherence of the Aristotelian view. In modern naturalism, the immanence of ideals is no longer interpreted as their inhering completely in a factual phenomenon. The immanence of ideals should be understood as referring to the basis of ideals in reality. In pragmatism the connection between ideal and reality is softened again: the basis in reality becomes a basis in the problematic aspects of social practices. In general we can understand the ideal's inherence as follows. The interplay between ideal and reality can be seen as a variety of the connection between the possible and the actual, with this difference, that the ideal is not merely a possibility but a desirable possibility.[28] The ideal sets out a direction, a possibility, for improvement of an actual situation. But not everything is a genuine possibility: the actual sets boundaries on what can appear as an option for improvement. In the same way that the possible is constrained by the actual, the ideal is constrained by the reality out of which it originates. The debate within the tradition of the immanent concept is over the heaviness of this constraint. The reality of ideals should be viewed in terms of this connection to actual situations and practices: it arises out of and is effective in existing situations.

Apart from the inherence of ideals, there are a number of other characteristics of the immanent concept that should be discussed here. On some aspects of the concept there is agreement between the theories discussed here, but about others there is debate similar to, and to an extent following from, that about inherence. The features that can be seen as shared among all versions of the immanent concept are the identity between ideal and value, the realizability of ideals, and their implicitness. Whether ideals are universal and enduring is a matter of debate, as is the question of the objectivity of ideals.

The identity of ideal and value and the realizability of ideals are best treated together, because they are closely connected. Seeing ideals as immanent in practices makes ideals and values indistinguishable. This is because, in comparison to the transcendent concept, the unrealizability of ideals is diminished significantly by connecting ideals to developing phenomena and practices. As ideals are part of those phenomena, they cannot rightly be said to go beyond them very far. To be sure, ideals indicate desirable possibilities and in that sense reach beyond the factual situation. But this is a temporary condition: they are again absorbed in the situation when they are effective. The immanent concept sees ideals as essentially realizable, although this does not mean that they are always realized. The core meaning of ideals is that they point the way towards a desirable development of a real practice. In the three different accounts of the immanent concept this implies that the right end can in principle be reached, either because it is part of a natural course of development or because it is a feasible answer to a problem. This does not necessarily mean that they are always practically realizable: ideals present aspects of what is good, but they do not set out a course that leads to the good overall. In concrete situations ideals conflict with each other, and trying to realize an ideal brings about problems that could not be foreseen when it was formulated. Because ideals in the immanent concept lack a

[28] Characterizing the ideal as possibility is an idea borrowed from Dewey (1920, 150): "[The ideal and rational] represent intelligently thought-out possibilities of the existing world which may be used as methods for making over and improving it" (also 1929, 227).

transcending and unrealizable character, there is no reason for a distinction between ideals and values: ideal and value have the same characteristics and perform the same functions.

All three theories defend the idea that ideals are implicit or latent in factual phenomena. This characteristic of ideals is derived directly from their being an inherent part of factual situations, but something more is meant by it. That ideals are latent in existing situations means that they are present before they are explicitly referred to, and that the articulation of ideals is a matter of formulating and elaborating on what was already there in a rudimentary form.[29] This idea has two important corollaries: explicit ideals have to build on their implicit precursors, and ideals have a role to play even if they are not explicitly recognized.

The first point conveys that the idea of latency does not purport to imply that ideals are present in a full-blown shape; articulating an ideal fills in a vague idea of it, which not only adds to the implicit meaning of the ideal but can also modify it. The argument about the relation between implicit and explicit ideal makes both a descriptive and a normative claim. The descriptive claim is that the idea of implicit ideals is the best explanation for the recurring but temporary significance of ideals. When tension arises between ideal and practice, the need arises to articulate the ideal in the light of the perceived problem. The alternative description would be to say that ideals only come into existence when they are proposed in answer to a problem. The latter description, however, is less able to account for the arising of the problem than the former. With the idea of implicitness we can explain that the move away from the ideal creates a problem and makes formulation of the ideal necessary. The normative claim is that explicit ideals function best when they are based on the implicit ideals of a practice. Ideals that are formulated while ignoring their relation to practical concerns are sterile and lack guiding power; they do not work because they underestimate the constraints and demands of the practical situation. The implicit ideals of a practice are intertwined with and evolve along with that practice, but explication is necessary to clarify the ideal and to determine its exact meaning. However, explication can have drawbacks when the intuitive appeal of an ideal is interpreted wrongly (Blok & Vedder 1998, 195).

This brings me to the second point: the role of implicit ideals. In the immanent concept of ideals, there is room for a guiding role of ideals even when they are not the subject of conscious deliberation or affirmation. One of

29 The idea of latency is an important element of Selznick's theory of ideals and will be treated extensively in Chapter 6.

the features of experiential knowledge is a learnt intuitive insight in how things are done. Without being able to formulate what it is that he does, a pianist can have superb knowledge of an interpretation of a piece of music. Similarly, a guiding value can exercise influence when it is intuitively known or felt as good. Implicit ideals are unproblematic ideals: as long as a practice runs smoothly, its guiding values can remain unarticulated. When problems arise, the need to articulate the ideal surfaces. Things are experienced as problematic because the right course to take is not immediately clear. In such situations, explicated ideals can provide propositions for solutions of the problem.

There is difference of opinion on the extent to which ideals can be said to be universal and enduring. In the naturalist version, ideals appear as more enduring than they do in the pragmatist version of ideals. A pragmatist theory stresses the revisability of ideals or values by referring to such standards as hypotheses to be tested (Dewey 1929, 221). As they are tied to concrete problems, ideals are valid as long as they help to guide a practice. Ideals are justified by their success in improving ways of life and keeping them satisfactory. When they no longer have a role to fulfil in practical deliberation and action, they lose their validity. The ideal of the self-reliant, land-owning citizen, which was central to republican thought, is an ideal which no longer has meaning in twentieth-century society where democracy and government function very differently from the seventeenth and eighteenth centuries of republicanism. To make the point in full, a much longer argument would be needed, but the core idea is clear. Ideals change along with the historical circumstances; different circumstances and contexts give rise to new or altered ideals. A naturalist theory by taking the nature of man as its starting point is committed to a view of ideals as more enduring. The point of connecting values to nature is to give them a firm foundation so that such values retain their relevance as long as human beings are the same kind of creatures. Of course, this does not exclude the correction of the empirical judgments about human nature. It is very well possible that certain features have been interpreted wrongly, which can entail that the accompanying values also turn out to have a different meaning. It then of course depends on theories of knowledge and truth what is viewed as a correct new interpretation,[30] but in a naturalistic view such matters affect facts to the same extent as basic values.

[30] The two extremes are correspondence theories and coherence theories of truth where the first in short tells us that true knowledge is determined by correspondence between propositions and the world 'out there' and the second that true knowledge is determined by the coherence of theory and observation.

The values that depend upon facts of human nature are as enduring as those facts themselves.

A similar, but less acute, difference can be discerned regarding the universality of ideals. If one sees ideals as dependent on human nature, they must be valid in respect of every human being. As we saw above, naturalists only defend universality of a limited number of basic values, which can be worked out differently in local contexts. A pragmatist view, focusing on the connection between ideals and particular situations, is more inclined to stress the differences between values according to the situation at hand. Such a view does not necessarily rule out the possibility of values with a universal scope, but these have relatively little practical relevance. If the validity of ideals is dependent upon their success in improving problematic situations, vague universal values have an indeterminate status because they often do not point out a specific course to take. For pragmatism the central category of ideals is that of ideals closely connected to specific practices.

In this description of the immanent concept of ideals, the emphasis on the connection between ideal and reality creates the impression that ideals are seen as objective. Ideals are seen as aspects of the natural and social world. On the other hand, the focus on experience as the source of knowledge might be interpreted as pointing in the opposite direction, that is, locating values in the subjective experiences of people. The ontological objectivity of ideals is directly related to the degree to which ideals are seen as inherent in reality. An Aristotelian view of ideals makes a stronger claim for ontological objectivity than a pragmatist view. In a pragmatist view the subjective quality of ideals comes more to the fore: for a pragmatist an individual's creative mind has the crucial role of formulating and developing ideals. This does not mean, however, that pragmatism denies that ideals have a basis in reality: they arise out of a situation to which they remain related. Similarly, the emphasis on the real objective basis of ideals made by naturalism does not mean that naturalism denies the importance of a subjective component in formulating and recognizing ideals. Immanent accounts of ideals try to combine objectivity and subjectivity by locating ideals in human experience, which has objective and subjective components. The objective aspects of experience are the real interactions between a person and the world around him, while the subjective aspects are that person's intelligent appreciation of these interactions and the creative thinking that guides them. The different versions of the immanent concept recognize both sides of experience, but differ on the precise relation between ideals and experience. Naturalism emphasizes the latency of ideals, the roots ideals have in real interactions, whether these roots are recognized or not. Pragmatism puts more emphasis on the intelligent input of the subject, the person using and testing ideals in problematic situations. The ontological objectivity of ideals thus becomes less important in pragmatism, but this does not mean that pragmatism distances itself from a conception of the validity of ideals as objective. We saw that subjectivism denied the possibility of establishing the validity of ideals: these cannot be justified or criticized. In a pragmatist account, ideals can be justified by their contribution to practical situations. An ideal that works to improve a situation has objective validity for that reason. Although we saw that the pragmatist arguments to justify ideals are not entirely satisfactory, retaining an objective basis for justification is valuable and can possibly be used to construct better arguments.[31]

## 4. THE MERITS OF THE TWO CONCEPTS

*The Ideal Dimension of Values*

The two concepts of ideals are developed on the basis of different ontologies, but this does not mean that there is nothing they share. There are features that both concepts have in common, and amongst those there are the features that justify referring to the two concepts as concepts of ideals. The first, most basic, feature that is shared by the two concepts is that ideals are seen as values. The main difference between the two concepts is that the transcendent concept sees ideals as a specific kind of value, while the immanent concept sees ideals and values as identical. The features of perfection, abstraction, impossibility of complete formulation, and inherent unrealizability figure in most versions of the transcendent concept as the characteristics distinguishing ideals as a subcategory of values. In the immanent concept the characteristics of ideals and values are the same. That ideals are, a subcategory of, values is the main reason why ideals are deemed worthy of striving for. Ideals suggest what should be, and by that token call for realization. That ideals or values are something to be realized is the second feature on which the two concepts are in agreement. This feature has a third feature as a corollary, that ideals or values transcend reality, at least in a minimal sense. If values are to be realized, they must extend beyond what is the case now, which means they transcend reality. These second and third features provide the reason for referring to the concepts as concepts of ideals. Demanding realization and a transcending quality are the ideal aspects of values. Even though these are the

[31] I will return to this point in Chapter 6, where I discuss Selznick's combination of pragmatism and naturalism, and in Chapter 7, where I try to improve the pragmatist theory.

aspects whose meaning is among the most contested by the two concepts, they do justify talking about ideals instead of values.

We can speak of ideals when there are conceptions of states of affairs that have not been realized yet, but are worth pursuing. However, that values have an ideal dimension, in the sense that they are as yet unrealized, has not been demonstrated. Here we leave the common ground between the two concepts, for the ideal aspect of values has a different basis in the two types of theories. Seeing ideals as transcendent relates the ideal aspect of values to their non-real character. Value conceptions guide the arrangement of social reality, and thus attempts are made to realize them, but however successful this is, true realization is impossible because the nature of values is such that they defy a transformation into something innerworldly. We have seen that they do influence reality, but the result of rearranging the world in the service of values is never more than the reflection of these values. In this sense then, transcendent values are inherently unrealizable, and necessarily ideal.

The story from the view of ideals as immanent is more subtle. If values are just aspects of reality they would seem to be realized already, because they are simply part of what is there. This is only true to a certain extent, or rather at certain times. In problematic situations, what is desirable diverges from what is the fact: then values become propositions about the direction to be taken to reach a better situation. Only then do values reveal their ideal side; in satisfactory circumstances the existing situation has value. Values are sometimes realized, sometimes unrealized, but not inherently unrealizable. It is possible, however, that large projects or complex practices — oriented towards ideals as practices are — are never perceived as completely satisfactory: the ideals of that practice may retain aspects that are not completely realized. Law seems to be such a complex practice in which, whether because of changing circumstances or its complex character, ideals never turn out to be completely realized. Even if values are not inherently unrealizable, in such cases of practical unrealizability referring to them as ideals makes clear how the values at stake continue to be one step ahead of the practice.

*Problematic Aspects*

In my discussion of the two concepts of ideals, I have paid little attention to objections that can be raised against them or to the problems to which the concepts are prone. In the two previous sections, I have examined the various characteristics of two concepts of ideals, but that leaves part of my main question unanswered: to what extent are these concepts defensible and what is their exact role in legal theory? Both of these questions can only be answered in full after detailed examination of specific theories using the concepts, that is, of the theories of Radbruch and Selznick.

Regarding the role of ideals in legal theory, I can only give an indication of my basic understanding of ideals and law, which contributes to my assessment of the way ideals are portrayed and used in these legal theories. First of all, it is important to keep in mind that law is a social institution that is meant to answer certain shared concerns in a society, e.g. to coordinate behaviour or to resolve conflicts. For the role of ideals in law this means that they have to function in a shared institution. Whatever else this entails, two minimal requirements follow: ideals have to be capable of justification in the context of that institution, and ideals should have a meaningful role to perform in law, otherwise they would be dispensable. A concept of legally relevant ideals should include an account of their justification and specify what role ideals have in law.

On the basis of the discussion in the previous sections, I can suggest possible answers to the question of the strengths and weaknesses of the two concepts. The points made here can then be used as hypotheses in the examination of the arguments of Radbruch and Selznick. Generally speaking, the two concepts of ideals each have one main problem area. For the transcendent concept, it is a problem of the knowledge of ideals; for the immanent concept, it is a problem of the justification of ideals. In both cases, these problems take different forms in different versions of the theory. The epistemological problem is the most urgent for a Platonic version of the transcendent concept of ideals. Somehow we know what ideals of goodness, of justice, of beauty are, but how does that process work? Some kind of rational intuition is supposed to be at work, but it is very hard to understand what that amounts to.[32] Kantian conceptions take this objection into account by redefining ideals as mental entities, which solves the mystery of intuition but still places much weight on rational insight in a different way. Its arguments on the necessity of accepting ideals as valid still require that all see this reasoning and its results as justified. It requires that everyone can in principle reproduce the argument and end up with the same ideals. This can only be done for ideals in a formal sense, which cannot perform their role of

[32] A theorist who accepts the rational intuition of Platonic Forms is T. K. Seung. He sees ideals as abstract and intuited, these ideals then need to be concretized by construction. However, his defence of Platonic ideals is based on a purely negative argument: there is no other way to develop critical standards, so these must have a transcendent source (Seung 1993, especially xii-xiv and 194-196).

evaluative standards because for this they need content. Ideals in this sense are heavily underdetermined.

It is not surprising that the constructivist and the subjectivist versions of the transcendent concept drop the claim to knowledge of ideals and make less ambitious claims based on intersubjective agreement and subjective preference, respectively. A subjectivist view of ideals does not connect ideals to any kind of objectivity but also reduces ideals to intra-personal considerations. They cannot be used as standards of evaluation to criticize or justify shared arrangements or the views of others because their meaning is confined to one person's beliefs. In the context of law, this is especially problematic because law is always a shared institution. A subjectivist view of ideals can only serve to point out false claims of objectivity (when legal arrangements are based on values) or serve to support arguments to bar values from the field of law.[33] It cannot give values a place in the institution of law as such.

The constructivist view of ideals, which replaces objective knowledge with intersubjective agreement on a coherent theory, seems to fare better. It can incorporate a range of ideals, from very abstract and general to relatively context-specific ideals; and it can also bring ideals into line with factual knowledge. However, it has its drawbacks as well. First of all, the epistemological status of ideals remains unclear. By replacing knowledge of ideals with agreement about their fit in a coherent whole, the question is left open how we arrive at the construction of ideals. Some additional account of their status seems needed. One might even say that the question of the ontology of ideals is side-stepped completely. A constructivist theory can in principle incorporate any theory of the nature of ideals that leads to a coherent whole. The Rawlsian version I have discussed here, is Kantian in its inspiration and defends a Kantian conception of ideals. One could imagine a different version, however, that includes an immanent ontology. This point means that constructivism cannot provide answers regarding the nature of ideals that I need for a satisfactory account. It needs to be supplemented to yield a complete view. Secondly, the justification of ideals suffers from circularity: because it is based only on coherence, the elements of the construction are justified in terms of each other. This problem of the circularity of justification is something a constructivist view shares with theories using the immanent concept of ideals.

The problems of the immanent concept stem from the difficulty to justify

[33] I will return to these issues in Chapter 8.

ideals. The naturalist view tries to do this by appealing to a natural teleology; it makes ideals follow from a view of natural human development. It presupposes a unified theory of what human nature is and its aspirations, comprising a natural tendency to realize ideals, which is not initially credible to all. Other conceptions of nature are possible, and a naturalist theory carries a burden of proof to show that a robust theory of human nature, which can give rise to ideals, is to be preferred. On a slightly different level, the problem of unified conceptions surfaces again. Naturalist theories connect ideals to social practices, thus linking an ideal to a particular kind of factual arrangement. But by this focus on the latency of ideals in social facts too little attention is paid to the variety of interpretations that can be given to a certain ideal in specific cases. If a naturalist wants to maintain that one kind of practice generates only one specific conception of its accompanying ideal, he needs to argue what that conception is and why other interpretations will not do. On the other hand, if he acknowledges this variety as legitimate, he needs to specify what the natural basis of ideals comprises. In the second case, the question also arises whether these various interpretations can really be said to be expressions of one ideal or are best seen as different ideals. If ideals are seen as providing unity to practices, interpreting variety as difference is problematic.

The problem of variety does not arise in a pragmatist theory because such a theory connects ideals to specific problems, and thus sees ideals as primarily context-bound from the start. However, there is a more general problem of the immanent concept of ideals that does affect pragmatism seriously, and that is the problem of circularity. Because a pragmatist view bases the justification of ideals on their contribution to the solution of problematic situations, it needs to specify what counts as a successful solution. That, however, again depends on standards of evaluation, that is, on ideals. This is a problem for any immanent concept of ideals, unless a convincing argument can be given for an independent justification of ideals, for instance the robust theory of human nature proposed by some naturalists.

On the basis of this inventory three theories offer promising lines of further investigation: Kantianism, constructivism, and pragmatism. However, because of its focus on coherence, the constructivist position does not really address the issue of value ontology, which is a central concern in this book. Therefore, I will concentrate on the Kantian and pragmatist views of ideals, which do provide interesting, different accounts of the nature of ideals. As was shown in this chapter, the Kantian view of ideals has the advantage of strong arguments for formal standards, but it remains to be seen whether it can be supplemented convincingly to provide meaningful standards of evaluation. The pragmatist view of ideals is an adaptive theory, which can react adequately to changing circumstances and provides means to examine personal opinions on ideals critically without reference to controversial eternal standards. However, the circularity of justification forms a serious problem for which a solution must be found to arrive at a completely satisfactory theory of ideals.

I will not, however, compare these theories in terms of general philosophy alone. What I am interested in, is the way Kantian and pragmatist theories can be related to the field of law. The context of law highlights specific issues with regard to a theory of ideals. Law is a special kind of institution, and addressing the role of ideals in law creates a number of new questions about ideals. How do ideals function in the field of law? What is the relationship between ideals, principles, rules and facts? What role do ideals play in determining the connections between law and other domains of society? These are some of the questions which arise in a consideration of a legal theory of ideals. The best way to address these and the way the two concepts of ideals work in legal theory is to examine specific theories which propose views on ideals in law. Therefore, the next part of this study is concerned with the legal theories of Gustav Radbruch and Philip Selznick. The critical examination of these theories will lay bare the requirements of a satisfactory theory of legal ideals and the extent to which Radbruch and Selznick are able to meet these. Consideration of their theories thus provides the building blocks for my own view of ideals and law.

# CHAPTER 3

# THE THEORY OF GUSTAV RADBRUCH

## 1. INTRODUCTION

The subject of this chapter is the theory of Gustav Radbruch. Radbruch, who lived from 1878 until 1949, was a prominent philosopher of law, criminal law jurist and social-democratic politician in Germany. Most of his life he taught at German faculties of law, in Königsberg, Kiel, and Heidelberg, but he also served as minister of justice for a short period in the Weimar Republic. In 1933 he was fired as a professor in Heidelberg by the Nazi regime and he led a private life until his rehabilitation in 1945, when he became Dean of the Heidelberg faculty of law.[1]

Radbruch was a scholar with a wide range of interests, whose writings vary from a draft of a criminal code (1922) to essays on Shakespeare and Goethe. His main interests were legal philosophy and criminal law theory, both of which he pursued throughout his career.[2] His political interests are not only apparent from his career as a social-democrat, but also from his writings on socialism and his contributions to public debate. During the Nazi regime he was unable to pursue his usual subjects because these were deemed threatening to the state. He turned to more historical and literary themes, writing a biography of Feuerbach and a collection of essays on biographical and literary subjects: *Gestalten und Gedanken*. As the result of a year in Oxford, he wrote a short account of English law: *Der Geist des Englischen Rechts* (1947).[3]

However, what interests me here is Radbruch's work on ideals and law,

1 For more biographical information, see Kaufmann's introduction to the *Gesamtausgabe* (GRGA 1, p. 7-88), his biographical study of Radbruch (Kaufmann 1987), and Radbruch's autobiography *Der Innere Weg* (Radbruch 1951).

2 His dissertation on the concept of action in criminal law is witness to both (Radbruch 1903). See volumes 7-10 of the *Gesamtausgabe* for his work in criminal law.

3 For the Feuerbach biography (*Paul Johann Anselm (von) Feuerbach: ein Juristenleben erzählt*, 1934) see GRGA 6; the essays in *Gestalten und Gedanken* (1944), depending on their subject, are to be found in GRGA 5 (literary writings) and GRGA 16 (biographical writings); *Der Geist des Englischen Rechts* in GRGA 15 (comparative law). On Radbruch in Oxford (1935-1936), see Vulpius 1995.

which for Radbruch was a subject of legal philosophy. His methodological point of view entailed that there is a separation in the subject matter and method of legal philosophy and legal science, the first of which is occupied with the values of law. Since Radbruch saw legal science as separate from legal philosophy, it seems warranted to focus on his philosophical works.[4] The reader will notice that references in the following discussion are predominantly to the *Rechtsphilosophie* of 1932.[5] The reason for this is that the *Rechtsphilosophie* is Radbruch's most complete account of his legal philosophy. Although he has elaborated on many of its themes and has revised some of its tenets, the fundamental ideas of his theory, especially those on values, are presented most clearly in the *Rechtsphilosophie*. Therefore I have opted to concentrate on this book and to confine the discussion of other works to points where these provide important additions or changes to the argument.

The structure of this chapter is as follows. I will start with an explanation of Radbruch's philosophical principles, his methodological dualism or triadism and his relativism, and relate those to theorists who influenced Radbruch's thinking. I will then turn to Radbruch's theory of law and try to show how his philosophical position shapes his legal theory. Finally, I will discuss the famous issue of Radbruch's turn from legal positivism to natural law and consider the relevance of this issue for this study.

## 2. RADBRUCH'S GENERAL PHILOSOPHICAL VIEWS

In this section I will discuss Radbruch's views on general philosophical questions, such as his ideas on method and the nature of philosophy and science.[6] I will relate these general ideas to law in the next section. Radbruch builds his philosophy on two pillars: methodological dualism and relativism. I will first discuss his account of dualism and go on to examine related themes that seem to relax the dichotomy involved in his dualistic view. I will conclude

4 Page references are to the *Gesamtausgabe* (GRGA). Here I have used the first three volumes of the GRGA, which deal with his legal philosophy. I refer to the year of first publication and the page in the GRGA. Thus, the *Rechtsphilosophie* is 1932, p. 205-450 (in GRGA 2). In the edition prepared by Dreier and Paulson, there is a table comparing the page numbering of the different editions of the *Rechtsphilosophie* (1999, 234).

5 The 1932 edition was the third, but the first two editions appeared under the title *Grundzüge der Rechtsphilosophie* (1914) and were so much revised in 1932 that the two can be regarded as separate works.

6 Science is the translation of *Wissenschaft*, which is a broad notion of science, including all academic disciplines.

this section with a discussion of Radbruch's relativism.

*Methodendualismus & Methodentrialismus*

Radbruch's methodological starting point is the Kantian distinction between is and ought (*Sein und Sollen*) (1932, 230). Because there is a strict separation between what is and what ought to be, arguments concerning the ought, or the realm of value, can only consist of value statements. Any conclusion about values can only be justified by appealing to higher value statements, not by using statements of fact. This is what Radbruch calls methodological dualism (*Methodendualismus*). We should preserve the clear distinction between is and ought in all our scientific pursuits and never base judgments of value on factual judgments or vice versa.

The dualism of is and ought was given great emphasis by the neo-Kantian school of thought at the end of the nineteenth and the beginning of the twentieth century. The Heidelberg or Southwest-German neo-Kantian school,[7] of which Wilhelm Windelband, Heinrich Rickert, and Emil Lask are the main exponents, developed the distinction between reality and value (*Wirklichkeit und Wert*) into a doctrine about the nature of philosophy and science. Radbruch goes beyond the ideas of the neo-Kantians in many respects, especially in regard to law, but some of his basic philosophical tenets are based on the ideas of Windelband, Rickert, and Lask.[8] The Heidelberg neo-Kantians saw the distinction between reality and value as the basis for the distinction between science and philosophy: science is concerned with realities and philosophy with values. The three traditional branches of philosophy — logic, ethics, aesthetics — can be seen as examining the determination of value in relation to the three highest values: the true, the good, and the beautiful (Windelband 1903, 27-28). While philosophy is the critical examination of the validity of values, science is the examination of empirical realities. These, however, are not all of the same kind: there is nature and culture. The two are distinguished by their relation to values: nature has nothing to do with values, while culture designates the reality that is oriented towards values. Examples of this are art, which pursues the value of beauty, and law, which strives for

7 Contrasted with the Marburger neo-Kantian School of Cohen and Natorp, which was an important influence on the legal philosopher Stammler. Hans Kelsen is also regarded as influenced by neo-Kantianism, although opinion is divided which school exercised the most profound influence (see Dreier & Paulson 1999, 237n). Generally on neo-Kantianism, see Ollig 1979.

8 See Radbruch's own references in the foreword to 1914 (GRGA 2, 13) and the first footnote in 1932, 221. On neo-Kantian influences in Radbruch's work, see further Kim 1966 (6-47), Seidel 1999 (62-69), König 1999 (222-229).

justice. Therefore, there is an important distinction within the sciences between natural and cultural sciences (Rickert 1926, 14). Basically, the cultural sciences have human pursuits and constructs as their object, and history is the prime example of a cultural science. The neo-Kantians emphasized the differences in method between these two types of science, but that is not something Radbruch makes much use of in his legal philosophy.[9]

What is important to dwell on, are the different ways of regarding the world that Radbruch develops on the basis of this systematization. There are four, which Radbruch describes as follows: the value-blind perspective of natural science, the evaluating perspective of philosophy, the value-relating perspective of cultural science, and the value-overcoming perspective of religion.[10] The value-blind and the evaluating perspective are each on one side of the gulf between reality and value. Natural science is only concerned with facts, while philosophy is concerned with values. The other two perspectives are attempts to bridge that gap: the value-relating perspective studies those realities that mean to realize values, while the value-overcoming perspective goes beyond fact and value because religion values everything equally in the last instance. In Radbruch's view, religion is forgiveness: the willingness to see the value even of sin and error (1914, 52). Going beyond value and disvalue is not the primary way to regard law: law is a reality meaning to realize value, and therefore the proper subject of the value-relating perspective (1932, 227). Because the perspective of religion does not have a very prominent place, Radbruch omits the value-overcoming perspective when he characterizes his method in legal philosophy as *Methodentrialismus* (1932, 251).[11]

Since Radbruch characterizes his method both as *Dualismus* and as *Trialismus*, the question arises which of the two characterizations is the more fundamental. Although a full answer can only follow after a closer examination of the idea of value-related reality (see 4.3), I can here point to indications that Radbruch did not see the value-relating perspective as really

9 Windelband and Rickert saw the cultural sciences as primarily concerned with particular events, while natural sciences aimed at the development of general laws. Rickert referred to 'die individualisierende Begriffsbildung' and 'generalisierende Begriffsbildung' (1926, 56-57). History is the prime example of an individualizing cultural science. Only in his discussion on the character of legal science does Radbruch characterize legal science as individualizing (1932, 355).

10 In German: wertblindes, bewertendes, wertbeziehendes, wertüberwindendes Verhalten, respectively (1932, 222).

11 He does pay attention to the religious perspective: in the section on the religious philosophy of law (1932, 325-329). It also underlies his ideas about mercy (1932, 410-413).

bridging the gap between value and reality. The value-relating perspective studies realities that are related to values in that their meaning is to realize values, but it still studies empirical cultural realities. The cultural science of law (*Kulturwissenschaft*) studies facts, but only those facts that have meaning in relation to values (1932, 356). To understand cultural phenomena, it is necessary to see that their meaning is value-realization, but the value-relating perspective is not concerned with the meaning of the values as such, that is the subject of philosophy. Science is concerned with reality, and philosophy with value: this methodological distinction also holds for legal science and legal philosophy, of which I shall say more in section 3.3.[12]

*Stoffbestimmtheit der Idee/ Natur der Sache*

The value-relating perspective is not the only element in Radbruch's theory that appears to soften the dichotomy of is and ought. Two other elements that can be regarded in that light are the *Stoffbestimmtheit der Idee* and the *Natur der Sache.*[13]

The idea of the *Stoffbestimmtheit der Idee* plays on the double meaning of 'bestimmt', which can signify 'determined by' as well as 'meant for'. *Stoffbestimmtheit der Idee* means that the idea is *determined by* the matter to which it is related, because it is *meant for* that matter. Radbruch gives the example of sculpting to make this clear: a sculptor will make a different sculpture when he uses marble than when he uses bronze (1932, 231). The material in which a sculptor works in part determines the idea he has of the work of art he wants to make. This relation between matter and idea is true of every idea. Justice is not a free-floating value, it is related to its matter, law, and therefore it both determines and is determined by the reality of law. However, this mutual influence does not entail that both idea and matter are of equal importance. For Radbruch the logical priority of the idea is clear: it is only because the idea is meant for a certain kind of matter that this matter has a role to play in the determination of the idea (1932, 232). It is not

12 Very critical of Radbruch's use of methodological dualism is Bonsmann (1966, 81-84), who attributes Radbruch's designation of value as completely outside of reality to a (neo-Kantian) misinterpretation of Kant's epistemology. I will address the puzzles of the unreal character of values in section 4.2.

13 This is a subject that became gradually more important during the course of Radbruch's work: it is absent in the *Grundzüge der Rechtsphilosophie* (1914), then in 1923/24 the *Stoffbestimmtheit der Idee* first receives serious consideration. Both ideas appear in 1932, but the most extensive treatment of *Natur der Sache* is to be found in two post-war works: *Vorschule der Rechtsphilosophie* (1948a) and *Die Natur der Sache als juristischer Denkform* (1948b).

warranted to conclude that the idea must be of a certain kind just because the matter on which it works displays those features. To do so, would be merely intuitive and cannot be a method to gain knowledge. Radbruch makes a distinction between the logical and the causal relations between facts and values: causally facts influence the formation of a value judgment but facts can never logically be used in the justification (*Begründung*) of the value judgment (1932, 232).

Therefore Radbruch warns against inductive reasoning — seeing the idea present in the matter — as a danger of reasoning based on the *Natur der Sache*. This legal doctrine is essentially the idea that existing factual relations in part determine what rules should regulate these relations. Radbruch believes it goes too far to draw conclusive evidence from the *Natur der Sache*, although other than that it has important uses. First of all, the idea of the *Natur der Sache* makes us sensitive to the conservative element in law (1948a, 140). When new regulations are made, one has to reckon with existing natural, social and legal facts which limit the freedom of designing new rules. Secondly, the *Natur der Sache* can make us aware that our very ideas about law are limited by the historical era in which we live (1948a, 141). And thirdly, every idea is meant for, and is in its essence partly determined by, its matter: *Stoffbestimmtheit der Idee* (141).

Thus, the doctrine of the *Stoffbestimmtheit der Idee* is seen by Radbruch as a part of the theory of the *Natur der Sache*. It is also the essential part of the theory to understand the extent of the relaxation of the dualism of fact and value. Radbruch holds on to that dualism in the last instance. He says himself that the *Natur der Sache* narrows the gap between fact and value, but in the end the idea is determinative:

> (...) in its relation to the Natur der Sache, which, as meaning of the given, is located on the side of Being, the idea of law should have the last word. Although the Natur der Sache confronts the idea of law with the demand to shape the given legal matter meaningfully, the ultimate judgement belongs to the idea of law (1948a, 141).[14]

Radbruch is unwilling to see the *Stoffbestimmtheit der Idee* as a complete reconciliation of fact and value. In the light of our topic, the nature and role of ideals, it is of eminent importance to know how far the relaxation of the

[14] My translation. In German: "Auch gegenüber der Natur der Sache, die sich als Sinn der Gegebenheit auf der Seinsseite bewegt, hat die Idee des Rechts das letzte Wort zu sprechen. Die Natur der Sache tritt zwar der Idee des Rechts mit der Forderung sinnhafter Gestaltung des gegebenen Rechtsstoffes entgegen, jedoch gebührt die letzte Entscheidung der Rechtsidee."

dichotomy goes, and whether values are seen by Radbruch as completely contained in their own realm. We should allow for the possibility that a detailed examination of the doctrine of the *Stoffbestimmtheit der Idee* shows that fact and value are brought together more than Radbruch acknowledges. However, the pursuit of this question is best reserved for the next chapter, where Radbruch's ideas on the nature of values will be treated in more detail (see 4.3).

*Relativism*

Besides the distinction between reality and value and its methodological consequences, the other crucial aspect for understanding Radbruch's theory is his view on value relativism. His central thesis on relativism is that it is impossible to find a theoretical basis from which to judge the ultimate worth of a value statement (1932, 235). There are no scientific criteria to decide which ultimate values have the highest worth; thus, from the standpoint of a philosopher, all value systems have equal worth. I speak in terms of ultimate values and value systems deliberately. In Radbruch's theory, value relativism is about the ranking of ultimate values and value systems are characterized by the order this ranking takes.

Radbruch's specific kind of relativism is a relativism of differing political doctrines. In the context of philosophy of law, the important value systems are political systems. An individual has the choice to commit himself to one of these value systems. Radbruch categorizes political value systems according to their highest values: individual, collective or work-related values (1932, 279). Thus, such value systems subordinate everything to either the individual good or the collective good, or to the work (not person-related) values of truth and beauty. Radbruch classifies the different political doctrines current in his days according to this scheme as individualistic, transindividualistic or transpersonal. Thus liberalism and social democracy are varieties of individualism, while conservatism is a transindividualistic doctrine.[15]

This way of ordering demonstrates the first main task of a relativist philosophy in Radbruch's view: it is to systematize value judgements into coherent systems and to demonstrate the real meaning of such value systems (1932, 233-234). A philosopher should think value judgments through, and lay bare and assess the assumptions on which they are based. Secondly, the task

[15] The third, transpersonal, type of doctrine is not represented by any existing political doctrine, but it would be a view that saw the goal of society as serving other values than a form of the good, for instance, devoted to the truth-finding of science. For a good discussion of Radbruch's systematization of political doctrines, see Dreier 1999.

of a philosopher is to devise a typology of value systems, such as the three types of political doctrines formulated by Radbruch (234). Such a typology involves giving an account of the connections between different value systems. Thirdly, a relativist philosophy can also show the connection between the ends of a given system and the means employed and show the effects of pursuing these ends (233). What the ultimate values are, is not a question but a given for Radbruch: the good, the true, and the beautiful.[16] His relativism does not question the status of these ultimate values, but the way they are employed in systems of belief which rank them differently.

Radbruch did not only endorse relativism from a theoretical standpoint; he also thought it had practical consequences. These consequences, however, concern political arrangements, not one's personal beliefs. Endorsing relativism as a scientific doctrine does not mean that one should be guided by relativism in one's own practical pursuits and daily action. Even if there is no theoretical ground for a choice, one should live one's life guided by a chosen value system. Relativism is a theoretical requirement, but not an ethical requirement:

> Relativism, however, belongs to theoretical and not to practical reason. It implies a renunciation of the scientific establishment of ultimate decisions and not a renunciation of the decision itself (1932, 235-236).[17]

A relativist should still believe in his own opinion as the right one, even if he knows that it cannot be proven to be so.

Radbruch does attach practical significance to scientific value relativism in the political realm.[18] He believes that certain substantive claims follow from his type of relativism. In an article entitled 'Der Relativismus in der Rechtsphilosophie' (1934) he expounds this substantive content. Its claims are

[16] In this respect, he follows the neo-Kantian tradition, see Windelband 1903, 41-42. Windelband, however, did not regard these values as the object of relativistic choice (see Seidel 1999, 70).

[17] Translation Wilk (1950, 57-58). In German: "Der Relativismus gehört aber der theoretischen, nicht der praktischen Vernunft an. Er bedeutet Verzicht auf die Wissenschaftliche Begründung letzter Stellungnahmen, nicht Verzicht auf die Stellungnahme selbst."

[18] Baratta and Seidel characterize Radbruch's relativism as 'positive relativism' because of the political ideas Radbruch derives from it (Baratta 1959, 515; Seidel 1999, 95). Baratta points out that Radbruch's relativism finds its inspiration in Goethe (1959, 510). For Brecht, the political aspect of Radbruch's relativism is reason to argue that Radbruch saw democracy as the highest value. He rightly points out that Radbruch's claim that substantive political values follow from scientific relativism is problematic (Brecht 1959, 337).

more far-reaching than one would at first sight expect. First of all, relativism establishes the validity of positive law (1934, 18). Because there is no knowing which opinion about what the law should be is right, we need another ground for deciding which rules to follow. This ground is the fact that a rule is positive law. But relativism also determines some of the content of law: since there is no way to decide which is the right opinion, all opinions should be heard. Therefore, relativism leads to liberal rights, such as the freedom of speech and the freedom of religion (19). The next step is that relativism, by proclaiming opinions equal, also demands the equality of the bearers of the opinions, which in our political reality means demanding a democratic state with majority rule (20). By way of these examples Radbruch wants to show that it is not necessary to adhere to traditional natural law doctrines in order to ground substantive claims about the law.[19] It is debatable whether pure relativism indeed gives rise to all these claims, but an investigation of that question will have to wait until the next chapter. Here we can conclude with the observation that for Radbruch relativism is not a cynical doctrine of indifference, but a view which is closely connected to strong ethical opinions.

## 3. LEGAL PHILOSOPHY AND LEGAL SCIENCE

We have arrived at the point where we should turn to Radbruch's legal theory in detail. I have touched upon aspects of his legal philosophy in the discussion of relativism and as an example in the exposition about philosophy and science. Now I will show how these general points shape his legal theory and how he builds on this foundation. But before we start, there is one point that should be clearly kept in mind. In his manner of reasoning Radbruch is very much a Kantian. He often uses the Kantian scheme of constructing a priori concepts which are necessary preconditions of reasoning. This means that there are things we cannot think or say without presupposing the existence of a certain more fundamental idea. A famous example is Kant's idea that we need to presuppose our own freedom in order to think of ourselves as moral beings. Radbruch accepts this type of reasoning, deductive arguments based on a priori concepts, as a matter of course. This should be kept in mind to

[19] That Radbruch felt the need to emphasize these substantive claims can be explained in light of the political situation at the time. With this paper (first presented in France and first published in French; most German journals did not accept his work in those years) he distanced himself from the Nazi regime shortly after it came to power (Kaufmann, GRGA 1, 79).

understand Radbruch's argument for the relations between law, its idea and its concept.

*Legal Science as a Cultural Science and a Normative Science*
I sketched the neo-Kantian distinctions between philosophy and science, and between two types of empirical science and I touched upon their use by Radbruch. How do these distinctions bear upon the legal sciences? The domain of legal philosophy is the evaluating perspective on law, i.e. legal philosophy is concerned with the meaning of the legal values. Legal science, on the other hand, is concerned with the reality of the law. And, because law is one of the realities which means to realize values and thus a cultural reality, legal science is a cultural science. These are the basics, but Radbruch adds a number of refinements.

Legal philosophy is not limited to studying the meaning of values, it is also concerned with the method and the prerequisites of legal science. And it is self-referential: in a legal philosophy its own method and starting points are subject of discussion as well. These points are most clearly made in Lask's *Rechtsphilosophie*: he distinguishes the methodological side of both legal philosophy and science, the value philosophy of law, and the cultural science of law (1905, 306-307). The "meta"-philosophy of method is very prominent in the general part of Radbruch's *Rechtsphilosophie*: the question of the proper tasks of legal philosophy and legal science runs through the whole of it. Radbruch relates the nature of legal philosophy closely to the nature of law as a cultural phenomenon; for him legal philosophy is first and foremost the cultural philosophy of law (1932, 251). It is a cultural philosophy because it endorses the idea of *Methodentrialismus*, of three perspectives.

Legal science is a cultural science, which means it makes use of the value-relating perspective: it understands the reality of law as having the meaning to realize the idea of law, which most importantly consists of the value of justice.[20] But there are different ways to regard this reality: one can concentrate either on its factuality or on its meaning. If one does the first, one can engage in different sciences which have factual aspects of the legal reality as their object: sociology and psychology of law, legal history, etc. If one does the second and concentrates on the meaning of the legal reality, i.e. the meaning of the positive legal order, one engages in legal science proper: "the science concerned with the objective meaning of positive legal orders" (1932,

[20] The construction of the idea of law will be discussed extensively later in this section.

343).[21] Thus, legal science proper differs from other cultural sciences related to law in employing the method of a normative science,[22] by studying the objective meaning of legal norms. But it does not go beyond the law in force, the positive law, so its object is not the purely normative, its object is the law as it is. This way Radbruch identifies legal science, in the narrow sense, with what we usually refer to as legal doctrine (*Rechtsdogmatik*), the study of the meaning of an existing legal system (Dreier & Paulson 1999, 238). Legal science is devoted to that part of reality that is law, but how do we determine what that is, how do we recognize law? For that we need the concept of law, to which I will now turn.

*The Concept of Law and the Idea of Law*

For Radbruch, the concept of law depends on the idea of law. Since both of these notions have remained unclear so far, I should explain them here. Radbruch takes three steps in developing the concept of law in relation to the idea of law (Dreier & Paulson 1999, 240-241). First, the idea of law is that at which the reality of law is oriented. The idea of law is the value that is specific for law, while the concept of law is based on this idea. It is a concept of law as the reality which means to serve the idea of law: "Law is the reality the meaning of which is to serve the legal value, the idea of law." (1932, 255).[23]

The second step is to identify the idea of law as *Gerechtigkeit*. The idea of law is thus used by Radbruch as a synonym for the value towards which law is oriented. The only candidate for this position of the idea of law is *Gerechtigkeit*, justice. This value is an absolute, axiomatic, value which cannot be derived from any other value (256). Radbruch considers the possibility of reducing justice to a form of the (moral) good. He rejects this view because the moral good is a value of the individual human being, only a human being can be morally good, while justice does not have the individual

21 Translation Wilk (1950, 140). In German: "... die Wissenschaft vom objektiven Sinn positiver Rechtsordnungen."

22 In German: Normwissenschaft (Radbruch 1932, 355). Normwissenschaft is distinguished from Seinswissenschaft. Again Radbruch invokes the distinction between 'is' and 'ought' but now to distinguish two aspects of legal rules: the factual aspect of being an imperative or command and the normative aspect of establishing an 'ought' (354-355). He also uses this distinction to establish the connection between law and morals (see below).

23 Translation Wilk (1950, 73). In German: "Recht ist die Wirklichkeit, die den Sinn hat, dem Rechtswerte, der Rechtsidee zu dienen."

as its object but the relationships between people (256).[24] Radbruch uses a second meaning of the idea of law, not as a synonym for justice, but as a notion composed of different elements which all play a part in determining the law.[25] I will give an account of these elements under the next heading.

The third step is to describe the features of law as the reality oriented towards justice. First, the concept of law points out a reality that is both positive and normative, a characteristic this reality shares with other kinds of, what Radbruch calls, psychological factualities. This is a term Radbruch uses to point to phenomena that are part of factual reality, but which at the same time apply standards to other parts of reality. An example Radbruch gives is the conscience, which he sees as a factual psychological faculty which judges other factual occurrences as good or bad (1932, 260). In the context of law, this factuality is the precept (*Anordnung*). Because it is oriented towards justice, it shares that value's social character; both justice and precept are concerned with the relations between people. They also share the characteristic of being general. Thus, law can be defined as "the complex of general precepts for the living-together of human beings" (261).[26] From its relationship to justice, Radbruch derives the characterization of law as a positive, normative, social and general order.

The concept of law is derived from a philosophical characterization of the reality of law, in conjunction with the idea of law. The features of law in the definition above are based on the characteristics of the value of *Gerechtigkeit*. Thus, the concept of law is an a priori concept which constitutes what law is. We can only recognize certain aspects of reality as law by using that concept. Law is not something that comes neatly packaged and labelled, it is constructed on the basis of the concept of law. The concept of law is the criterion for separating law from non-law (1932, 261). The concept of law is a necessary concept: without it, there would be nothing recognizable as law.

As a consequence of this, the concept of law is not a part of legal science, but precedes it. Legal science takes law as it is as its object, but the question

24 Radbruch held a different view in the *Grundzüge*, where he did not see *Gerechtigkeit* as an absolute value (he reserved that qualification for goodness, truth, and beauty) but constructed it as a derived value that has *Gemeinschaftsleben* as its substratum, which serves the highest values (1914, 57-58). Remnants of this view are still visible in the 1932 *Rechtsphilosophie*. See also Bonsmann 1966, 19-22 and 39-41.

25 Kaufmann refers to *Gerechtigkeit* in a broad sense, as the idea of law, and *Gerechtigkeit* in a narrow sense, as one of the three elements of the idea of law (1997, 154-155).

26 Translation Wilk 1950, 76; in German: "der Inbegriff der generellen Anordnungen für das menschliche Zusammenleben". Radbruch's later definition of law is slightly different: "... der Inbegriff genereller, positiver Normen für das soziale Leben" (1948a, 151).

what law is can only be answered by looking at the world from the point of view of the concept of law (1932, 261).

*The Elements of the Idea of Law*

Maybe the most important part of Radbruch's legal philosophy is his development of the idea of law. We saw earlier that the idea of law as the specific value of law had to be justice. Justice is the value which has the relations between people as its substratum. Radbruch uses the Aristotelian distinction between commutative justice and distributive justice to argue that distributive justice is the basic form of justice (1932, 258). Commutative justice is the absolute justice of goods, e.g. a certain pay for a certain job. The second is the relative justice between people, e.g. reward according to someone's merit. Distributive justice provides the principle of equality, while commutative justice presupposes that those concerned have an equal right. If two workers both deserve to be paid for their jobs, commutative justice requires that if they both do their job, they both ought to get paid. Determining whether their two jobs have equal merit and deserve equal pay is a question of distributive justice. Thus, distributive justice precedes commutative justice.

That makes distributive justice the basic form of *Gerechtigkeit*, but it is only a formal value. Distributive justice requires equal treatment of those who are equal and unequal treatment to the degree of inequality. It does not specify, however, whom to regard as equal or unequal and how to treat them (1932, 278). Therefore, justice may be the value that is specific for law, but it merely determines its form. It needs to be supplemented in order to determine the content of law: for this, Radbruch introduces the value of *Zweckmäßigkeit*.[27]

This second element determines the purpose of law. Because it is part of the idea of law it must be based on an absolute value like the value of *Gerechtigkeit*, that is either the true, the good, or the beautiful. For Radbruch it is obvious that the only one of these three that the law can serve directly is the good (1932, 279). However, there are many different views about the good and the purpose of law. Here, Radbruch makes use of his theoretical doctrine of relativism: the ranking of different goods and values depends on political doctrines. Therefore, the purpose of law cannot attain a final determination, it will differ according to the dominant political doctrine. This presents us with a problem: what should the law be if its content cannot be conclusively determined? This problem leads to the third element of the idea of law: legal

[27] This is hard to translate. Wilk gives 'expediency' but literally it says 'according-to-purpose-ness'. Its meaning is somewhere between 'purposiveness' and 'expediency'. I usually employ the German term.

security (*Rechtssicherheit*). Because a final determination of the purpose of law is impossible, but the law still has to provide one order to govern society, this order has to be posited (1932, 302). The value of legal security demands that the law be positive. This leads to the paradoxical tenet that the idea of the right law requires that it is positive law: "So, most oddly, the positivity of the law itself becomes a prerequisite of its rightness: to be positive is implicit in the concept of right law just as much as rightness of content is a task of positive law" (303).[28]

Although the element of *Zweckmäßigkeit* can only be regarded relativistically, the other two elements are unmistakable in their demands. The requirements that the law be positive and that like be treated alike, hold good whatever the political constellation is. There is one last question to be answered concerning the elements of the idea of law: how do they relate to each other, or, which of the three is the most important? This cannot be determined once and for all. Even if we know that justice and legal security have general validity and the determination of *Zweckmäßigkeit* does not, this does not give any indication about their ranking. Once again, the relativistic stance of Radbruch's philosophy confronts us. Both the determination of *Zweckmäßigkeit* and the order of the elements of the idea of law have to be regarded relativistically.

On precisely this point, the internal ordering of the idea of law, Radbruch's views have undergone a change over the years, which became the subject of an ongoing debate. I will consider the debate about his supposed change of views in section 4.

### *Law and Morals*[29]

For a clear understanding of Radbruch's legal philosophy, one essential part of his theory still needs to be discussed: his view on ethics and on the differences and connections between law and morals. Of all his ideas, Radbruch's ethical theory is maybe influenced the most by Kant. Radbruch

[28] "Die Positivität des Rechts wird damit in höchst merkwürdiger Weise selbst zur Voraussetzung seiner Richtigkeit: es gehört ebensosehr zum Begriffe des richtigen Rechts, positiv zu sein, wie es Aufgabe des positiven Rechts ist, inhaltlich richtig zu sein." (transl. Wilk 1950, 108)

[29] It is important to realize that Radbruch makes specific use of the terms *Moral*, *Moralität*, and *Ethik*. I use the English 'morals' as a translation for *Moral*, the cultural reality that is contrasted with law, and morality in its specific meaning as the quality contrasting with legality (*Moralität versus Legalität*). Ethics (*Ethik*) is the philosophical discipline concerned with questions regarding morals. For Radbruch, this is Kantian ethics. See also Dreier & Paulson 1999, 244.

follows Kant in seeing morality as something concerning the individual will and in using the notion of autonomy to indicate the essence of morality. Being moral means freely following the moral law, willing to do what is right. A moral agent is autonomous when he freely and rationally decides to do what is required by the moral law. Therefore, the true subject of ethics is the individual will: what is most important is the individual's inner disposition to do what is right. This entails that the relevant judge of an act's rightness or wrongness is the individual conscience. Radbruch uses these ideas as the ground for his view on the relation between law and morals.

First of all, this individualistic notion of morality shapes Radbruch's ideas about the distinction between law and morals. He discusses the distinction in terms of the internal versus the external (1932, 264). Radbruch points out that the contrast between law as concerned with the external and morals with the internal is ambiguous. He distinguishes four ways to understand it, and gives his own interpretation of each. First of all, the distinction can point to the subject matter of law and morals. Radbruch interprets this as referring to the main interest of each. The domain of morals is concerned with the individual and its inner motivation, while law is concerned with social life (*Zusammenleben*), which makes it interested primarily in the external conduct of the individual (1932, 265). Law is interested in the inner life of an individual only to the extent that it is relevant for conduct in the community. The second understanding of the distinction relates to the purpose of law. The legal value of an action is the good it does for others or for the community, while moral value is the intrinsic good of an action (267). As a consequence morals demand certain actions simply because it is one's duty to perform them, while law demands actions in the interest of someone else (267). Most important for Radbruch are the third and fourth understandings of the distinction, which concern the moral and legal duty. The third understanding connects morals to morality and law to legality (268); the fourth connects morals to autonomy and law to heteronomy (270).[30] Radbruch disagrees with both characterizations.

Here Radbruch makes an important move: for him, as for Kant, the only true duty is the pure, moral duty. This is because Radbruch characterizes a duty as the subordination of the will to a norm (1932, 268). In his

[30] These are all important notions in Kantian ethics and legal philosophy: morality refers to duty as being affirmed in the individual's conviction, while legality refers to duty as simple subordination to a norm; autonomy means that the source of a duty is one's personal will making a free rational decision, while heteronomy means the source of a duty is the will of another. For a clear discussion of Kantian ethics, see Korsgaard 1996.

individualistic ethics this can only be an autonomous decision. Why is this so important? Because only morality can give rise to duties, morality is in two ways the necessary complement to law. It is the ultimate source of law's obligatory force and the ultimate end of the law (271-272). The first point follows directly from the idea that the only true duty is a moral duty. Because law imposes obligations on the individual from the outside, such obligations are not an autonomous act of the will and are therefore not true duties. For an individual to incur a duty it is necessary that he morally accepts it as obligatory. Therefore, law needs morality to back it with a sense of duty. The second point, that morality is the ultimate end of the law, follows from this autonomous idea of duties in a more indirect way. Because a person can only be moral by deciding autonomously to subject him or herself to a norm, the law needs to create room to do that. The norms of the law must be such that it allows individuals to be free in order to be moral. It is therefore important that the law gives the individual rights which guarantee freedoms (272). One of the more concrete examples which show how important the individual's morality is for Radbruch, is his view on *Schandgesetze* (shameful laws). To the individual conscience, a law can be so abhorrent that it cannot be regarded as valid by that individual (1932, 315). This follows from Radbruch's idea that the validity of law is in the last instance dependent on moral acceptance by each individual. All that law can be in such a case, is a heteronomous power (1932, 316). He extends this reasoning in his article on relativism (1934) where he also discusses conscientious objectors: he believes the criminal law should contain special norms to deal with this category of offenders, because their transgressions are motivated by their moral convictions (1934, 19). Theirs is a tragic conflict between a legal demand for compliance and a moral duty, which the law should recognize as special even if it cannot allow such conduct to go unpunished.

In short, the relationship between law and morality is such that law should enable people to be moral. But because this is essentially something only an individual can do out of free will, by creating the possibility of morality, law also creates the possibility of immorality. The content of law and morals may differ greatly, but their relationship is vital even though it is full of tension (1932, 273).

## 4. FROM LEGAL POSITIVISM TO NATURAL LAW? RADBRUCH'S TURN[31]

In textbooks on legal philosophy, there is little consensus on the characterization of Radbruch's position. Sometimes he is regarded as a legal positivist, sometimes as a natural law thinker. Often, both characterizations are used for the argument that his pre-war views were positivistic, while his post-war work is a defence of natural law.[32] This thesis, that Radbruch's philosophy of law underwent a major change in response to the Nazi regime, is the subject of the debate on Radbruch's turn.

In the English-speaking world Radbruch is best known as the subject of a debate between H.L.A. Hart and Lon L. Fuller. In 1958 Hart wrote an article about the separation between law and morals in which he reproached Radbruch for a naive rejection of the separation between law and morals as a reaction to the horrors of the Nazi regime (Hart 1958, 31). Fuller replied that Hart had gravely misunderstood Radbruch and that Radbruch provided a better account of the dilemma of unjust law than that given by Hart (Fuller 1958, 656-657). The debate between Hart and Fuller and their interpretation of Radbruch has been analysed by various authors,[33] so there is no real need to repeat it here. Moreover, the Hart-Fuller debate is more about the consequences of positivistic and natural-law responses to Nazi law than it is about Radbruch's position.

While both Hart and Fuller focused on Radbruch's postwar writings, their approach differs from the debate in German legal philosophy, which concentrated on the change in Radbruch's position itself. The main question in the German debate was and is how we should interpret Radbruch's views and whether his postwar writings form a coherent whole with his earlier work. The central text in this debate is 'Gesetzliches Unrecht und übergesetzliches Recht' (1946) in which Radbruch proposes his famous formula:

> Preference is given to the positive law, duly enacted and secured by state power as it is, even when it is unjust and fails to benefit the people [*unzweckmäßig*], unless its conflict with justice reaches so intolerable a level that the statute becomes, in effect, 'false law'['unrichtiges Recht'] and must therefore yield to justice. It is impossible to draw a sharper line between cases of statutory non-law and statutes that are valid despite their flaws. One line of distinction, however, can be drawn with utmost clarity: Where there

[31] In German: Umbruch.

[32] For a good discussion of the characterization of Radbruch's theory by interpreters, and of the thesis of his turn, see Seidel 1999 (112-115; 159-164).

[33] Two recent examples are Ward 1992 and Paulson 1994.

> is not even an attempt at justice, where equality, the core of justice, is deliberately betrayed in the issuance of positive law, then the statute is not merely 'false law', it lacks completely the very nature of law (1946, 89).[34]

This passage has generated endless debate among scholars. The question is whether the formula means that Radbruch converted to natural law theory. As I said, an affirmative answer is usually combined with the idea that Radbruch's earlier position was positivistic. The debate about Radbruch's turn therefore depends on specific interpretations of both his earlier and his post-war work. Before I go into the different positions, I should indicate what the common ground between Radbruch scholars is. There is agreement that Radbruch changed his views, probably in reaction to the terrors of the Nazi regime. He revised his ideas about the relationship between the elements of the idea of law. Instead of his completely relativistic account of 1932, in which he said that the ordering of the elements of the idea of law depended on differing political views, he now proposed a specific ordering of the elements. *Zweckmäßigkeit* should never be allowed to dominate, it should always be kept in check by the other two elements (1946, 88). Those two, *Gerechtigkeit* and *Rechtssicherheit*, he believed to have a closer connection: the security of the law is itself a requirement of justice, so that *Rechtssicherheit* is really an integral part of justice (compare Baratta 1959, 521). To find a way to determine which of the two should prevail in any particular instance, he proposed the formula of the degree of injustice. The formula is usually regarded as consisting of two components: the first component being the intolerability formula, the second the betrayal formula.[35] The second component sets a clear threshold, in Radbruch's view. When a statute does not even attempt to realize equality, it does not fall under the concept of law as the reality meaning to realize justice; therefore, it is not law at all. The first component is vaguer, because it says that the conflict between legal security

[34] Translation Paulson (1994, 317). In German: "(...) daß das positive, durch Satzung und Macht gesicherte Recht auch dann den Vorrang hat, wenn es inhaltlich ungerecht und unzweckmäßig ist, es sei denn, daß der Widerspruch des positiven Gesetzes zur Gerechtigkeit ein so unerträgliches Maß erreicht, daß das Gesetz als "unrichtiges Recht" der Gerechtigkeit zu weichen hat. Es ist unmöglich, ein schärfere Linie zu ziehen zwischen den Fällen des gesetzlichen Unrechts und den trotz unrichtigen Inhalts dennoch geltenden Gesetzen; eine andere Grenzziehung aber kann mit aller Schärfe vorgenommen werden: wo Gerechtigkeit nicht einmal erstrebt wird, wo die Gleichheit, die den Kern der Gerechtigkeit ausmacht, bei der Setzung positiven Rechts bewußt verleugnet wurde, da ist das Gesetz nicht etwa nur "unrichtiges Recht', vielmehr entbehrt es überhaupt der Rechtsnatur."

[35] In German: Unerträglichkeitsformel und Verleugnungsformel. See e.g. Dreier & Paulson 1999, 245; Seidel 1999, 165.

and justice can be so great that the positive law, the statute, which serves legal security, has to yield to justice and not be applied. The first component has been used by German courts, most recently in cases against former DDR border guards (see Seidel 1999, 40). It has been made applicable by interpreting the demands of justice to recognize human rights, as laid down in international treaties.

There is a group of authors who believe that the change in Radbruch's conception of the idea of law constitutes a major break between Radbruch's earlier, more positivistic ideas and natural-law flavoured postwar views.[36] They defend this idea with reference to Radbruch's earlier conception of the role of the judge. In 1932, Radbruch said that an individual citizen could conscientiously object to a shameful law, but that the judge has the duty to serve legal security and to uphold the law (315). It is clear that he no longer thought so in 1946, in regard to extreme injustice. Opposing this interpretation are those who believe that Radbruch's postwar position is simply part of an ongoing elaboration of the idea of law.[37] They defend the view that Radbruch always considered *Gerechtigkeit* as the element specific for law and had always thought it more important than *Zweckmäßigkeit*. The change they see is mostly a shift in accentuation of *Gerechtigkeit* instead of *Rechtssicherheit* (Kaufmann 1987, 153). They also deny that the change in the position of the judge constitutes an clear break; Paulson, for example, regards it as a correction of an earlier mistake (1995, 500).

But even if this debate is the key in which most Radbruch studies are set, this does not necessarily mean it is important in the context of my study about the role of ideals. Does an understanding of Radbruch's shifting views tell us anything about the role values play in his theory? I do think Radbruch's turn is relevant for this study, mainly because the turn is about the central idea of his legal philosophy: the idea of law. However, it is not necessary to discuss the issue exhaustively; it does not relate to our concerns in all its aspects. There are three questions regarding Radbruch's turn that need to be answered. First of all, we need to know whether Radbruch's turn entails a change in his opinion about the character of the elements of the idea of law: does Radbruch

36 Apart from Fuller and Hart, important proponents of this view are von Hippel (1951, 37-39) and Dreier (1981, 37-39), although Dreier in the 1999 article with Paulson seems to have changed his view to the unity thesis. Also Tjong (1967, 85-88), Seidel (1999, 186-196) and Brecht (1959, 361), who see his later views as incompatible with his earlier relativism. In the article by Paulson there is an overview of those for and against the 'Umbruch' theory (1994, 318-319), similarly in Seidel 1999 (159-164).

37 For example: Wolf (1959, 498-503), Baratta (1959, 537), Kaufmann (1987), Paulson (1995).

have a different conception of the nature and the role of these values? This leads us to a second, broader question: does Radbruch's turn imply that he gave up his relativism about values? Thirdly, there is a more specific question about the element of justice: does Radbruch move from a formal to a substantive view on justice?

First of all, it is clear that the shifting meaning of the elements of the idea of law does not affect the character of the idea of law itself or its connection to the concept of law (1948a, 150-151). About the role of values as such we can be brief, insofar as this issue is connected to Radbruch's turn: the change in views concerns the relations between the elements of the idea of law, not the importance of values altogether. Throughout his work, Radbruch maintained his dualistic method and his view of law as a value-related reality. The view that values have a constitutive role in law is neither strengthened nor weakened. The shift concerns the relative status of the three elements of the idea of law: they are each awarded a more specific place within the idea of law. The absoluteness of justice is reaffirmed: justice is the most important element in determining the law. Like justice, legal security retains its status as a universal component of law, but it is more directly connected to justice itself: since legal security demands the repeated, and therefore equal, application of the laws, it can be seen as a part of the value of justice. I will return to the changing conceptions of justice and legal security in a moment, but now I want to focus on the value of *Zweckmäßigkeit*. Of the three elements of the idea of law, the changes in the role of *Zweckmäßigkeit* are the most fundamental. Radbruch emphasizes that this element should be kept in check by the other two: because the content of *Zweckmäßigkeit* is determined by the political theories of the day, it is dangerous to let it rule completely. We should notice here that Radbruch does not change his account of the nature of *Zweckmäßigkeit*, but is instead tracing the consequences of the value thus conceived. Because the content of *Zweckmäßigkeit* cannot be determined once and for all, its power needs to be limited.

And that brings us to our second question: how much of his value relativism does Radbruch retain in his postwar ideas? We saw that it was the relativistic account of the nature of *Zweckmäßigkeit* that led him to a change in the relations between the three different values, so that this part of his relativism is still fully endorsed. As we know, Radbruch applied his relativism to the idea of law at two points: to the determination of the element of *Zweckmäßigkeit* and to the ranking of the three components of the idea of law. The first part remains unchanged, but what about the second, the relativistic account of the relations between the components? This is the main point of change in Radbruch's views. Unlike his ideas in the *Rechtsphilosophie,* in which he was unwilling to prescribe any preconceived ordering, but let it depend on political world views (1932, 306), he now explicitly ordered them. *Zweckmäßigkeit* should never dominate and becomes the least important, *Gerechtigkeit* should reign supreme, and *Rechtssicherheit*, being interpreted as a part of *Gerechtigkeit*, follows closely. This move is not completely surprising because Radbruch had indicated in 1932 that all three elements are determinative of law (303), so that a complete disregard of justice and legal security, to which the Nazi focus on expediency had led, made a renewed focus on all three elements necessary. This can be interpreted as a reminder not to forget that all three elements are determinative of the idea of law, or as the claim that a rearrangement was now necessary in order to restore the balance within the idea of law. Paulson points out that the latter interpretation that Radbruch simply shifted the accent to accord with different historical circumstances makes his post-war views as relativistic as his pre-war views: maybe another change of circumstances might lead to a different arrangement of the three elements (1995, 499). Such an interpretation neglects the changes in Radbruch's conception of justice and the central place in his postwar account of the ordering within the idea of law.[38]

This leads to my third question: did Radbruch move from a more formal to a more substantive account of justice? At first sight, it seems that, because of the more rigorous task of justice, Radbruch extends the meaning of justice to a substantive account of what is just. His ideas about the degree of injustice that determines the limits of legal security suggest that he has a substantive view of what constitutes (in)justice: one needs to know what counts as injustice to see when the balance between legal security and justice tips in favour of the latter. And indeed Radbruch appears to think justice is something more than a purely formal notion of equality: in the *Vorschule* he characterizes the conflict between legal security and justice as an inner conflict of justice. Legal security demands the equal application of unjust laws and thereby serves the equality demanded by justice, while at the same time contradicting justice by supporting unjust laws (1948a, 150). In extreme cases the second aspect of justice should prevail, but what that second, substantive, aspect of justice is, remains unclear. On the other hand, in the *Vorschule* Radbruch still describes

[38] Seidel sees a definite ordering of the elements of the idea of law as conflicting with Radbruch's doctrine of the antinomies between the elements, because he sees that doctrine as logically entailing that the three elements have equal weight (1999, 189). Such an interpretation is unduly restrictive; I will present my own interpretation of Radbruch's antinomies in the next chapter (4.4).

justice as a purely formal notion, a notion unable to indicate who is equal or how to treat people equally (1948a, 143). The clearest indication that Radbruch did move towards a more substantive conception of justice, is found in the first short post-war paper, 'Fünf Minuten Rechtsphilosophie'. Here he interprets justice as moral equality, as applying the same measure to all and guaranteeing human rights to all (1945, 78-79). He no longer leaves the criterion of equality to be completely determined by *Zweckmäßigkeit*, but gives justice a substantive core. Human rights are not interpreted completely ahistorically, however: Radbruch refers to a growing consensus on human rights with a historical basis (1945, 79).[39] Therefore, it seems to me that Radbruch definitely extended the meaning of justice, but did not himself consider it a major break with his previous ideas.

It is time to assess the results of this discussion of Radbruch's turn. As far as is relevant in the context of this study, Radbruch's position does not change drastically. His views on the nature of values do not seem to have changed: his account of the idea of law and of its elements remains similar. Likewise, values have the same central, constitutive role in his theory. The major change is in his relativism: this admits of more side-constraints, but is not thrown overboard in his description of the value of *Zweckmäßigkeit*, nor as a general philosophical principle. His views on justice seem to have moved a little in the direction of a substantive role of justice, but since Radbruch still describes his conception of justice in formal terms in connection to the concept of law, it seems unwarranted to interpret this as a serious shift in position. In the next chapter I will look more closely at Radbruch's conception of values and I will come back to the issues that have arisen here, especially to the question of relativism and the absolute nature of justice.

[39] See Dreier & Paulson 1999, 245. Several authors (e.g. Tjong 1967, 88; Seidel 1999, 195-196) point out that Radbruch does not develop his post-war views systematically: it is unclear what the exact consequences of a more substantive conception of justice are for his other ideas.

# CHAPTER 4

# RADBRUCH ON IDEALS

## 1. INTRODUCTION

After discussing the main components of Radbruch's philosophy of law, it is time for a specific consideration of his view on ideals. In the last chapter, some of the issues to be raised here were already hinted at. Radbruch's methodological dualism commits him to a specific view of values. His view on the relation between value and reality is influenced by the idea of value-related realities and the *Natur der Sache*. The change in his post-war view led to consideration of the relation between the three elements of the Rechtsidee and Radbruch's conception of justice. But before I turn to examination of these issues, let me give a short overview of Radbruch's view on ideals.

Radbruch's theory of values[1] starts from the idea that fact and value should be sharply distinguished, that is, from the premise of methodological dualism. Values are not part of the factual reality we perceive, but go beyond that reality: they are *überwirklich* (1923/24, 453). What they are cannot simply be derived from factual situations; their nature is of another kind than that of facts. About values we do not have scientific knowledge, which means that their validity is not susceptible of proof. Values are ultimately a matter of choice depending on someone's world view. Therefore, Radbruch characterizes his position on the nature of values as relativistic. The background of these ideas is formed by the theory that the world as it confronts us appears as a chaotic whole in which we perceive things as possessing or lacking value. In our immediate experience we do not realize that things do not possess value but that it is our own consciousness which assigns value to things (1932, 221). But because we are thinking creatures that become aware that our own self is something distinct from this given world, we come to recognize that it is our own mind that assigns value. It is important to recognize that for Radbruch value is not part of the way things are. Instead, valuing is seen as a uniquely human feature, as something we use to make, and to make sense of, our world.

1 The concept of values, not of ideals, is the basic concept for Radbruch. Whether a meaningful distinction between the two can be made, will be considered later in this chapter.

In Radbruch's philosophy values have a dual role: they are constitutive of realities and at the same time they are the standards with which we evaluate those realities.[2] However, not all of reality is formed with the help of values. The physical world as such, which is the subject of the natural sciences, has nothing to do with values. The realities that are created with values as their constitutive principles are cultural realities, which together form the whole of human activities. Cultural realities are value-related (*wertbezogen*): they aim at realizing some human good and they should be understood as meaning to serve the values which are at their basis. Therefore, those values are also the evaluative standards for the given reality: they are the standards by which we assess the success of a given reality at what it tries to do.

The domain to which Radbruch primarily applies these ideas is, of course, the law. The part of reality that we see as law is set apart by being related to the value of justice. This means that our concept of what law is, is based on the value of justice and that we use justice as a standard of assessment for law. Radbruch refines this account of law as a cultural reality by distinguishing three values that together form the idea to which law is related: expediency and legal security in addition to justice. Here, Radbruch's value relativism plays an important role: the relation between the different values of which the idea of law consists differs according to world views.

A number of conceptual questions present themselves when we connect this account of Radbruch's theory of values with the general questions of this study. First of all, Radbruch uses the terms 'value' and 'idea'. Does he also distinguish between values and ideals, or are these basically the same in his theory? I have discussed the idea of law and its constituting values and we have come upon the concept of idea and the concept of value in other contexts. How do these two concepts relate? Radbruch makes a fairly casual use of the terms 'idea' and 'value', sometimes appearing to distinguish between them, sometimes using them as synonyms. For the time being I will follow him in this, but at the end of this chapter I will attempt to construct a more precise distinction between these terms, on the basis of the substantive issues that I will discuss first.

What are the issues we need to get clear to be able to use Radbruch's ideas for the construction of a theory of ideals in jurisprudence? First of all, we need to know what values are, that is, what ontological status of values follows from Radbruch's philosophy. More precisely, we need to examine the meaning and consequences of his dualistic and relativistic method. This will be the subject

2 In German: "das konstitutive Prinzip und zugleich der Wertmaßstab" (1932, 227).

of section 4.2. Secondly, the relationship between values and reality needs to be considered. Two parts of his theory, *Stoffbestimmtheit der Idee* and the idea of *Wertbezogenheit*, are used by Radbruch to establish links between the realms of fact and value, but it is still unclear how strong those links are and what this entails for the nature of values. Section 4.3 will be devoted to these issues. Thirdly, there is the question how values are interrelated. To that end, in section 4.4 I will examine, in detail, Radbruch's views on the relationship between the different elements of the idea of law. The fourth substantial question, which will be treated in section 4.5, is what role values perform in Radbruch's theory of law. The two main issues to be dealt with are the way values operate in enhancing or reducing the autonomy of the law, and whether there are values which can be regarded as specifically legal. Section 4.6 will provide the promised reconstruction of the concepts of ideal, value and idea. Finally, I will evaluate Radbruch's theory in the light of the leading questions of this study and consider which aspects of it are promising or problematic for the development of a jurisprudential concept of ideals.

## 2. THE NATURE OF VALUES

In order to find out what Radbruch's views are on the nature of values, it is best to return to his methodological dualism. From the antithesis of fact and value we may not get a precise idea of what values are, but we can at least gather information about the differences between values and facts. As we saw, the basic idea of dualism is that statements concerning the 'ought' cannot be derived from statements concerning the 'is'. This entails that ought or value statements can only be justified by a deduction from higher value statements. This in turn leads to the conclusion that there are some axiomatic ultimate values, the end or starting point of any justification of a value judgment (1932, 233). These ultimate values Radbruch regards as absolute (256). This means, first of all, that they cannot be derived from any other value, i.e. that they function as axioms. Secondly, Radbruch takes it to mean that they have absolute validity (*absolute Geltung*) (279). In neo-Kantian philosophy, validity is contrasted with existence (Rickert 1926, 21; Lask 1905, 280). While factual reality exists, values transcend concrete existence: values cannot be said to exist, to be, but only to be valid, to have *Geltung*. Thus, dualism entails that values have a mode of "being" that transcends reality, and this mode is described as validity. The absolute validity of ultimate values should be read as indicating an independent source of validity: ultimate values are not valid by virtue of a relationship to another value, but in their own right.

An essential difference between facts and values is that we can know the first category (*Erkenntnis*), but can only avow our values (*Bekenntnis*) (1932, 233). Complete knowledge — implicitly understood by Radbruch as scientific knowledge — is only possible regarding the realm of fact, the realm of values is ultimately a matter of choice and allegiance. The denial that values can be known, which Radbruch sees as following from the dichotomy of fact and value, is the basis of Radbruch's value relativism. Because values cannot be known, the only way to ground value judgments is by retracing them to the fundamental values of the world view in which they are embedded. Which ultimate values are part of that world view, or which are the most important components of it, can only be chosen by the person who holds it. We know that Radbruch saw as the task of a relativistic philosophy to clarify and systematize world views. He believed many things can be said about the coherence of beliefs and about their consequences and presuppositions. Moreover, he thought that there are only so many distinct and coherent views possible, which philosophy can spell out. This optimism about the achievements of philosophy indicates that Radbruch wants to limit his relativism to core values. There is no way of correcting someone's belief that the community is more important than the individual, because that is something which is susceptible to choice only. It is possible, however, to show that one cannot hold the community and the individual both to be the ultimate locus of value without contradicting oneself; or to show that certain more specific values, for example intrinsic value of the family, only fit with the view based on community value. However, the core values, which can only be chosen, do form the ultimate basis of the different world views. As a consequence, Radbruch's relativism has far-reaching effects: the basis of the different world views, to which all value judgments can be retraced, is insusceptible to knowledge, proof or argument. Because all opinions concerning values depend on such a world view, any examination of the role of values in phenomena that are value-related — such as law — will need to look at those values in relation to the world views of which they are part. Radbruch illustrates this in his discussions of specific legal subjects in the second part of the *Rechtsphilosophie*. For instance, in the chapter on the legal conception of the person, Radbruch traces different theories of the legal person back to their origins in the three basic philosophical positions he distinguishes (1932, 366).

Thus, there are two important currents in Radbruch's value theory: the recognition of absolute, ultimate values and the relativistic choice of those values as the basis of a value system. What complicates matters, is that Radbruch uses two catalogues of highest values: the four absolute values of the good, the true, the beautiful, and the just, and the three possible understandings of the good: individual, collective, and work values (1932, 256; 279). The values of truth, beauty, goodness and justice, the elements out of which world views are built, are not in need of further justification: they are independent and self-evident (*selbständig und selbstverständlich*) (1924, 461). Additionally, Radbruch holds that there are only three categories of objects capable of being valued: human individuals, human collectivities, and the products of human work. The individualistic view sees the individual good as the ultimate object of value; the transindividualistic view sees the collective good as ultimate object, for instance the nation or the community; the transpersonal view sees cultural works, for instance works of art, as the ultimate object of value. The reason why Radbruch limits the range of value systems to these three, is that he believes that all things valuable must be connected to human beings:

> In the whole world of experience, there are only three kinds of subjects susceptible of absolute worth: individual human personalities, human collective personalities, and human works. According to these substrata we may distinguish three kinds of values: individual values, collective values, and work values (1932, 279).[3]

For Radbruch it is evident that only what is human, understood in a broad sense, can have value of itself. At its basis his philosophy is thoroughly humanistic.[4] These two sets of highest values are related, but it is not immediately clear in what way.

In the *Grundzüge der Rechtsphilosophie* Radbruch consistently adhered to the traditional three ultimate values, goodness, truth, and beauty, which he related to a specific part of reality (1914, 57). Truth and beauty attach to human works, goodness to human personalities. Justice is not an ultimate value, but a derivative value which supports the ultimate values. Radbruch uses Lask's theory of the differentiation of meaning (*Bedeutungsdifferen-*

3 Translation Wilk 1950, 91-92. In German: "Es gibt im ganzen Bereich der Erfahrungswelt nur drei Arten von Gegenständen, die absoluter Werthaftigkeit fähig sind: menschliche Einzelpersönlichkeiten, menschliche Gesamtpersönlichkeiten, menschliche Werke. Wir können nach Maßgabe dieser ihrer Substrate drei Arten von Werten unterscheiden: Individualwerte, Kollektivwerte und Werkwerte."

4 It is humanistic in the sense that human beings are at the center of his philosophy (see also Baratta 1959, 506, who emphasizes Radbruch's humanism as the unifying theme in his philosophy). This anthropocentrism may seem less adequate in our present age, now that we have come to recognize that nature and animals are also worthy of concern.

*zierung*): values are classified according to the subject to which they apply ('auf die sie hingelten'). Justice applies to the relations between persons, but such relations cannot be the subject of absolute value.

In the *Rechtsphilosophie*, Radbruch makes two important changes. He distinguishes between the individual and the collective as human personalities, and accordingly between the individual good and the collective good as highest values. Secondly, he includes justice among the ultimate values. Both can be explained in line with the idea of differentiation of meaning: Radbruch widens the scope of the reality that can be subject of absolute value to include communal life and relations between people. The puzzle that now comes up is how these are related, and especially how justice fits in the system of highest values. Radbruch still adheres to the old scheme that only human personalities (now as two types) and human works can be subject of ultimate value: this leads to the conclusion that justice is not an ultimate value. On the other hand, Radbruch includes justice among the ultimate values of beauty, truth, and goodness. How to resolve this puzzle? The answer can be found in Radbruch's formal conception of justice. He believes that this cannot determine the content of law and he then appeals to a different set of values, entering the idea of law via the value of *Zweckmäßigkeit*. This element of the *Rechtsidee* can be understood as the gateway through which other values enter. Only at this point does Radbruch introduce his typology of value systems based on the highest values of individual good, collective good, and work values (beauty and truth). In the context of legal philosophy, justice has a different function (as the basic constitutive value of the concept of law) and does not appear in political value systems.

I now want to turn to the other important role of ultimate values, as the points of orientation for different cultural realities. The relationship between value and reality will be discussed in the next section; here I want to draw attention to the fact that Radbruch uses truth, beauty, goodness and justice as the necessary standards for specific cultural realities. Again, it is seen as self-evident which specific value a value-related reality means to serve.[5] When Radbruch tells us that law is a value-related reality and asks to which value law is related, it needs no argument that its value must be justice (1932, 255). Thus, the four ultimate values are in two respects necessary: they are part of the ultimate basis of people's value systems, and they are the necessary points of orientation for cultural realities.

We can now distinguish two, apparently opposed, characteristics of

[5] This can be explained by Radbruch's reliance on Lask's theory of the differentiation of meaning: each value is specified according to the reality which it guides.

Radbruch's value philosophy: on the one hand, relativism of ultimate values, on the other, a number of necessary and self-evident values. Radbruch believes that world views are ultimately a matter of personal choice, but he also defends that there is a specific, limited set of views and of absolute ultimate values to choose from. Moreover, these absolute values serve as constitutive values of cultural realities. If one denies, as Radbruch does, that knowledge about ultimate values is possible, how does one know that his proposed typology of ultimate values is the right one? How does one establish which value belongs with a certain reality? We need to consider if and how these two aspects of his value theory can be reconciled.

The first thing that needs to be clarified is the exact character of Radbruch's relativism. The term relativism can stand for a number of positions regarding the nature of values.[6] Radbruch's value relativism should not be confused with a form of subjectivism, i.e. the idea that values are simply a matter of subjective preference. According to Radbruch, the opinions people have about values can be traced to the objective ideas they express. He believes in a true meaning of value statements which can be uncovered by a philosophical investigation. Such an investigation finds its limit when it has uncovered the specific constellation of values that form the world view of which the value judgment under consideration is part. This must, of course, be one of the three world views he has described. Unlike many contemporary versions of relativism,[7] Radbruch does not see values primarily as relative to the culture to which people belong. For him, different value systems are first of all represented by different political parties. In his legal philosophy that is what matters, because different political views enter the domain of law by way of the value of *Zweckmäßigkeit*.[8] Where Radbruch differs from many present-day relativists like Rorty is in limiting his relativism to values. While relativism now often includes scepticism about all claims of true knowledge, Radbruch thinks only knowledge of values is impossible to achieve. Additionally, Radbruch limits his relativism in two further ways: first of all, it only concerns ultimate values and secondly, it concerns them only in their

6 See section 1.2 and 2.2.

7 For example: the view of Richard Rorty. See his chapter 'From Epistemology to Hermeneutics', in: Rorty 1980, p. 315-356.

8 One could say that Radbruch focuses on the different value systems within a culture, although he himself does not mention cultures in this sense. However, his philosophy can easily accommodate the view that values differ over cultures. His typology of individual, collective and work values could also be applied to different cultures. The argument that no decisive evidence can be given in favour of one set of values also holds in relation to whole cultures.

role as the core of world views, not when they are constitutive of cultural realities. It is doubtful, however, whether relativism can be contained in this way.

The appeal of a limited relativism depends on the plausibility of the combination with the non-relative elements of the theory, and on the persuasiveness of that part. In Radbruch's case this is the combination of a relative theory of the good with other absolute values, most importantly justice, which perform the important role of constituting parts of reality. The arguments he gives for the absolute values are tenuous: absolute values are self-evident, they must necessarily be accepted. I think the absence of elaborate arguments can be explained from Radbruch's philosophical method. Radbruch appeals to a neo-Kantian tradition of regarding values as being beyond reality and having validity instead of existence. His arguments for these transcendent values are transcendental, that is, they concern the preconditions of our knowledge and cultural reality. Thus, the argument for the self-evidence follows a Kantian scheme: as a human being, one can only understand the point of law by seeing it as oriented towards justice. Such an argument depends on the possibility of every rational being reproducing the argument and finding it inescapable, because it is the only way that the reality of law makes sense. However, the argument that law can only be understood as oriented towards justice is not as self-evidently clear as Radbruch would have us believe. Only in a philosophical system that grounds the idea of law in transcendent values (a neo-Kantian system) does justice as the constitutive value of law appear inevitable. In a philosophy denying this type of *Wertbezogenheit*, law can as easily be understood as an instrument of power or of efficient co-ordination. Seeing law as necessarily oriented towards justice depends on the presupposition that such values are transcendent absolutes.

Moreover, it is not clear why Radbruch does not extend his relativism to justice. If the absolute value of the good can be interpreted differently according to the object that is deemed most important, why not extend this line of argument to interpretations of the absolute value of justice? Radbruch emphasizes that our relation to values is one of *Bekenntnis*, not of *Erkenntnis*, but he does not apply this insight to justice: the value towards which law is oriented can be no other than justice, and justice can be interpreted only as equality. However, this is exactly what is contested in theories of justice. Such theories question what the core meaning of justice is — equality or fairness? — and whether justice should be seen as the supreme value of law or politics. Because opinion is divided over such issues, it would seem to be in line with Radbruch's relativism to extend it to conceptions of justice as well. That would mean that his relativism would have a broader scope than he is willing to award it. In the light of Radbruch's methodological starting points, that would yield a more coherent theory of values. The problems of such a theory arise in the account of the relations between values and reality, to which I now turn.

## 3. VALUES AND REALITY

In the last section the distinct character of values was the focus of discussion, and for a proper understanding of that character we needed to get a firm grip on Radbruch's dualism. However, as we already noted in the discussion of *Stoffbestimmtheit* in the last chapter, there are parts of Radbruch's theory that go a long way towards bridging the gap between 'is' and 'ought'. Apart from the *Stoffbestimmtheit der Idee* and the related doctrine of *Natur der Sache*, one can also regard the idea of cultural realities and the accompanying value-relating perspective[9] in that light. So this section concerns the relationships between the realm of fact and the realm of value. More specifically, the question to be answered here is whether 'values *and* reality' should be read as a primarily disjunctive relation — values on one side, reality on the other — or as a basic connection — values *in* reality. To that end, I will discuss the two main leads in Radbruch's work for an exploration of this question: first, the doctrines of the *Stoffbestimmtheit der Idee* and *Natur der Sache,* and second, the idea of cultural realities with the related value-relating perspective.

### *The Relationship between Idea and Matter*

In the last chapter I left unanswered the question whether the doctrine of the *Stoffbestimmtheit der Idee* leaves the dichotomy of fact and value intact as Radbruch claims. If ideas or values are truly determined in part by the realities with which they are connected, the assertion that there is an unbridgeable gap between the two becomes untenable. The answer to this question is of great importance in the context of this study, because the success of such bridging would make a combination of transcendence and immanence possible: ideals could then transcend reality and yet, at the same time, be grounded in reality. From his dualistic perspective, in which anything belongs to either the realm of being or the realm of value, Radbruch denies that values can both transcend and be based in reality. However, the idea of *Stoffbestimmtheit* does seem to

[9] In German: 'das wertbeziehende Verhalten' (1932, 95).

provide a real grounding of values. Radbruch devotes an early article to the issue of Stoffbestimmtheit, 'Rechtsidee und Rechtsstoff. Eine Skizze', which provides a helpful account of the connections between idea and matter (1923/24).

Radbruch argues that, although the idea can logically be seen as the form, which shapes matter, we can only think the idea in relation to its matter. The distinction between idea and matter can only be achieved by abstracting the idea from the reality in which it works (1923/24, 454). Thus, Radbruch adheres to the distinction between the causal influence of reality and the logical priority of the idea, but by making clear that logical relations can only be conceived by departing from the given interrelatedness of idea and matter, he seems to soften the distinction between the causal and the logical.

Radbruch makes his doctrine of *Stoffbestimmtheit* more concrete by examining the interaction between legal idea and legal matter. Here we see that the influence of ideas remains the key feature of his conception of legal matter. In his discussion of the *Natur der Sache* Radbruch tells us that one of the meanings of this doctrine is that, when making new rules, the legislator has to reckon with existing natural, social and legal facts. These facts, the matter to which the idea of law is applied, limit what can be achieved with new rules based on the idea of law. The thing to notice here is that Radbruch conceives of facts, or reality in a broad way: not only natural facts, but including social and legal facts. What is peculiar about the latter is that they have already gone through a process of meaning being attached to them. Social facts are not simple, raw data; such facts already mean things to us because we look at them through a conceptual framework. The reality to which the idea of law is applied has been preformed with the help of other concepts and ideas (1923/24, 459).

I believe it is this meaning (*Sinn*) which reality already possesses which forms the bridge between matter and idea. By discovering the meaning of some fact we separate the conceptual and ideal side of a phenomenon from its raw factuality. The meaning of facts derives from their being formed with the help of ideas and concepts. So clarifying a fact's meaning is essentially the same as discovering the ideas and concepts that had a part in the creation of that particular fact. This creates the possibility of connecting it to other ideas, in our case, the idea of law. The relation between legal idea and legal matter can be reinterpreted as the relation between the ideas determining the legal matter and the idea of law. The legal method of the *Natur der Sache* focuses on the meaning of the legal matter and reconstructs the political and social ideas that shape it and tries to reconcile these with the idea of law (see 1948b,

235). The concept of *Sinn* can therefore be used as the bridge between matter and idea, because it allows us to uncover the ideas present in the matter. The connection between legal idea and legal matter is mediated by other ideas. However, the concept of *Sinn* is not unproblematic in itself. How do we determine the meaning of a factual situation? How should we conceive of that meaning; is it part of reality or not? For answers we need to consider the nature of the realities Radbruch is interested in, the realities which have meaning, that is, cultural realities.

*Cultural Realities as Value-Related*

We already touched upon the subject of cultural realities in the last chapter when the study of law was characterized as a cultural science. In Radbruch's system, cultural sciences are those concerned with the kind of reality which means to realize some value (1932, 225). Cultural realities always involve human activities: because human beings are the ones who assign value, only human enterprises can form cultural realities. The concept of a cultural reality is broad: every human activity is guided by ideas or values and thus comes under the category of cultural reality (227). Everything people do is done according to some idea, however vague, of what the action undertaken should be like or result in. The important point about cultural realities is that they are only *oriented* towards values, a relationship which should be understood as rather loose. One of Radbruch's examples, the practice of science, illustrates this best. Science can be characterized as the search for truth, but to merit the name of science, research in no way needs to succeed in this quest. A completely erroneous enquiry still deserves to be called scientific as long as truth is the value to which it aspires. We need to be able to understand the enquiry as aiming to get closer to the truth.

Here we have reached the core of the idea of cultural realities: their meaning (*Sinn*) is to realize values. Cultural realities are always meaningful and their meaning consists in being value-related. Therefore, the most important way to discover the meaning of a factual phenomenon is to find out which value it is oriented towards and in what way. In some cases, for instance science which is related to truth, there is one value which is the point of orientation in a fairly straightforward manner. But more often — and this might even prove to be the case in a seemingly simple case like science — there are more values which guide the reality in question in a complex way. The prime example here, of course, is law and its threefold idea. The way in which the different guiding values of the law interact will be the subject of the next section. Here I want to pursue the question how to determine which values a given reality means to serve, because I believe this is a problematic aspect of Radbruch's theory.

Radbruch takes for granted that there are obvious links between certain realities and corresponding values. The idea to which law is oriented can only be the value of justice (1932, 256), and art must be striving for beauty (222). Radbruch sees the relation between such a reality and a value as a necessary connection. Art can only be understood as meaning to realize the value of beauty. But what about art that is meant as an expression of the identity of the artist, or art which only means to convey a conceptual point? In these cases, beauty does not seem to be at issue, while we would still want to call the object a work of art. The problem is that Radbruch takes orientation towards a specific value to be the defining criterion without arguing why we should accept such a necessary connection between this value and this domain of reality. The only argument for a necessary connection he gives is the general argument that we need ideas or values to generate concepts with which we can order the given reality around us. He does not provide an argument why we should accept justice as the guiding value of the law or beauty as that of art. The example of art illustrates the problem well: over the course of the twentieth century we have seen a move away from the value of beauty towards other values, e.g. the value of authenticity, the work of art as an expression of the individuality of the artist, and of articulation, the work of art as the vehicle of ideas. It is doubtful whether beauty can still be regarded as the unifying value towards which art is oriented, and orientation towards beauty is certainly not the defining characteristic of art. It can still be defended that art is necessarily oriented towards values — this could even be the basis of an argument about the controversies over what art is — but it is not necessarily oriented to one specific value. If one extends this argument about beauty to other domains, it leads to a relativized conception of values. The problem that then remains is how one can account for shared practices and common conceptions of social reality, if the values on which they are based are manifold. Making the understanding of reality dependent on specific values is problematic when these values are subject to radical reinterpretations or can be exchanged for other values.

Now we can also see in what way the concept of *Sinn* is problematic: what does the meaning of a cultural reality signify other than orientation towards the value with which it is constructed? And how do we determine that meaning if it is unclear towards which value a cultural reality is oriented? Radbruch relies on the possibility of determining the objective meaning of a cultural reality (1932, 344) to account for the meeting of value and matter in social and legal facts. But if the value on which that meaning is based is not univocal, the meaning of social and legal facts becomes indeterminate and will not be indisputable and objective. The heavy duty laid on value and idea as determining meaning and thereby reality creates tension in the account of cultural reality, once Radbruch's concept of value is shown to be questionable.

## 4. THE INTERACTION OF VALUES

In this section I would like to discuss the way values are related to each other. Values cannot be regarded as isolated entities: realizing one value may obstruct realization of other values, or attention for one value may assist or demand the realization of another. How these relations should be conceived of, and whether values really can and do interact, needs to be investigated. I believe Radbruch's theory can provide valuable insights into these problems, particularly his theory of the idea of law.

Here we should recall some of the things Radbruch says about the role and the structure of the idea of law. Central to Radbruch's views on the idea of law is that it is both constitutive principle and standard of evaluation (1932, 227). The first role points out the way the idea of law is the basis for the concept of law, the second expresses that we use it to evaluate the legal reality. At times it may seem a little artificial to separate two roles, because the evaluative and the constitutive function reinforce each other to a large extent. It is, however, important to separate the way values are the basis for evaluation of reality from the way values determine our perception and constitution of reality. The reason for stressing this double role of the idea of law is that I believe Radbruch uses it as the basis for two arguments about the internal structure of the idea of law. The first argument is that the three values are necessary to make the idea of law work as a constitutive principle; the second argument is that the three values complement each other as evaluative standards.

In short, the argument about the elements of the idea of law was as follows. The idea of law consists of three values — *Gerechtigkeit, Zweckmäßigkeit, Rechtssicherheit* — of which we already saw that they require each other. Justice as a formal standard of equality needs supplementation by *Zweckmäßigkeit* because it cannot by itself determine the content of law. *Zweckmäßigkeit* in its turn cannot give a final determination of what is to count as law because the purposes law can serve are many. The value of legal security is therefore needed as the basis for a decision mechanism, as a basis for the validity of legal norms. Together these three values form the idea of law as it should be; they determine the character of the legal system.

As constitutive principle, the idea of law needs its three elements because each on its own is inconclusive about the nature of law. Although justice suffices to generate the concept of law,[10] it does not give us a complete idea of what law is about. Radbruch only gives reasons why justice cannot stand on its own, but one can construct arguments why *Zweckmäßigkeit* and legal security cannot either. *Zweckmäßigkeit*, because it derives from the value of the good, does not provide a clear boundary between law and other realities. Legal security suffers from a similar shortcoming as justice: it is too formal to give law true content, because it only demands positivity. For instance, the principle that prohibits the retroactive effect of rules does not say anything specific about the content of those rules. A legal system can be identified as such, when it observes formal equality, has a purpose and claims to give determinative decisions.

As standard of evaluation, the three elements are necessary because only together do they give a complete idea of what law should aspire to. Each value on its own is one-sided and can never give good direction. If a legal system were oriented towards only one of these values instead of towards the idea of law as a whole, it would become a one-dimensional system and a caricature of law (1948a, 147). This is so because each value exerts a pull in a different direction. *Gerechtigkeit* creates a tendency towards general rules that abstract from concrete inequalities between people, while *Zweckmäßigkeit*, representing the idea of the good, demands a solution that is tailored to the specific needs of the situation (1932, 304). For instance, equal application of environmental rules to all factories may clash with the concrete needs of one specific community with such a factory. Legal security requires that law is practical, easily applicable and understandable, with clear rules and sharp boundaries, which can come into conflict with the demand for proportionality made by justice and the demand for individuality made by *Zweckmäßigkeit* (304).

The three values are thus precariously balanced: each tends to pull the idea of law in one direction but is checked by the countervailing forces of the other two. To know what the idea of law demands is not easy, since it requires the assessment of opposing ideals. In combination with the notion of *Stoffbestimmtheit*, this idea of conflicting values generates a dynamic conception of the idea of law. In every new situation we need to rediscover the exact meaning of the three values and it may well be that the balance among

10 This theme will be treated more extensively in the next section.

the three values shifts a little because of this reconsideration in the light of the meaning of new facts. Radbruch rightly points out that the attempt to achieve a balance between the different values can never have a completely satisfactory result. The attempted realization of one value conflicts with the realization of another: the gain in one direction will therefore entail losses in regard to other values. Radbruch believes these conflicts between the different components of the idea of law to be irresolvable (1932, 307). This has both negative and positive effects: the negative consequence is that full realization of values is impossible, the positive effect is that undesirable overconcentration can be avoided as long as one remains aware of these conflicts.

Radbruch constructs the idea of law on the basis of an a priori argument of the different components requiring each other. The thesis that the idea of law as the reigning evaluative standard of law consists of conflicting values is appealing. It can account for conflicting interpretations of what law should be in two ways: because of a different assessment of what the governing values of law are, and because of a different interpretation of the relations between governing values. Again, the difficulty of Radbruch's conception lies with the argumentation for the components making up the idea of law: on the one hand, a relation of necessity, but on the other, subject to relativistic interpretation. Fortunately, this does not seem to be the only way to argue that the governing values of law are a set of related but conflicting values. There is also the possibility of an inductive argument: pointing out that a legal system in fact is committed to a conflicting set of values and using this empirical knowledge to argue that these values make up the governing ideal of law. That would mean giving up Radbruch's strict adherence to logically acceptable deductive arguments, and moving in the direction of a more immanent account of ideals. I will attempt to incorporate Radbruch's ideas of the interaction of values in such an account in Chapter 7.

## 5. THE ROLE OF VALUES IN LAW

In previous sections we more than once came across the dual role of values in Radbruch's philosophy. We examined Radbruch's general idea of the connection between values and reality and uncovered the structure of ideas and cultural realities. Now, since the ultimate object of this study is to construct a concept of ideals relevant in the context of law, it is time to focus more specifically on the role values have in the domain of law. The guiding question will be what Radbruch sees as the possibilities and limits of a value-oriented approach when law is the object of study. Especially I want to examine what one can learn from Radbruch about the role of values in determining the character of the law as an autonomous system.

*Justice as Constitutive of Legal Reality*

By describing law as a cultural reality, Radbruch draws attention to the value-laden character of law. Law, as part of the cultural world, is formed by the value it purports to serve. The idea of law as a cultural reality is a straightforward application of Radbruch's *Methodentrialismus*, which conceives of man-related reality as partaking of the realm of value. All human activities are done with leading ideas or values in mind, which is therefore also true of law. None of this is surprising in the light of what we have seen of Radbruch's theory, but it does yield strong conclusions about the significance for law of values in general, and, more importantly, of the specific values law serves. To put it crudely, the existence of law depends on values, and the nature of law is derived from the nature of justice. It is the idea of law, not the value of justice alone, that determines the reality of law, but of that idea justice is the part that gives law its specific character (1932, 259). The concept of law, which enables us to separate the legal from the non-legal, is based on the value of justice. As Radbruch puts it himself: "Our discussions have shown that justice is the specific idea of law, sufficient to unfold the concept of law, but that it does not exhaust the idea of law"[11] (1932, 278). The concept of law is our tool to recognize and to make law. Because it is based on justice, understood as formal equality (treating like cases alike), law is characterized as the totality of general norms for social life (1948a, 151). General norms, because the idea of justice as equality requires that rules are applicable to all alike; norms for social life, because the idea of justice concerns the relationships between people. Radbruch thus uses values as the very basis of legal reality. Of the values that determine the law, justice has a special place because it provides the characteristics that distinguish law from the other parts of value-related reality.

I believe that this use of justice as the specific constitutive value of law commits Radbruch to a conception of justice that is at times at odds with the way he uses justice as a value standard. In its constitutive role, justice

[11] Translation Wilk (1950, 90). In German: "Aus unsern Betrachtungen ergab sich, daß Gerechtigkeit zwar die spezifische Rechtsidee ist, genügend, um aus ihr den Begriff des Rechts zu entwickeln, daß die Idee des Rechts sich aber in der Gerechtigkeit nicht erschöpft."

determines the form of law. In this capacity, justice needs to be formal, because it serves to distinguish law from other parts of reality and is not meant as a standard of the quality of law. Radbruch wishes to avoid the natural law idea that the quality of a legal norm, assessed by the standard of justice, decides whether the norm is law or not. This is in part realized by seeing law as a reality that only means to serve justice, but does not necessarily serve it in fact. In addition, Radbruch needs room to allow for historical changes in the idea of law, while at the same time providing a necessary criterion to determine what law is. That is why he uses a formal idea of justice as the basis for the concept of law, but brings in relativized elements in the idea of law. If the idea of justice itself were more substantive, the concept of law would be too restrictive. However, the idea of law as a whole determines more precisely what the reality of law is like. One could say that justice is used to draw the lines and the idea of law to complete the picture. That the exact characterization of justice is a crucial element in Radbruch's theory becomes apparent when we once more consider Radbruch's postwar writings.

We saw that Radbruch in his postwar work gives justice a more prominent position.[12] Justice appears as the central element in the idea of law, the one element that can never be set aside completely. The famous formula features justice as the standard by which positive laws are assessed: when the discrepancy between a statute and justice becomes too great, the positive law has to give way to justice, and to be rejected as unjust (1946, 89). Here we see that Radbruch uses justice in a different role than its constitutive one: justice is regarded as the value standard by which existing laws are assessed. Instead of the basis for an a priori concept of law, justice is now a standard applied afterwards to legal norms already established as such. Radbruch combines this test with another that is more in line with the argument that sees justice as constitutive (1946, 89). That supposedly legal norms are not really law if they do not even mean to serve justice, is consistent with the idea of law as a value-related reality. If no link between justice and the norm in question can be discerned, that norm cannot be part of the domain of law. But because justice is no more than formal equality, this criterion is easily satisfied. As long as the norm is general, positive and meant for social life, it can be brought under the concept of law. The question is whether justice as formal equality can also serve as the standard of *richtiges Recht* (right, lawful law). At first sight the answer seems to be that it can. Something counts as law if it satisfies the concept of law: it means to serve the value of justice; and it counts as right law

[12] See the discussion in section 3.4.

if it realizes justice: it succeeds in serving that value.[13] However, it is doubtful whether formal equality suffices to provide an idea of *richtiges Recht*. As Radbruch shows himself in the discussion of the idea of law, justice as formal equality needs supplementation by other values to give a complete idea of law. Justice alone does not generate enough content; it only demands generality and proportionality. It can be used to condemn inequality before the courts or unwarranted exceptions, but it needs more substance to provide a standard with which a legal rule can be fully evaluated. In 'Gesetzliches Unrecht und übergesetzliches Recht' Radbruch emphasizes the tension among the three elements of the idea of law and uses justice as an independent standard of evaluation for positive law. That means he has to choose between using the notion of justice as formal equality, which means having an incomplete standard of lawful law and expanding the notion of justice to incorporate a substantive idea of equality.[14] The article is not conclusive about the choice he makes, but an argument for a more substantive notion of justice can be made on the basis of other post-war papers (see 3.4). Although the idea of justice as formal equality is consistent with Radbruch's theory as a whole, a more substantive idea of justice would strengthen the non-relative elements of his theory. Radbruch's relativism would commit him to an idea of law that depends on political views for its exact content, also when this political view is as abhorrent as that of National Socialism. However, we have seen that an understanding of justice as demanding observance of human rights is part of Radbruch's post-war views (1945, 79). Such a stronger notion of equality could be a standard that transcends the political views of the day. A theory with Kantian inspirations such as Radbruch's could base such a view of equality on Kant's idea of treating people as ends, never as means only.

This lengthy discussion of the idea of justice was meant to show that the two different roles that values have in Radbruch's legal philosophy create tendencies to conceptualize values differently. Justice as constitutive principle works best when it is regarded as formal equality, while justice as standard of evaluation is more powerful when seen as substantive equality. The constitutive role of values, requiring a necessary relation between a specific value and a part of reality, demands an unambiguous conception of justice, best realized by seeing justice as formal; the role of evaluative standard,

[13] In the literature on the use of Radbruch's formula in German court cases, these two distinct parts of the formula have become known as the criterion of renouncement and the criterion of intolerability. See Mertens 1998, p. 275.

[14] Ronald Dworkin's idea of equal concern and respect is an example of what I have in mind here (Dworkin 1978, 180).

requiring a robust criterion, demands a more substantive conception, that is inevitably more controversial.

*The Autonomy of Law*

There is one aspect of the relation between values and law that deserves more detailed attention, which is the way values operate in the connections between law and other parts of cultural reality. We know that Radbruch regards law as a distinctive cultural reality with its own specific characteristics, but we have not yet discussed to what extent and how values function in law's relation to other realities such as politics or the economy. We have just seen that Radbruch's basic idea is that justice shapes the specific nature of law. Being related to justice guarantees law its autonomous character, because justice is a specific value that is the basis of the separation between the legal and the non-legal. But although law is a system with its own unique features, Radbruch sees a number of ways in which it is influenced by other realms of human activity, two of them in connection with legal values: the *Natur der Sache* and the relative elements in the idea of law.

First of all, the *Natur der Sache* establishes relations between law and other parts of life. We saw that law has to reckon with pre-existing social and legal facts: law cannot ignore settled social arrangements (1948a, 140-141). It means that law needs to be sensitive to the way people are accustomed to think and act, and to mould legal norms in keeping with the ways of a society to a large extent. Of course, this does not mean that progressive legal regulation is ruled out. Radbruch simply warns of the impotence of legal rules that are too distant from existing ways of life: there is a fair chance that a rule that aims to overturn established arrangements will accomplish nothing at all (1948a, 141). The conservative tendency of the *Natur der Sache* does not work exclusively as social reluctance to change. It can be equally inhibiting when a legal reform affects ingrained legal habits. It is a resistance to change both within law and society. Similarly, the idea of law is bound by historical circumstances. The idea of what law should be is always dependent on the *Zeitgeist*, on presuppositions that are unchallenged in a certain historical period (1948b, 237).

However, the elements of the idea of law are not all subject to those changing ways of thinking to the same extent. Radbruch conceives of the elements of justice and legal security as necessary. And even if doubts can be cast upon Radbruch's conceptualization of justice, the idea of a close relation between law and justice is appealing. The elegance of Radbruch's idea of law lies in his careful distinction between elements that are open to influences from other domains and elements that protect law from such influences. It is through the value of *Zweckmäßigkeit* that different conceptions of the good enter the idea of law. Radbruch sees this primarily as the political influence on the idea of law, which is of course most important because the lawgiver is a political body. But the same reasoning can be applied to, for instance, views about morals or economics. The ordering of the different elements is relative to political views as well, so that Radbruch's theory can both accommodate changes in the historical climate which influence the idea of law and competing views which defend different versions of the idea of law. Although the thought that justice and legal security are more intimately connected to law than these political values is appealing, his arguments for justice as equality as the necessary value element are inadequate. The statement that the value of law can be no other than justice (1932, 256) does not suffice for a convincing argument. The distinctions between different values influencing the law which identify some as specific to law and others as external to it are useful, but the neo-Kantian account of the nature of those values is not satisfactory.

## 6. THE CONCEPT OF IDEALS

It is time to attempt an answer to the conceptual questions I have put off until now, and to assess Radbruch's relevance for the development of a jurisprudential concept of ideals. One of the leading questions in conducting my research into the concept of ideals has been how to view the relation between ideal and value. If, as was my starting point, ideal and value are related concepts, in what way exactly are they related? Are these two concepts identical, and if they are not, what are the differences between them? What does Radbruch have to say on these issues?

For Radbruch, the basic concept is that of value (*Wert*). That is the concept he uses as one of the two opposed poles set up by his dualistic principle: value against reality. His main concern is to explain the differences between the two realms which the concepts of value and of reality designate, not to distinguish among different concepts within these realms. In the first instance then, value, idea, ideal, and norm are all used to refer to the sphere that transcends reality, or fact, or being. On the dualistic model, all these terms refer to those things that should be spoken of in terms of validity instead of existence. The terms ideal and value are not used in any distinct sense, both appear as indicators of the same realm, as opposites of nature (*Natur*) and reality (*Wirklichkeit*) respectively (1932, 226). If at all, Radbruch appears to distinguish between different terms only in order to draw attention to the different aspects of the realm of value which differentiate it from the realm of fact.

This is most apparent where he uses the term idea[15] in the place of value. Radbruch uses the term idea primarily in relation to concept (*Begriff*), more precisely, concepts are seen as related to ideas. We saw that the concept of law is based on the idea of law. Broadly, ideas designate the conceptual tools of the human mind that are used to recognize and generate things in reality (1932, 227). To use Radbruch's example, tables are made with a certain idea in mind that comprises the purpose for building a table. In using the term idea, Radbruch stresses that our conceptual apparatus is mind- or thought-related and the way in which this forms our reality. Value, on the other hand, is the term that emphasizes the normative, or to put it slightly redundantly, the evaluative, character of this sphere: it provides us with standards of evaluation. Now these characteristics, highlighted by the term idea and the term value respectively, do not seem to reflect a difference in subject matter: so far, the two terms are merely means of viewing the same thing from different angles.

However, from his discussion of the idea of law we can gather a more significant difference between idea and value. In this context, Radbruch distinguishes between the idea that is composite and values that are its constitutive elements. Here, the idea is used to refer to the whole to which law is oriented, while values provide the different directions of orientation. Seeing law as serving one idea, although consisting of three elements, makes clear that it is the whole value complex that determines law. It conveys the insight that the three values cannot be isolated because it is their interaction that makes the idea of law. At the same time, conceiving of that idea as comprising three elements allows us to recognize that the idea consists of distinct standards with very different characteristics.

The most significant differentiation within the realm of value is made between values and norms.[16] Although both are expressions of what ought to be (*Sollen*) and are normative standards that transcend the reality to which they

[15] The term idea or *Idee* has a rich philosophical history to which Radbruch alludes occasionally. The example of the table which Radbruch uses is a classic in the explanation of Plato's theory. In German philosophy both Kant and Hegel made use of the term, although attaching rather different meanings to it. In Kantian philosophy, the idea is a necessary concept of reason, while in Hegelian philosophy it is a fully realized or actualized concept (Inwood 1992, 123-24). Radbruch's use differs from both, it is not as stringent as Kant's and it does not connect idea with a realized state as Hegel's.

[16] The most extensive discussion of norms is in Chapter 5 of the Rechtsphilosophie (1932, 269-270). Radbruch distinguishes between the empirical working of a rule (*Rechtssatz*), the rule as imperative, and the normative meaning of a rule, the rule as norm.

are applicable, the category of norms has a closer connection to that reality. Law is the reality in which this is most obvious, because law can be considered as a system of norms. That is what legal science is concerned with. Legal norms are the directly value-related content of the legal order, as opposed to legal facts which are related to that order and thereby are indirectly related to values (1932, 343-344). There are therefore three levels in play: legal values, legal rules (*Rechtssätze*) and legal facts. The intermediate level of rules can be regarded as norms — because their meaning is part of the realm of value, or as imperative — because they have effect as empirical commands. In this way, Radbruch expresses the double character of law as both an empirical reality and a normative order.

In many modern theories the category of norms is divided in the subcategories of rules and principles.[17] In Radbruch's theory there is no direct need to distinguish between rules and principles, because his system conceptualizes all norms as directly related to values. There is a possibility, however, of modifying Radbruch's theory to incorporate a distinction between rules and principles. The point of departure for constructing such a distinction is Radbruch's view of norms as intermediary between values and facts. If we can see norms as directly serving values, we can maybe characterize them as guidelines to action that prescribe how best to realize values. However, it needs to be further examined, first, whether all norms can be seen as serving values, and second, whether there are degrees or different modes of the value-related character of norms. If there are, that may be a key to a distinction between principles and rules. In Radbruch's system (legal) norms are necessarily value-related because being part of the same realm of values they are based on the ultimate values that form the basis of that realm. The second point, whether there are degrees or modes of value-relatedness, is harder to answer, because there are no direct starting-points in Radbruch's theory to work with. Because of his deductivist model, however, there is reason to believe that the degree of distance to ultimate values can vary: more general, less fact-related norms are fewer steps removed from ultimate values. This means that a concept of principles as more general guidelines than rules is compatible with the spirit of Radbruch's philosophy. If we relate Radbruch's ideas to contemporary distinctions between principles and rules, Alexy's characterization of principles as *Optimierungsgebote*[18] seems the closest to

[17] See the discussion in section 1.4.

[18] "Der für die Unterscheidung von Regeln und Prinzipien entscheidende Punkt ist, daß Prinzipien Normen sind, die gebieten, daß etwas in einem relativ auf die rechtlichen und (continued...)

Radbruch's ideas, if we interpret the optimizing demanded by principles as the optimizing of legal values. The determination of the actual content of legal principles, though, would be the proper task of legal science, as the science concerned with the meaning of positive legal norms (1932, 209).

## 7. CONCLUSIONS

After this examination of the different aspects of Radbruch's theory of values I should now connect that discussion to the questions I have formulated in Chapter 1. Here I will consider what Radbruch's answers are regarding the three issues that I distinguished as components of the main question, how to conceptualize ideals in the context of legal theory. The first issue concerns different aspects of the ontology and epistemology of values and the relation between values and reality, the second issue is the distinction and interaction of different values, which in Radbruch's theory leads into the third issue, the relation between values and law.

First of all, the ontological status of ideals is at issue. In Radbruch's view, ideals are not in any way distinguished from values. Values or ideals form a realm separate from reality, seen as transcendent. The transcendence of values means that they go beyond factual reality; they are *überwirklich*. Other than this non-real and therefore transcendent character, Radbruch does not say much explicitly about the nature of values. However, from his discussion of the separation between reality and value we can gather that values are subjective, in the sense that they are products of the human mind (1932, 221). It is important to see that this does not mean that the validity of values is dependent upon subjective preferences of individuals. Additional evidence can be found in Radbruch's epistemological claim that a person's relation to values is one of *Bekenntnis*: although Radbruch sees the significance of this relation in the consequence that one cannot know values, it also implies that values are something to which a person commits him or herself and are not identical with someone's feeling or preference. The validity of values is based on their relation to ultimate values, to which all values can be reduced. These ultimate values have the character of irreducible axioms, whose validity is absolute. Radbruch treats the characterization of values, as transcendent

[18](...continued)
tatsächlichen Möglichkeiten möglichst hohen Maße realisiert wird. Prinzipien sind also Optimierungsgebote." (Alexy 1985, 19)

entities whose mode of being is validity, as self-explanatory. However, the meaning of validity and transcendence is not clear, let alone the ontological status of values.[19] Therefore, his conception of values needs to be reconstructed. I think a likely definition of values in Radbruch's sense would be the following: values are the necessary postulates of our normative thinking, transcending physical reality and with a subjective basis.

Such an initial definition leaves many questions to be answered. The first question concerns the transcendence of values: if we think of values as transcending reality, does this necessarily mean that they are in no way grounded in that reality? Radbruch's answer here is ambiguous: on the one hand, he uses the doctrine of the *Stoffbestimmtheit der Idee* to establish that values are influenced by reality; on the other hand, he speaks of the transcendence of values as complete. He tries to reconcile these two propositions by distinguishing between the causal influences of reality on ideas and the justification of ideas. Causal influences can be recognized, but cannot be used for the justification of ideas, because ideas can never be justified by factual evidence. And even this causal connection between values and reality is downplayed by attributing the meaning (*Sinn*) of social facts to the influence of other values. This manoeuvring with the relations between facts and values shows that, in spite of the difficulty of combining it with a genuine connection between value and reality, Radbruch holds on to a strict interpretation of his methodological principle that 'is' and 'ought' must be distinguished. Although he tries to account for the links between the two realms with the idea of *Stoffbestimmtheit*, the reduction of the meaning of social facts to their value-relatedness makes that idea rather an empty formula, so that a real basis of values evaporates and the gap between fact and value remains unbridged.

A second question concerns the dynamics of values: what does a conception of values, as transcendent necessary postulates, entail regarding the changeability of values? Here too, Radbruch's answer has two sides to it. The ultimate values he distinguishes, the axioms of value systems, are necessary or absolute, but the value systems that are based on them are relative to personal convictions. This means that the basic values themselves remain unchanged, but the weight that is given them is liable to change: different constellations of values are adhered to in different historical circumstances and

[19] Compare Kaufmann: "...(eine nicht zu klärende Frage ist, als was Radbruch die "Werte", die "Rechtsidee" angesehen hat: schwerlich als etwas real Existierendes — aber als Axiom, Postulat, Hypothese, transzendentale Bedingung?)..." (Introduction in Radbruch GRGA 1, 74)

according to different political views. This is also true of the idea of law: it is seen as containing necessary and enduring elements, but as a whole it undergoes continual changes because of the relativistic nature of the exact mix of values that constitute the idea of law.

This brings us to a third question left open by the initial definition: does Radbruch distinguish between different types of values? Radbruch first of all distinguishes the ultimate values that form the irreducible starting points of value systems: the value of the good with its three alternative substrates — individual, group or work — and the values of truth, beauty, and justice. These ultimate values differ from values that are derived from them, as for instance legal security derives from justice. Secondly, a distinction can be made between composite values, which I termed 'ideas' following the idea of law, and their constituent values. The category of constituent values overlaps with that of ultimate values, but only to a degree. The idea of law consists of the ultimate value of justice and the derived values of expediency — derived from the good — and legal security — derived from justice. Not all values are therefore necessary postulates of world views, but that is the most important category in Radbruch's theory because it forms the basis of the realm of values. Radbruch does not pay attention to the exact relation between ultimate values and other values; he seems to believe that value systems can simply be deduced from a few ultimate values. That leaves open the question how to reach the content of more specific values: perhaps from a combination of values, perhaps by relating values to reality. Radbruch does not give a direct answer. Probably because he sees deduction as an unproblematic method, he does not specify what other factors enter into the determination of specific values nor in what way: for instance, whether and how factual information is incorporated.

One of the questions leading to this research was whether a meaningful distinction can be made, in the context of law, between ideals and principles. This is something which is not a direct issue in Radbruch's framework, but something that can be derived from the distinction between values and norms, which to him is the central distinction within the normative realm. From Radbruch's distinction between values and norms it follows, granted that we should see principles as a type of norms, that ideals (as identical to values) and principles have a completely different character. Radbruch does not make any distinction within the category of norms, comparable to that between rules and principles. What is interesting, however, is that Radbruch sees norms as intermediary between values and facts. Pursuing this line led to the suggestion that principles could be seen as norms that are more general and more directly related to ultimate values than rules. Following Alexy, principles can thus be regarded as having a more open character than rules, because they directly require optimization of legal values.

Now there is a basis for a slightly revised account of Radbruch's conception of values, distinguishing between absolute and derivative values. Derivative values are those elements of our normative thinking, transcending physical reality and with a subjective basis, that can be deduced from the absolute values that are the postulates of this normative thinking.

Because of Radbruch's dualistic method distinguishing value from fact, the question arises what the relations are between value and reality. In 4.3 I have shown that Radbruch tries to save both his dualistic and triadistic principles by focusing on the meaning of reality. He uses the concept of meaning (*Sinn*) to keep the separation between value and reality intact, while at the same time accounting for the value-laden character of the factual social world. By understanding meaning as the previous influence of value on factual situations Radbruch reduces the relations between values and reality to one-way traffic: there is no significant role for reality in the determination of values. Nonetheless, in the other direction the relations between values and reality are tight: values determine the character of all cultural (man-related) reality. Radbruch thus defends a very strong thesis regarding the significance of values for the human world: being value-related is the main defining characteristic of human reality. The important thing to see is that this does not mean that values are necessarily realized: the cultural world is organized with the purpose of value-realization but this is not always successful. In a simple way, Radbruch's idea can be put like this: people do things and organize their society from their view of what is right and good, but when trying actually to work on the basis of these values, they find that existing arrangements, factual circumstances and the attempted realization of other values frustrate the realization of the values they support. The main problem that arises from this view of values and reality is how to allow for different appreciations of values, while at the same time accounting for the perception of a shared cultural reality. Radbruch solves this by combining a necessary relation between a domain of reality and a particular value with relativism of other values. However, what he fails to establish is why the proportion between absolute and relative elements should be regarded the way he does, more precisely why the relative aspect of his theory does not affect truth, beauty, and justice the way it affects the good.

The second main issue concerns the interaction between different ideals. From the discussion of the three elements of the idea of law we learnt that values can at the same time require each other and conflict with each other. They require each other because each alone is an incomplete guide to law, but they also conflict because each leads into a different direction. Because the three values of the idea of law conflict, they keep each other in check. Radbruch sees the tensions within the idea of law as a guarantee against dangerous overemphasis on one value. From this idea of a balance of values we can also learn that even though these values may not be inherently unrealizable, they are in effect unrealizable: each prevents the complete realization of the others. Radbruch gives a convincing account of why complete realization is something to be wary of. The three values can both reinforce and impede each other's realization, but Radbruch deems the latter more important. His ideas on the interaction of values can be used as the basis of an argument about both positive and negative consequences of interaction, but in order to complete such an argument the issue of positive interaction needs work. It will also be interesting to see if his view on the interaction of values can be given broader application than the idea of law: maybe other constellations of values can be discerned in more specific fields of law. In his own applications of his ideas to specific fields of law,[20] Radbruch points to the direct influence of the *Rechtsidee* and its three values; he does not develop more specific value notions. For example, in his discussion of criminal law he shows how the different theories of punishment emphasize one of the three different values, but also how the other two values constrain the development of such theories (1932, 402).

The subject of interaction, leading to discussion of the *Rechtsidee*, is primarily interesting in regard to the issue I identified: the role of values in law and legal theory. We saw that justice is fundamental to the understanding of law because it gives law its specific nature, distinguishing it from other parts of cultural reality. Radbruch uses the different elements of the idea of law to account for the only partly autonomous character of law: *Gerechtigkeit* and *Rechtssicherheit* are the elements that are specific to law, while *Zweckmäßigkeit* is the value through which political and social influences enter the domain of law. The autonomy of law is therefore guaranteed by the first two values, but this is counteracted by the influence of *Zweckmäßigkeit*. In effect how open law is to societal influences, depends on the relative weight of the three values in the idea of law.

20 This is based on the second part (*Besonderer Teil*) of the Rechtsphilosophie (1932, 358-444).

The idea of law is also the standard of evaluation for the existing legal system. The legal system can be assessed in the light of the idea of law, which is the idea of law-as-it-should-be. The idea of law can thus be used both as a source for criticism and as a source for justification of existing legal arrangements. However, because the exact content of the idea of law is a matter relative to world views, there is not much that can be said about the standard of criticism other than that it will contain the three elements mentioned before. Because of this relativistic notion of the idea of law, Radbruch's theory does not give concrete answers about the critical potential of values. To what extent values are used to criticize or justify the law depends on the conception of the idea of law defended by the different political views.

In Radbruch's system of values, the set of "distinctively" legal values form a category that is derived directly from justice. For Radbruch each domain of cultural reality seems to have its own specific value, the value that sets that part of reality apart. But the same values that perform this role of constitutor of one cultural reality are also influential in other domains. Thus, the value of justice is the specifically legal value, from which everything that is specific to law (including the value of legal security) is ultimately derived. But the content and concrete character of law are also determined by other values, *Zweckmäßigkeit* or the good, which are not specific to the legal domain at all. In a sense, the only truly legal value is justice, and other values are only "legal" by virtue of their being related to justice.

Finally, we need to assess how convincing is Radbruch's argument about the nature of values and their role in legal theory. At first sight, his view of values as transcendent and subjective, necessary postulates, seems acceptable. There are, however, three aspects of his theory that make this view of values problematic. First of all, there is Radbruch's use of the dichotomy between is and ought. Radbruch presents it as a methodological principle, but also uses it as a category distinction between fact and value. As a methodological principle it is acceptable, because it reflects the importance of remembering the difference between judgments of what is the case and judgments of what ought to be done. But Radbruch absolutizes this distinction to the principle that ought judgments can *only* be justified with reference to higher 'oughts' and connects to it a dichotomy of the radically different nature of facts and values. Trying to combine this dichotomy with the establishment of links between the realm of value and the realm of fact, Radbruch erodes the doctrine of *Stoffbestimmtheit* and places undue emphasis on the influence of values on reality, neglecting the influence of reality on values.

The second problem concerns Radbruch's method of reasoning. Radbruch's theory can convince someone, like himself, who is devoted to a deductivist method of justification, and who accepts the rational necessities of the a priori reasoning of Kantian philosophy. A deductivist method is problematic, however, if we accept that value notions are complex notions which for their explication depend on the meaning of other such value notions (Vedder 1998). Legal security is not simply a requirement derived from the value of justice; the meaning of the value is also connected to, for instance, notions of personal freedom. The complex character of values is denied when the relations between them are seen as straightforward deduction from higher values. Radbruch can hold on to the deductive model because he strictly separates causal from logical arguments. The influence of facts and of other values is then seen as merely causal and insufficient for a good justification, which can only be achieved by a logical deductive argument. The problem of such a priori reasoning is that it depends on strong premises regarding the rational necessity of accepting certain arguments: a rational human being must accept such an argument as the basis for understanding the world. Such reasoning relies on the self-evidence of such arguments and the idea that rational deliberation leads to inevitable conclusions. Leaving general criticism aside, the relation between specific values and law is not self-evident nor rationally inescapable. Arguments are needed that are declared unnecessary in a Kantian approach.

The third problem is the most fundamental to my mind: Radbruch's combination of absolute and relative elements in his account of values. In their role of constitutive values of cultural realities, ultimate values function as absolute and necessary reference points. But the absolute value of the good is subject to relativistic interpretation in the context of competing world views. Similarly, the exact make-up of the *Rechtsidee*, the relation between its elements, differs according to world views. This limitation of the relativistic aspects of a theory of values seems arbitrary. It is not such a matter of course as Radbruch seems to believe, that only expediency and the good have to be interpreted relativistically, and that justice and legal security are beyond relativistic interpretation. His a priori arguments for necessary relations between values and reality depend on universal acceptability, but precisely on that point his relativistic principle sheds doubt. If we take his relativism seriously, all values become subject to relativistic interpretation. The main problem then — if one accepts the constitutive role of values for cultural reality — is how to explain the shared experience of one legal reality. The most plausible reason why Radbruch tries to contain the relativistic aspects of his theory is to avoid a completely relativized view of cultural reality and law. To do that, he needs non-relative and necessary elements which cannot really be combined with relativism to form a coherent theory.

I am sympathetic to what Radbruch tries to do with his theory: to give an account of the role of values in law, which combines the idea that law is necessarily oriented to certain values with an account of changing and historically situated interpretations of those values. However, his combination of absolute values with radical relativism does not provide a convincing solution. If we want to account for the experience of a shared legal reality and a flexible interpretation of values, it seems wise to explore another conception of ideals in law. It may be that a theory starting from different philosophical tenets is more successful.

# CHAPTER 5

# THE THEORY OF PHILIP SELZNICK

## 1. INTRODUCTION

Philip Selznick (born in 1919) is an American sociologist and social theorist. He holds a Ph.D. in sociology from Columbia University, New York. In 1952, he became a professor in sociology at the University of California, Berkeley, where he worked until retirement. He was one of the founders of the Center for the Study of Law and Society at Berkeley, and the first chairman of the Jurisprudence and Social Policy program at the Berkeley Law School. His main fields of interest are organizational sociology, the sociology of law, and general social theory. Over the last twenty years he has also been involved in the debate between liberalism and communitarianism.

The main components of his work on the sociology of organizations, *TVA and the Grass Roots* (1949), *The Organizational Weapon* (1960, orig. 1952), and *Leadership in Administration* (1957), all deal with prominent features of organizational life: co-optation, strategy, leadership. The first two are case studies, dealing with the Tennessee Valley Authority (1949) and the Russian Bolshevik party (1960). The third (1957) deals with administrative leadership in a more general fashion. Important works on the sociology of law are the articles 'The Sociology of Law' (1959), 'Sociology and Natural Law' (1961), 'The Sociology of Law' (1968), *Law, Society and Industrial Justice* (1969), and *Law and Society in Transition* (Nonet & Selznick 1978). His interest in general social theory culminated in *The Moral Commonwealth* (1992), which brings together the different themes of his earlier work. It is held together by the commitment to communitarianism, which is also expressed by its subtitle: *Social Theory and the Promise of Community*.

This chapter aims to introduce those aspects of Philip Selznick's work that are necessary to understand his theory of ideals. This chapter is descriptive in character, I will turn to the evaluation of his ideas in the next chapter. Selznick's background in sociology and his interest in social theory are important factors in his understanding of ideals, but even more important is his philosophical outlook: his endorsement of pragmatism. Pragmatism is the main subject of section 5.2, where I discuss the theory of John Dewey and its implications for Selznick's method. Sociology and social theory figure in section 5.3, where I discuss his understanding of the two key theoretical components of his theory that are most relevant to his view of ideals in law: the sociology of law and communitarian social theory. I will then turn to his particular view of law in section 5.4, which deals with the developmental model of law and society and with Selznick's approach to the nature of law: legal naturalism.

## 2. THE INFLUENCE OF PRAGMATISM: SELZNICK'S METHOD

In many of his works, Selznick acknowledges the profound influence that the work of John Dewey has had upon his own theory. In no aspect of his ideas is this influence as far-reaching as in his method. His manner of reasoning and his theoretical points of departure express his allegiance to Dewey's pragmatism most clearly. For a clear understanding of the extent to which Selznick can be seen as a follower of Dewey it is necessary to have a general idea of what Dewey's theory amounts to. Therefore I will start with a broad sketch of Dewey's theory. In Chapter 2 I have already indicated what the core of a pragmatist theory of ideals is. Here, my main point is that Dewey's ideas about normativity and about moral and social philosophy can only be understood when they are related to his views about science, especially about scientific method. In the second part I will pay attention to specific aspects of Selznick's theory that are based on pragmatist philosophy. I will conclude this section with a discussion of methodological themes in Selznick's work that do not have direct roots in pragmatism.

### *Dewey's Theory*

Pragmatism, the theory advanced by Charles Sanders Peirce, William James, and John Dewey, is most famous for its theory of truth and scientific method. They argued against the correspondence theory of truth, truth as reflecting a given eternal reality, and replaced it by a theory of truth as the effective guidance of action.[1] The truth of a proposition is revealed in the consequences it has for our actions. A proposition is true if acting upon it is successful. This entails that scientific method is experimental: hypotheses have to be tested to know their truth. Here, I want to focus not so much on the theory of truth, but

1 See Joas 1993, 19: "The concept of reality no longer expresses a correct representation of reality in cognition, which can be conceived of using the metaphor of a copy; rather, it expresses an increase of the power to act in relation to an environment."

on Dewey's method of inquiry and its application to all human concerns.

In Dewey's work a major theme is the continuity between inquiry in the natural sciences and inquiry in social and moral subjects (1929, 201; 1920, 178). His belief that both physical science and moral 'science' would benefit immensely from the realization that knowledge of physical goods and knowledge of moral goods are interrelated is his main drive for developing a theory of experimental inquiry in the normative realm. His theory can be described as an extension, a broadening, of the method of physical inquiry into a much wider field. His reason for thinking that the scientific method is worthy of being applied more generally, is that it has advanced enormously whereas beliefs about morals or religion or politics are still determined in the same way they have been for thousands of years (1929, 200).

In scientific inquiry, the emphasis is on doing, instead of contemplating. A scientist confronts a problematic situation, formulates a solution of the problem, and tests this hypothesis in an experiment. For Dewey, the first and the last steps are especially important. The first step because it means an inquiry starts with a genuine problem: it is not something done for its own sake, but to help us on in practice. The last step, because experimentation means an active manipulation of conditions; the fact that in science experiments are done, instead of passive observation of natural phenomena, means that our own activity is seen as an influential factor. Science is an active practice, not a passive contemplation of nature. But scientific inquiry is not simply an active process, it is *intelligent* activity. Dewey introduces his concept of intelligence as qualifying activities to replace the traditional concept of reason. In his view, reason suggested an eternal natural order that can be grasped in a purely rational manner (1929, 170). Such a concept of reason demeans experience and activity. Because it searches for order at a deeper level of reality, it does not fit scientific inquiry as Dewey sees it.[2] Dewey's concept of intelligence has a much broader meaning than the traditional notion of reason:

> We may, . . . , give the name intelligence to these directed operations. Using this term, we may say that the worth of any object that lays claim to being an object of knowledge is dependent upon the intelligence employed in reaching it. In saying this, we must bear in mind that intelligence means operations actually performed in the modification of conditions, including all the guidance that is given by means of ideas, both direct and symbolic (1929, 160).[3]

2 See also Raymond Boisvert's work on Dewey's metaphysics (1988, 119).

3 See also 1929, 204: "intelligence in operation, another name for method".

Intelligence in operation means making use of ideas and acquired knowledge in carrying out inquiries. The exercise of intelligence directs the course of changes (171), and it demands judgment with regard to the selection of means and the choice of ends (170). Intelligence as the exercise of judgment can be interpreted as a reflection upon means and ends before you act. The important point to keep in mind is that knowing is a form of doing (1929, 170). Acquiring knowledge is a practice, an activity, and this practice must be conducted intelligently in order to result in sound knowledge.

The connection between knowing and doing can also be taken to mean something quite different: that knowing, in Dewey's interpretation as the practice of inquiry, is extremely important for doing in its traditional sense, as praxis. In this sense, connecting the two means that practical judgment, or moral judgment, can benefit from application of the experimental method. According to Dewey, inquiry is called for in problematic moral situations as much as in other problematic situations. In a moral context, inquiry also means intelligent application of an experimental method. This includes: the analysis and clarification of the moral situation; "(...) tracing the consequences of the various modes of action that suggest themselves; regarding the decision reached as hypothetical and tentative until the anticipated or supposed consequences which led to its adoption have been squared with actual consequences" (1920, 173). This view of moral decision-making as the result of inquiry in a specific situation makes morality much more flexible than it was traditionally. There is no fixed set of moral laws or a predetermined collection of ends or human goods. What is right or good is determined by consideration of the consequences of proposed actions. Acts to be performed are specific, and therefore the moral judgments about such acts have to be specific and concrete (1920, 175).

The most important consequence of the pragmatist view, that there are no fixed ends, but a plurality of goods, is that the means of attaining ends become much more important. Dewey himself stresses the point time and again: adopting the experimental way of thinking "(...) would place method and means upon the level of importance that has, in the past, been imputed exclusively to ends" (1929, 222). Pragmatism is easily misunderstood as being mainly concerned with means, with what works, but for Dewey attention to means is meant as the joint and equal attention to both means and ends. For him, "the problem of philosophy concerns the *interaction* of our judgments about ends to be sought with knowledge of the means for achieving them" (1929, 30).

His rejection of the separation between means and ends also leads him to stress the connections between instrumental and intrinsic good (1920, 178). Things such as bodily health and economic prosperity are usually seen as having merely instrumental value, as belonging to another order than the higher ends of aesthetics or religion. This separation between the two types of ends is damaging in two ways. On the one hand, the separation can lead to a spirit of unreflected materialism, if the instrumental comes to be viewed as the only end there is (1929, 215); whilst, on the other, ultimate ends that are rightly called higher, have much richer meaning when they are part of human life, when they are supported by effective means. This all requires that means are seen to have intrinsic value as well and that the continuities and interrelations between means and ends are always kept in mind.

The irrelevance of the distinction between different types of good follows from Dewey's focus on problematic situations. When we are faced with a problem, it does not matter whether it concerns a moral good or a natural good; what is important is solving the problem. And in order to find the solution to the problem all considerations should be taken into account: even when a problem can be characterized as moral, non-moral considerations are just as relevant as moral ones. Since we cannot know beforehand which considerations will be most helpful, none should be ruled out. This is one of the occasions where the pragmatic character of Dewey's philosophy clearly shows: we should never rule out a potentially helpful notion beforehand just because the notion is not in the category we are currently working with. Categories and classifications are tools to order our thinking, they should never be regarded as absolute realities.

*Dewey's Influence on Selznick*

Having a general idea of Dewey's thought, we can now consider how Dewey has influenced the work of Selznick. Many methodological and structural features of Selznick's theory can be understood as a result of the anti-dogmatism that Selznick adopts from Dewey. Throughout his work Dewey sought to expose the fallacious separation between means and ends, moral and non-moral qualities, theory and practice, thinking and doing, the ideal and the real (1929, 19; 1920, 149). Although it makes sense to distinguish between the partners of these pairs conceptually, it is a mistake to think that these distinctions point to ontological certainties. Too often the distinction is turned into a dichotomy, a strict separation by which the links between the two distinguished concepts are lost from sight. It is this rejection of dichotomies that is the most pervasive influence of Dewey in Selznick's theory (1992, 21).

Both Dewey and Selznick criticize the kind of dogmatic thinking that has produced dichotomies out of distinctions. Their own motto, in Selznick's words: "We must avoid all dogma that blocks inquiry" (1961, 94; 1992, 21). Selznick continually criticizes theories with absolutist tendencies.[4] If we find that people are immensely influenced by the culture they are part of, this does not warrant the conclusion that there is no such thing as a common human nature (1961, 93). If one cause or one relation is found to be of large importance, that is in itself no reason to conclude that it is the sole determinant of the studied phenomenon nor that its counterpart has no role to play.

Selznick does not only apply this insight in empirical cases, it also determines the way he handles conflicting theories. The most noticeable reconciliation, upon which I will elaborate in section 5.3, is that between communitarianism and liberalism, which led him to a position that he himself calls "communitarian liberalism" (1992, xi). While retaining the basic values of liberalism, Selznick emphasizes their cultural roots and framework, and the limits that should be observed when these values are taken as guidelines (1995b, 489). He underpins liberal values with a communitarian theory of the person and society. But although communitarianism and liberalism play the most prominent role in Selznick's work, they are not the only theories Selznick tries to combine. Universalism and particularism, 'nature' and 'nurture', natural law and legal positivism, are all positions that are incorporated in Selznick's theory.[5] His strategy is to point out in which way the truths of these positions are partial truths or are relevant for different aspects of the problem at hand. It makes Selznick's pragmatism an inclusive theory: he always looks for the valuable aspects of theories under consideration and looks for ways to give them a place in his own view.

Thus, a pragmatic way of thinking shapes the general outlook of Selznick's theory and gives it a reconciliatory tone. There are, however, also more specific themes in Dewey's work that are taken up by Selznick. Selznick disputes two dichotomies that were also the subject of Dewey's writing: the separation between fact and value and between means and ends. Both distinctions are important in the contexts of this study. Ideals are often equated both with values and with ends, so that a criticism of these two dichotomies will also have consequences for the position attributed to ideals.

4 Dewey's most direct attack on absolutism is *Reconstruction in Philosophy* (1920), the lectures in which he criticized the dichotomies of traditional philosophy.

5 For the combination of universalism and particularism, see 1992, 193-201; for nature and nurture, see 1992, 133-134; for natural law and positivism, 1992, 442-445. I will return to the last theme in section 4.

In Selznick's work, the fact-value distinction is raised in the context of the proper way to conduct sociological research (1961, 85-86). It surfaces in two ways: in connection with the subject-matter of research, and in the approach of the researcher himself. By the first I mean that the distinction between fact and value can be applied to the research material: one can decide either to focus only on facts or to study the combination of facts and values.[6] By the second I mean that the distinction is used to reflect upon the position of the researcher: how do his own values influence his work — is it possible to attend to facts without letting one's own values interfere?

Selznick primarily relates the fact-value distinction to the subject-matter of research. Although he acknowledges that it is important to distinguish facts from values, he does not see the distinction as reflecting an ontological separation. He rejects the ontological claim that facts are something different and disconnected from values. He sees facts and values as elements of the same reality: values are immanent in reality. In conducting sociological research this means that facts and values cannot be studied separately because they deeply influence each other (1992, 21). In his view, social reality cannot be genuinely understood without studying the interplay of facts and values. This leads to the central theme of the next chapter: Selznick's doctrine of master ideals. These are the ideals guiding the normative systems which make up social reality. Social behaviour cannot be understood without knowledge of these master ideals (1961).

The researcher's ability to be entirely objective is a problem generally recognized in science. Selznick follows Kuhn in seeing scientists as heavily influenced by their membership of a particular community and grants that this determines their outlook and background theories (1992, 83-84). Scientists share scientific ideals such as accuracy, scope, consistency, and these are the ideals that influence their research. They have a common basis, but they are not completely determinate: "Scientific ideals are neither impotent, nor arbitrary, nor mere preferences. But they do allow for disagreement, and they must be balanced against one another when a choice of theories is to be made" (1992, 86). The general guidelines are agreed upon but they are interpreted differently. And so they should, in the interest of the advancement of science. Selznick does think the researcher's values influence his study of the facts and the choice of theory and method, but this is not really problematic because the researcher's values are more than his own whims or preferences. Science cannot be value-free, but the values that are influential have an intersubjective

6 In social science, the first alternative is associated with behaviourism, the second by interpretivism (see Tamanaha 1997, 59-90).

basis: they are seen as justified by the scientific community.

The other distinction that merits discussion is that between means and ends. Stressing the continuity between means and ends was a permanent concern of Dewey's[11] and it is also one of Selznick's main examples when demonstrating the futility and dangers of dichotomies. Selznick values Dewey's views on means and ends because of three insights in particular: that both ends and means are instrumental, that both ends and means are valuable in themselves, and that ends cannot be determined without assessing means at the same time (1992, 328). The first idea, that both means and ends are instrumental, entails that ends have a provisional status similar to means: both are assessed in the light of the broader consequences they have. An end or goal is not beyond scrutiny. On the other hand, the means by which an end is pursued are not valuable simply as the instruments for the end. For instance, a parliamentary debate may be instrumental in reaching the goal of establishing a certain policy. However, it is at least as important that there is an open discussion about policy, and as such the debate has intrinsic value.[12] The third idea, that ends and means have to be assessed in combination, entails that both ends and means can be criticized for the consequences they have upon each other. A goal should not be pursued if the means to reach it are undesirable, and similarly means should lead to a desirable end. The most important aspect of these views on the character of means and ends is that ends are not taken as given and that their acceptability depends on the instruments used in their implementation. Ends are not final but subject to constant reassessment in the light of the means necessary to achieve them.

For both Dewey and Selznick this conception of means and ends informs their ideas about the role of reason or rationality. However, their focus on excesses resulting from the place awarded to reason or rationality is different. Dewey criticized the traditional concept of reason because it underrated means, while Selznick criticizes the contemporary concept of rationality because it ignores ends.

Selznick finds fault with many ordinary uses of rationality as such uses see rationality as instrumental, i.e. relating to the ways to reach a pre-existing goal. The methods used to attain the goal or end can be assessed using standards of rationality, but the goals themselves are not subject to this assessment. Ends may be based on deep belief, democratic decisions, considered preference, or mere fancy, their character or worth does not enter in the rational calculus.

11 See e.g. 1920, 121; 1939, 227-230.

12 On intrinsic and instrumental value, see Raz 1986, 177-78.

This neglect of ends from the standpoint of rationality can have serious consequences. An important instance of such a use of rationality is a technocratic way of thinking. It leads to domination by technology and to what Selznick calls "the tyranny of means" (1992, 55-56). This expression describes the way that means tend to determine the course of action completely, once ends disappear from sight. The best example of the tyranny of means is the way technological possibilities determine what is done: advanced weaponry is made because it can be made (1992, 56). The tyranny of means shows to what excesses the divorce of means and ends can lead. In order to keep both ends and means in check, the two should always be related to each other. Where Dewey wished to refute the saying 'the end justifies the means', Selznick also warns of the reverse: means should not be allowed to create an end. In Selznick's view, both ends and means are subject to rational assessment.

*Basic Methodological Principles*

Now that it is clear how pragmatism forms the core of Selznick's theory and how he interprets pragmatism's central tenets, we can turn to the way Selznick develops his own methodological theory. Four distinct but related ideas are especially important in the context of this study: the idea of variability, normative theories, the distinction between weak definitions and strong theories, and the distinction between baseline and flourishing.

Selznick extends the pragmatic idea that dichotomies should be avoided, to the idea of variability. This idea consists in the recognition that empirical phenomena only answer to characterizations and classifications to a degree and that there are always variations among the phenomena placed in a certain category. For instance, categorizing a procedure as democratic does not mean that a choice has been made between two alternatives which completely settles the democratic character of the procedure studied. At least as important a question as *whether* the procedure is democratic is *to what degree* it is democratic. Selznick applies the idea of variability both in his criticism of various theories and in his description of important social phenomena. In theoretical criticism, recognition of variability is the counterpart of the rejection of absolutist claims. Subjectivism is one of the main targets of this criticism. Selznick recognizes the importance of subjectivity as a part of empirical reality, but rejects the sceptical and emotivist doctrines of subjectivism (1992, 81). Subjectivism has often been guilty of absolutist statements which ignore the existence of variation, such as the thesis that perception is theory-laden:

> But to say that a perception is "theory-laden" or "theory-impregnated" *suggests* more than it necessarily asserts. Such characterizations do not say precisely how far the process goes or just what takes place. In any inquiry some observations and classifications are more theory-dependent than others (1992, 89).

Such theories forget that such sweeping statements cannot be made while doing justice to the variety of empirical reality.

Selznick not only wants to say that there are always variations to be found when attention is payed to the facts, but also that the most important differences are differences in quality. In his own work, a central place is given to the normative side of social phenomena: in organizational theory the institution is the key concept, in legal theory it is the rule of law, or legality. Paying attention to qualitative variability means that organizations are assessed according to their institutionalization, i.e. to their infusion with value. For law, it means that legal systems are evaluated on the basis of their realization of legality, i.e. the progressive reduction of arbitrariness. Institutionalization and legality are variable achievements (1992, 233; 1969, 13).

This interest in qualitative difference is the main exponent of Selznick's evaluative approach to research, an approach that is based on his conception of normative theories. I just pointed out that the recognition of qualitative variability turns on the use of strongly normative concepts in sociological description. A comprehensive approach based on such normative concepts amounts to a normative theory. Selznick developed his idea of a normative theory in an early article written together with Gertrude Jaeger: 'A Normative Theory of Culture' (1964). In this article they fused the broad notion of culture used by anthropologists with the humanistic notion of culture as high culture. Their theory of culture is normative because it connects culture with the realization of values and its conditions. The distinguishing mark of a normative theory is that it is strongly evaluative:

> An understanding of the nature of the values at stake, and the conditions of their realization, must form a part of the theory of culture. It is in this sense a normative theory, one that does not shrink from identifying some cultures as attenuated, some symbols as emptied out, some experiences as truncated or distorted (1964, 666).

The concept of a normative theory applies not only to Selznick's understanding of culture but also to law and management. Law strives to realize the values of legality; management develops into the more demanding governance, into acceptance of "responsibility for the whole life of the institution" (1992, 290). Although a normative theory is evaluative, it does not look exclusively to values, it looks at them in context. The pragmatist's warning never to forget that things happen in experience, with specific conditions and consequences, has been taken to heart: Selznick continually reminds us of the limits of and conditions for the realization of values. So although a normative theory strongly evaluates — it assesses empirical situations according to their realization of values — it does this by examining both the potential and the obstacles for value realization.

Selznick distinguishes different normative theories: a theory of law, a theory of culture, a theory of management. These theories apply to particular social phenomena, but these phenomena must first be identified as such: when do we speak of law, when of management, when of culture? Selznick recognizes the need for a threshold to delineate the field to which a normative theory applies. Not all rule-guided behaviour is law, but when is the transition made from a loose form of social organization to a legal system? For this purpose Selznick distinguishes definition and theory: definitions mark the boundary of the field to which a theory is applied.[13] Definitions should be weak: potentially interesting objects of research should not be ruled out merely on the basis of a stipulated definition. Theories, on the other hand, should be strong (1969, 4). In his legal theory, he uses a weak definition of law based on criteria for authority: "The minimal elements of a legal order exist when there are accepted criteria for testing and certifying the authority of social obligations" (Nonet & Selznick 1978, 11).[14] His theory of law is strong because it sees law as directed towards the ideal of legality, which demands ever higher levels of achievement (1969, 12), and because most of his theory is dedicated to an understanding of the value of legality and to the conditions and complications it involves.

Selznick's idea of a strong theory is closely related to the idea of a normative theory. To my mind, a strong theory is not necessarily normative in the strong sense explained above: a strong theory need not be about the realization of values. But in the light of the broad commitments of Selznick's project we can say that for him strong theories are normative in the sense of being value-oriented (1992, 360).

Selznick thus approaches his research subjects with a dual strategy:

13 In 1969, 4, it was 'concept shading into theory', but the term concept can be confusing because others (e.g. Hart or Dworkin) use it as a more inclusive term, closer in meaning to definition. Therefore, I will use 'theory' instead of 'concept'. Selznick himself also prefers 'theory' over 'concept' in his later work (See 1978, 11; 1992, 266, 358).

14 The criteria Selznick has in mind are Hart's secondary rules. He uses these as criteria providing a weak definition of law throughout his work (see also 1969, 5; 1992, 442).

delineating with a weak definition and arguing with a strong, normative theory. This dual strategy is parallelled by another: the combination of baseline and flourishing. Here the focus is different, although the structure is similar: where the combination of weak definition and strong theory is used for the purpose of lucidity in the theory as a whole, the combination of baseline and flourishing operates within that theory to support a moral appeal to give them equal attention. The idea of baseline and flourishing attaches both to social systems — groups, cultures, moral systems — and to values. On the one hand, there are basic conditions ensuring the survival of a system or value; on the other, there are the promises and appeal of the highest level of achievement (1998, 25; 1961, 91). In order to avoid the excesses of pessimism and utopianism, one should always pay attention to both baselines and flourishings, and when the theoretical climate tends towards the one, one has to bring back the balance by focusing on the other.

One of the subjects to which Selznick applies the combination is the rule of law. Often the rule of law is viewed as a set of principles of restraint, a way to control the power of government and to prevent excesses. This is the baseline view of the rule of law, in which it comprises the basic values of accountability, liberty, regularity, and social peace (1998, 25). But the rule of law can also be viewed with an eye to its flourishing, and then more ambitious values such as rationality, equality, fairness, and integrity appear most important (1998, 17). To focus too intently on either the baseline or the flourishing of the rule of law is dangerous: complete concentration on the baseline values impoverishes the rule of law because there is no attention for its potential for growth. But a concentration on the flourishing only is at least as perilous because there is the chance that the most elementary and most necessary checks are omitted.

The rule of law example illustrates the moral import that the combination of baseline and flourishing has for Selznick. The well-being of a system, the existence of a value depend on a concern for both basics and aspirations.[15] It is only by equal attention to both that we can ensure the best development of social systems and their values.[16]

[15] The idea bears close resemblance to Fuller's morality of duty and morality of aspiration (Selznick 1992, 260n).

[16] See e.g. Selznick 1992, 431.

## 3. SELZNICK'S SOCIAL THOUGHT

In the introduction to this chapter, I have identified the four fields of social studies with which Selznick has been occupied. In this section I want to discuss two themes more closely which are important as a background to his theory of ideals and law. First, I will discuss how Selznick understands the discipline of sociology of law. I will then turn to his ideas on social and moral theory and discuss the extent to which these ideas are communitarian.

### *Sociology of Law*

Here I will outline Selznick's theory about sociology and law. I will not deal with his theory on the nature of law as a social phenomenon, but address his theoretical understanding of sociology in connection to law. This includes his general understanding of sociology.

In his 1959 article on the sociology of law, Selznick addresses the tasks and opportunities of sociological research in a legal context. He distinguishes three stages, from a very basic involvement with sociological truths, through a dealing with specific socio-legal themes, to a dedication to overarching problems of legal philosophy. At the first stage sociologists merely make available basic sociological insights to legal scholars. Since this has a limited, educational aim, it does not offer much opportunity for sociological research itself, which should therefore turn towards the second and third stages. The major task of the second stage is to derive hypotheses about law from sociological theory and develop socio-legal research to test these (124). In such research the most fundamental questions about the nature of law can be avoided, but such questions are central for the third stage of the sociology of law. At this stage, sociology of law moves towards legal philosophy and addresses perennial themes such as the role of reason in law or the meaning of legality.

This division into three stages is relevant in this context because it helps explain Selznick's own interest in questions of legal and social theory, questions of the third stage: he is interested in the meaning of legality or the rule of law (1969, 11), in the development of the legal system as a whole (Nonet & Selznick 1978), in the connections between social and legal theory (1992). This focus on theoretical questions has been condemned as the practising of sociological jurisprudence instead of sociology of law (Black 1972, 713). For Selznick himself this is not problematic, because he sees the subject-matter of legal sociology and sociological jurisprudence as a continuum and uses both the terms legal sociology and sociological jurisprudence for what he does. Again, we can recognize the pragmatist basis of his theory in the fluidity of this characterization. What really sets Selznick apart from a sociologist such as Black is the emphasis on normative theory and the continuity between empirical research and a normative standpoint. The debate between Selznick and Black is a debate between two very different views of social science. For Black, the only proper object of social science is observable behaviour, while Selznick deems it essential to connect behaviour to the values held by the actors.[17] According to Selznick, a social-science perspective on law should pay attention both to the social conditions that affect law and to the distinctively legal (1968, 50-51).

Selznick reproaches sociology in general with a preoccupation with informal structures. Although informal patterns are very important, they often occur within a formal setting and this setting both influences and is influenced by informal structure. In much of his own work, Selznick occupies himself with the interplay of formal structures, organizations and institutions, and informal and implicit patterns.[18] This is especially relevant to sociology of law, which deals with a field dominated by the formal structure of law. Selznick sees it as a task of legal sociology that it have an eye for the interplay of formal and informal elements, for example incipient law (1968, 55; 1969, 32-33). The idea of incipient law means that formal law can grow out of an informal social setting. Changes in the social setting can generate the need for new kinds of legal rules, rules which then emerge from the social circumstances (1969, 33). A good example is the trend towards strict liability for harm caused by manufactured goods (33). Through incipient law, changing social patterns feed legal change naturally: established social rules or expectations cannot be ignored by law and are incorporated. In *Law, Society*

17 For an extensive discussion of two types of social science research, behaviourism and interpretivism, see Tamanaha 1997. Black is usually regarded as a representative of behaviourism, while Selznick can be regarded an interpretivist. However, one should keep in mind that interpretivism has radicalized (e.g. in Critical Legal Studies) to a relativist position that is not Selznick's. The debate between Black and Selznick started with Black's review of *Law, Society and Industrial Justice*, to which Selznick reacted (Black 1972, Selznick 1973; see Nonet 1976 and Schuyt 1983, 94-109 for a discussion).

18 The connection between formal and informal patterns was also prominent in Selznick's organizational sociology. In his case study of the Tennessee Valley Authority (TVA), he described the importance of both formal and informal co-optation. The TVA was an administrative organization that had to work closely with pre-existing groups in the area. The way it found to do this can be described as co-optation. Co-optation can be a deliberate strategy of the organization's leadership, that, however, need not be the case. Deliberate and open co-optation is what Selznick calls formal co-optation, but there is also an informal type: uncalculated response to pressures from the community (1949, 14).

*and Industrial Justice* the continuity between law and other social institutions is highlighted by pointing out the internal affinity of organizations with principles of legality (1969, 17). Selznick shows how principles of fairness and due process already acknowledged in organizations form a basis for a broad law of governance, applicable to both public and private institutions.

Selznick sees a close affinity between sociology of law and legal pluralism, the idea that we can find law in a range of contexts not necessarily connected to the state. However, in order to identify these forms of law it is necessary to have an idea of what law is, so this is also a subject with which a legal sociologist must be occupied. The character specific to law is designated as 'the distinctively legal': "An adequate theory of law must identify the distinctive work done by law in society, the special resources of law, and the characteristic mechanisms that law brings into play" (1968, 51). For Selznick, a focus on the distinctively legal does not limit the study of law to state law. Law is based on authority, but authority can also arise in other settings than the state. The distinctively legal is also expressed in Selznick's idea of law having its own 'master ideal'. The ideal that governs law is legality, "the progressive reduction of arbitrariness in positive law and its administration" (1976, 233).[19] It is the specific aim of the law to realize legality, but as we saw, this ideal also has meaning in contexts where only the first rudiments of legal thinking can be discerned.

*Communitarian Social Theory*

Selznick's magnum opus is *The Moral Commonwealth* (1992), the book that weaves together almost all the themes that have interested him over the years. However, those themes are combined from one particular perspective: Selznick's version of communitarianism. Selznick had already contributed to the liberal-communitarian debate with a few articles (1987, 1989), but in *The Moral Commonwealth* he expounded his 'communitarian liberalism' in full with support from moral, social and legal theory (1992, xi-xii). His view is indeed a blend of communitarian and liberal ideas, but it has a definite communitarian grounding in his view of the person, his idea of culture, and his views on the values of community.

Selznick's view of the person is based on the idea of the 'implicated' and

[19] A recurring phrase, see also: 1961, 100; 1968, 52; 1969, 12; 1992, 445. I will discuss the ideal of legality at length in Chapter 6.

responsible self (1992, 201; 227).[20] The implicated self is a person with genuine attachments to the people around him: his sense of moral obligation primarily derives from relatedness and identity. In the relationships with significant others he is involved with his whole personality. "Out of this meshing of lives and activities there emerges an implicated self whose obligations are neither wholly voluntary nor wholly imposed" (205). According to Selznick, the implicated self is not only recognizable in one's responsibilities and ties to others, but also in a sense of responsibility for one's own character. A responsible person is characterized by integrity and self-governance guided by moral ideals (227-228). Being responsible combines care for others with care for one's own character: it is to a large extent in the relationships with others that the self develops. Thus, the person in Selznick's view is grounded in social bonds. Being a moral person starts with acknowledging the obligations to particular others, and although universal moral norms are equally important, these particular bonds are primordial (194).

The idea of the responsible self is combined with a strong notion of culture. Culture is that which is produced by, and sustains, shared symbolic experience (Jaeger & Selznick 1964, 663). Culture is created by human beings when they create symbols, when they give their ordinary, physical and instrumental, environment expressive and person-centred meanings (1964, 660). These are cultural symbols when they are shared by a group and are expressive of a common history. Culture is needed by human beings: they need a tradition that provides symbols and a sense of a shared background (1992, 395). Culture in this strong sense of shared symbolic experience is not necessarily present in all groups that we usually call cultures. Cultures in the latter, weak sense of any group with a similar background can very well lack the integration and shared values that are essential to shared symbolic experience. In fact, one of the losses of modern Western society is precisely the weakening of culture in the sense of shared symbolic experience (1992, 8). Thus, Selznick uses the notion of culture for communitarian criticism of modern society.

The third central concept in Selznick's theory is that of community. He defines it as follows: "A group is a community to the extent that it encompasses a broad range of activities and interests, and to the extent that participation implicates whole persons rather than segmental interests or

[20] The idea of an implicated self is one of the key elements of the communitarian criticism of liberalism. Extensive use of it was made by Michael Sandel, who criticized (Rawlsian) liberalism for using an atomistic theory of the person, "the unencumbered self" (1982, 175-183).

activities" (1992, 358). Community is not dependent on specific shared understandings, but, like his concept of culture, the idea of community is demanding because of the focus on involvement of whole persons. In order to achieve this, a community must realize an intricate balance of values (364). A good community allows for plurality and supports personal autonomy, but it also nourishes a sense of a shared history and of identity, and builds reciprocity, participation, and integration (361-64). The realization of these values is the key to community, and in the range of values we can see how Selznick blends liberal aspects into his communitarian views. Selznick makes the elements of autonomy and plurality, which have a definite liberal orientation, interdependent with elements that are characteristic of communitarianism, such as historicity and mutuality.

In the idea of community, liberal and communitarian elements are combined, which is indicative of a general strategy to use liberal ideas to counter the negative consequences of too strong an emphasis on tradition and social cohesion. Although the weakening of culture in modern times is mourned, it is also an opportunity to find new values, to emancipate oppressed groups, and to make decisions more rational. For Selznick, the regret for the loss of integrated, strong cultures is counterposed by the gains of modernity for liberal values such as autonomy and moral equality.[21] Similarly, the responsible self is built on a social basis of particular relationships, but moves on to extend moral recognition to all human beings. We should never be content with the conventional morality of the group, but should use critical morality to improve it (394). The important underlying reason for defending a communitarian liberalism is that the society to which Selznick belongs, the American community, should be understood as a liberal community, one in which liberal principles and values are part of the tradition and define the way of life. So loyalty to the particularity of his own culture and a genuine understanding of its values commit Selznick to liberal views. However, the basis of this liberalism is thoroughly defended in a communitarian way, and communitarian insights serve as a handle to criticize the excesses of liberalism. The values he defends are a blend of the liberal and the communitarian, but the basis of his theory — his account of the person and of society — is communitarian.

21 This makes Selznick more positive about modern society than many other communitarians, the most prominent pessimist about modern morality being Alasdair MacIntyre (1984).

## 4. LEGAL THEORY

Selznick's theory of law is an integral part of his broader social theory. This is reflected in his main theses about law: the development in the changing relations between law and society, and the importance of an empirically informed study of law's values. Both the development model and the doctrine of legal naturalism are important in this context, because they underpin Selznick's view of law as oriented towards the master ideal of legality.

### *A Developmental Model of Law and Society*

Selznick advanced his developmental theory in the essay *Law and Society in Transition: Toward Responsive Law*, written together with Philippe Nonet (1978). In this work they sketched a theory about the nature of law that distinguishes three stages: repressive, autonomous, and responsive law. Their theory is developmental because of the thesis that each stage of law generates the need for the next stage because of internal problems. The stage of repressive law is marked by a structure of law as command, in which law is the instrument of existing political powers. The state uses law to mould society to its will. Law is used as a pliable tool to secure the position of the ruling elites (1978, 51). The system of repressive law runs into problems because it depends on control by the state and its officials over society. Repressive law depends heavily on the use of sanctions to force people to comply. It does not pay enough attention to the need for the legitimacy of power, and by this lack of accountability fails to secure consent of the citizens (52). The pressures within the system of repressive law push the legal system in the direction of autonomous law. Autonomous law is characterized by a separation between law and the political state: the law has its own field of expertise, the application and refinement of rules. The shift from repressive to autonomous law shows in the shift of emphasis from legislation to adjudication; repressive law works by making and changing the rules, while autonomous law depends on procedure and the constraints of the rule of law. But autonomous law has its own problems: because it is isolated and contained in its own specialism, the links between the law and the society in which it operates are weakened. The law offers only formal justice, justice according to the rules, and this is often a far cry from substantive justice. This discrepancy paves the way for responsive law, in which law and politics are reunited in a flexible way based on general purposes, so that it can be sensitive to concrete problems (1978, 79). Law is responsive when it attends to the needs and values of society. Responsiveness is made possible because the law is based on generally formulated purpose instead of strict rules: the more general nature of these purposes allows adaptation of the law in response to people's interests.

This developmental analysis of law gives an instrument to characterize a legal system or field of law and thus a way to understand the problems or possibilities of a given system. The more interesting part, however, of the developmental model is its characterization of the dynamics of law. The changes in law occur because of an "inner dynamic", they are not forced upon it from the outside but result from an adaption of the legal system itself when it runs into problems (1978, 23). Each stage of the development has both merits and defects, solving some problems but creating others. None of the stages are balanced, they always lead to something else. The main danger of responsive law is overreaching: when the purposes of the law become too generalized they allow opportunistic interpretations and decisions (83). Finally, responsive law can lead to the loss of law's distinctive identity, when legal purpose and government purpose become one (116). The great risk then is a relapse from responsive law to repressive law, because both types of law are characterized by a large amount of official discretion (117). The main difference between the two is that responsive law tries to uphold political ideals.

In his later work (1992, 1998), Selznick stresses the way responsive law builds on the achievements of autonomous law, especially on the centrality of the rule of law. Both autonomous law and responsive law are committed to the ideal of legality. Responsive law does not depart from rule of law thinking, but changes the conception of the rule of law. Where autonomous law stresses procedural constraints and formal justice, responsive law focuses on broad principles and substantive justice. Selznick believes the promise of a responsive legal order is already contained in the common law tradition: the tradition of judge-made law that treats the law as given, yet adaptable (1992, 449). Common law judges take social usage as their key to adapt principles to new circumstances and are thus committed to "the integration of law and society" (463). Selznick argues that the Anglo-American legal climate was congenial to a shift from autonomous to responsive law, because the common law tradition contains the grain of a responsive approach. This sheds a different light on the dynamics between the three stages of law. Here, Selznick draws attention to the strands that can be found in a legal tradition that are congenial to responsive values. Even when the overall characterization of law as autonomous law is correct, the autonomy of the legal order need not be complete. It is possible that a change towards a new stage can build on certain elements that are already part of the tradition. This means the developmental model must be applied with caution, although the thesis that development is the result of an inner dynamic still holds: development is not abrupt but it is possible to trace the shifts of emphasis in the history of legal systems.

*Legal Naturalism*

In an early article devoted to sociology and law Selznick clearly took a position in the ongoing debate between legal positivism and natural law by giving the article the title 'Sociology and Natural Law' (1961). In it he argues that natural law shares with sociology its basic commitments, most importantly to scientific inquiry, to the centrality of ideals, and to discovering enduring truths (102). The combination of scientific inquiry with a central place for ideals and for enduring truths is specific to Selznick's interpretation of natural law thinking. He is able to connect his social science perspective to natural law, because he sees natural law thinking as dependent on the discoveries of the social sciences — discoveries about the nature of man, of society, of law. His affinity with traditional natural law thinking depends on the other two commitments, which they share: the quest for enduring truths and the focus on ideals. These ideas are not accepted wholesale either: Selznick interprets them in such a way that they accord with his pragmatist, scientific perspective.

Traditional natural law theory found its enduring truths in divine revelation or in self-evident truths about the nature of man (see Chapter 8). For Selznick, the source of truth is different: it is the result of (social) scientific research. In his pragmatist view, this means that enduring truths are objective and may be universally valid, but they are not absolute. Discoveries have been made about man, society, and law that can be applied — with caution — in all contexts, but their truth is subject to revision (1961, 101). They are the best we have got now, but we should always be prepared to revise them in the light of new evidence. Once again, the importance of scientific inquiry is asserted: inquiry is necessary for the critical examination of accepted truths. Not all enduring truths are universally valid: not all truths about men, societies, and legal systems have a universal scope, on the contrary, many are particular to one group or system. However, this does not make it true that there are no universal truths at all. Selznick thus accepts part of the natural law doctrine: he agrees with the search for universal principles, but he is cautious about their scope and he rejects the claim that they are true forever (103).

The other connection to natural law thinking is the attention he gives to the role of ideals or values; again he interprets a natural law idea in a sociological way. Selznick believes that social phenomena that are normative — what he calls "normative systems" — can only be understood in connection with leading ideals: normative systems are oriented towards ideals and in order to understand the social phenomenon the ideal must be understood as well (1961, 86-87). Law is one such normative system, oriented towards the master ideal of legality.[22] The idea that law is inherently connected with certain values such as justice or legality is a recurring idea in natural law theory. For Selznick this feature is something that law shares with other normative systems such as democracy, parenthood, or reason. All of these should be studied by the social scientist with a focus on the ideals that guide them. This does not mean that these ideals alone can give adequate knowledge of the normative systems: behaviour of the participants, norms of the system, factual circumstances are equally relevant, but they should be considered in relation to the governing ideal. Because of this view of the proper approach to social science, as an evaluative approach, Selznick believes in the possibility of combining social science and natural law and proposes a theory of law that is ideal-oriented and science-oriented at the same time.

Because of these differences with traditional natural law theory, giving Selznick's theory the label of natural law theory is misleading. To express the combination of pragmatism and natural law, another term to refer to his theory is needed. I will use legal naturalism, a term suggested by Selznick himself, coined in a book review on Lon Fuller, whose theory he also brings under this heading (1970, 1475). Selznick chose the term to emphasize the affinity between legal naturalism and the pragmatic naturalism of Dewey's (1477). Legal naturalism shares the pragmatist emphasis on scientific inquiry: "The objective of the naturalist is a social science of legal ordering" (1479). It is explicitly normative, concerned with legal values and ideals, but it sees the relations between law and ideals as variable. Although legal experience is intimately connected with values, it is an empirical question to what extent a given legal system realizes those values. Legal naturalism with its focus on empirical variability is able to assess the presence or absence of values in a legal system.

Although Selznick has a clear affinity with natural law he also uses elements from legal positivism. In *The Moral Commonwealth* he even tries to reconcile the two old enemies. He uses two main strategies to achieve this reconciliation, both familiar: a focus on values and a distinction between weak definition and strong theory. Selznick insists that both natural law and legal positivism are attentive to the values of the law, but they focus on different values. According to Selznick, natural law sees justice as the central value of

[22] I will discuss the notion of master ideals in detail in the next chapter.

the law, while positivism thinks clarity, certainty, and autonomy are central (1992, 435-36).[23] Selznick sees the values associated with positivism as important, but nevertheless as subordinate to substantive justice. When they cease to serve justice and enlarge arbitrariness, their worth should be reassessed (437). The other strategy to bring natural law and legal positivism together uses the definition-theory distinction. Legal positivism is interested in the question of the definition of law: what are the criteria for calling a system legal? Selznick has always used the definition of Hart, based on the existence of secondary rules, which is eminently suitable to set up a threshold (1969, 5;1992, 442). Legal positivism thus provides the weak definition of law that can form the basis of Selznick's legal theory. However, it is only the basis; to develop a strong theory of law he needs natural law which connects law and justice:

> Natural-law theorists counter that law need not be understood as a mere datum of social power or convention. They see in legal experience the development of expectations and constraints, standards and aspirations, that push law in the direction of justice, even though that push may not go very far at any given time (1992, 444).

Selznick follows natural law theory in the focus on substantive justice. In his theory of law, it is used as a critical standard in the sense that legal arrangements and legal values are assessed according to their contribution to justice in society (1992, 433-434). Selznick presents his theory as a reconciliation of legal positivism and natural law, but when we examine the combination it is apparent that natural law theory has influence on the more central points. Positivism has a very limited part in his theory: its values are subordinate to justice and its definition is no more than the threshold of the theory. And, more importantly, one of its chief tenets — the separation of law and morals[24] — is rejected completely. Therefore, Selznick's theory is better understood as a legal naturalism that owes a large debt to natural law, but to make it more empirically informed, interprets natural law by drawing on the pragmatist tradition.

The combination of pragmatism with natural law's focus on human nature is one of the key features of Selznick's view of ideals. In the next chapter, I want to examine what view of ideals his pragmatist naturalism entails and how successful this combination is between natural law's focus on enduring values and pragmatism's focus on context and provisionality.

[23] The attribution of value-orientation to positivism is not generally accepted by positivist theorists. Compare the discussion of legal positivism in Chapter 8.

[24] See Hart 1958, 18. I will go into the discussion about Hart's separation thesis in Chapter 8.

# CHAPTER 6

# SELZNICK ON IDEALS

## 1. INTRODUCTION

In the last section of Chapter 5 we saw that Selznick combines a pragmatist emphasis on empirical inquiry with natural law's search for enduring and universal ideals. In this chapter I want to examine in detail what this combination, that is, Selznick's naturalism, yields by way of a theory of ideals. This account of Selznick's views on ideals is a preliminary step towards my main aim: evaluation of Selznick's theory in the light of the leading question of this book. Does his theory provide a concept of ideals that is useful in legal theory? To that end, I will consider both the acceptability of the theory as such — its plausibility and consistency — and the usefulness of his concept of ideals in a legal context. The remaining part of this introduction will be devoted to Selznick's main argument about ideals.

Selznick introduced his theory of master ideals in his article 'Sociology and Natural Law' (1961). The main argument of the article is that sociology, and legal sociology in particular, can learn from the natural law tradition to give values a central place in its account of the social world. Selznick argues that important social phenomena, such as parenthood, love, scholarship, or citizenship, cannot be understood unless they are seen as oriented towards a master ideal. All of these are "phenomena in the social world whose very nature encompasses the realization of values" (1961, 86). The distinguishing feature of such phenomena, called 'normative systems' in this article, is that they are governed by a master ideal. Friendship, for instance, is an intricate mix of feeling, behaviour, thought, and norms that is held together by a commitment to the ideal of friendship (87). This means that one can never fully understand what friendship is, unless one knows what the ideal means at which this normative system is aimed.

However, Selznick's argument is not simply a plea to study the ideal in addition to the phenomenon in which one is interested. There are two important reasons for understanding these phenomena as governed by a master ideal: it gives an account of what is characteristic about them and it provides a standard of assessment. Seeing friendship as a normative system, or practice, governed by the master ideal of friendship explains what the different relationships called friendships have in common, that it is more than serving one's interest, that it involves commitment and trust, etc. But the master ideal can also serve as a tool to understand why some friendships are closer than others, and what is problematic about a certain friendship. When the ideal is related to concrete friendships, it serves as a standard of evaluation. A focus on ideals brings to light the tensions and problems normative systems generate while trying to realize ideals. Understanding how a normative system and its ideal interact gives insight in the functioning of the normative system that cannot be attained by looking at observable facts alone (1961, 87). Of course, it is possible to describe a phenomenon, for instance, parenthood, in a factual manner, without regard for the values involved. However, a purely factual approach cannot account for a parent's feelings of failure or for the satisfaction a good parental relationship gives. These and other aspects of parenthood can be readily explained by relating them to the ideal of a good parent.

These ideals are not some outside standard, invented by a theorist as a tool of analysis. Values have a natural basis: the ideal of parenthood arises naturally from the biological ties of a parent and a child. In other words, the ideal of parenthood is latent in that biological relationship (1961, 90). The latency of ideals does not mean that every parental relationship is actually realizing the ideal of parenthood or is even necessarily oriented towards it. Many things can go wrong, but in the normal course of things parenting will involve value orientation. The emergence of an ideal is likely, although not necessary. Moreover, parenthood is a more satisfying experience when it is guided by the ideal. Normative systems function more effectively when there is a commitment to the ideals that are latent in them.

A focus on the ideal provides a basis for criticism of specific norms within a phenomenon. This can be shown most clearly in the case of law. When law is seen as governed by an ideal, as it is in the natural law tradition according to Selznick, we see that realization of the ideal is the test for assessing specific norms: a legal rule can be criticized for frustrating realization of the master ideal of law. When the ideal is related to factual conditions, we can also see that in changing circumstances upholding a norm which was effective previously can now impede realization of the ideal (1961, 103).

When one studies normative social phenomena, it is necessary to pay attention to the ideal that guides a phenomenon, and ask what that ideal means and demands. But such a phenomenon should be studied as a living reality, which means examining the ways in which realization of the governing ideal is supported or undermined and the way the ideal interacts with other aspects of the phenomenon at hand. A firm understanding of what the ideal demands helps to get a grip on the problems within a practice. Knowledge of the standard of achievement is necessary to evaluate problems and solutions — without knowing the ideal, there is no way to determine which direction solutions should take — even though it is not sufficient to see what is right in the circumstances. Knowledge of the ideal needs to be supplemented with knowledge of facts and specific norms. However, the use of a master ideal as a central element of a phenomenon points to the difference and the connections between "the living reality" of a practice and the ideal that it aims to achieve (1961, 87).

In this chapter I will discuss and evaluate the four main aspects of Selznick's theory of ideals. I will first examine his argument about the ontology of ideals and examine his combination of pragmatism and naturalism (6.2). I will then focus on one central feature of ideals in Selznick's theory, their latency in the world of fact (6.3). In section 6.4, I will discuss his doctrine of the master ideal. That leaves the role of ideals in law (6.5) and, finally, my conclusions about Selznick's view (6.6).

Before I go on, I need to make one note about Selznick's theory in relation to my aims in this book. Selznick does not provide precise answers to the conceptual questions I raised in Chapter 1. This is most noticeable in relation to the distinction between ideal and value. Selznick uses the terms ideal and value as interchangeable, and does not seem to attach specific features to either ideal or value. The most promising aspect in this respect is his concept of a master ideal; therefore, I will address the issue of a possible distinction between ideal and value in section 6.4. Until then, I will follow Selznick's indiscriminate use of the terms ideal and value.

## 2. THE NATURE OF VALUES

This section deals with the ontological basis of Selznick's concept of ideals. It is important to realize that Selznick's approach to questions regarding the nature of ideals and their distinctive features is profoundly influenced by his sociological orientation and his pragmatist method. Selznick is not primarily interested in the development of a concept of ideals, but in a meaningful account of ideals in societal practices. He is committed to a view of ideals or values as situated in and determined by social reality, but a more precise description of the concept of ideals can be avoided with reference to empirical findings: the meaning of ideals is established by examining how they function in a factual situation. This neglect of conceptual work makes it necessary to reconstruct Selznick's argument about the nature of ideals that will at times move beyond the letter of his work.

Selznick's account of the nature of ideals is made up of both pragmatist and natural-law ideas. The pragmatist influence is apparent in his insistence on the provisional status of ideals and their basis in problem-solving experience. These are backed by the emphasis on empirical knowledge. The natural-law influence is apparent in Selznick's grounding of universal ideals in human nature and in his interpretation of the latency of ideals. In this section I will discuss the implications of these two strands in relation to the nature of ideals.

Selznick proposes four central theses about ideals or values that can be read as following from his commitment to pragmatism. First, values are the objective basis for the distinction between the satisfying and the satisfactory (1992, 33). Secondly, values have their basis in problem-solving experience (1992, 192). From this ontological claim about the immanent nature of values follows a third, epistemological claim: empirical knowledge is vital for understanding values (1992, 37). And, fourth, values should not be seen as having eternal validity (1961, 101).

All of these claims are more easily understood, if we return to Dewey for a moment and consider his ideas about values.[1] In Dewey's theory values have their origin in experienced enjoyments, but unlike a subjectivist account of values his theory takes felt enjoyments only as a starting point. Enjoyments are not always right or good: an alcoholic enjoys drinking, but no one would conclude that his drinking is therefore a good thing. Values come into the picture when felt enjoyments are problematic, when we need to ask ourselves what is good. Values are the standards "that are taken to have rightful authority in the direction of conduct" (1929, 204). How do we determine those values? Here we should recall Dewey's insistence on the unity of method between the (natural and moral) sciences. Values should be regarded as hypotheses which are assessed by the application of the scientific method (1929, 221). Their worth is determined by the consequences that are discovered in this process. Thus, the most important aspect of the method used in assessing proposed values is to review the consequences of adopting the value. Values are assessed by their conditions and consequences: the validity of a value is dependent on the means necessary to bring it about and on what

[1] This account of Dewey's theory is based primarily on the chapter "The Construction of Good" in *The Quest for Certainty* (1929, 203-228).

it results in when acted upon (1929, 212). Because values are determined in this process of reviewing conditions and consequences, they can be regarded as resulting from a methodical investigation. As the result of intelligent inquiry, values are objective standards of criticism and guidance: they have been tested and found sound.

Once through this process, values are reconnected with enjoyments: when values are acted upon, states of affairs are brought about, objects are made and chosen, that have genuine value. It is important to realize that in Dewey's theory the term 'value' is ambiguous: "Judgments about values are judgments about the conditions and the results of experienced objects; judgments about that which should regulate the formation of our desires, affections and enjoyments" (1929, 212). In the first sense, an object is a value when it is judged to have value, but in the second sense the standard that warrants this judgment is a value. For Dewey, the first sense of a value-object is primary: it is the problem of an object having value or not that triggers inquiry. However, we can say that this inquiry generates the value-standard: that by which one judges the object. When the object is judged valuable, standard and object coincide; when it is not, the value-standard remains a value to be realized. Thus, value-object and value-standard turn out to be closely connected but distinguishable. In general, the important point remains that values gain objectivity by being subject to intelligent inquiry, and this makes them crucial in criticizing and guiding conduct.

We can now return to Selznick's four pragmatist theses. All four can be understood in the light of Dewey's value theory, although it is not always entirely clear whether Selznick himself gives a consistently pragmatist interpretation to these ideas. He does in regard to the first thesis I mentioned. The distinction between the satisfying and the satisfactory — made by both Dewey and Selznick — is directly related to Dewey's concept of value as the result of inquiry. The distinguishing mark of the satisfactory as against a simple enjoyment is that the first has value in the sense of having stood the test of critical evaluation. Values can therefore be used to criticize judgments of states of affairs: even if a state of affairs is seen as satisfying, that does not mean that it is satisfactory in the light of the values concerned. With the distinction between the satisfying and the satisfactory the idea is conveyed that, although values are closely connected to direct, unreflected, feelings and judgments, values are not reducible to these, but have objective validity when they are warranted by intelligent inquiry.

A crucial point in the pragmatist argument is when to move from unreflected enjoyments to inquiry into values. This is necessary when an enjoyment becomes problematic: consideration of the value of the enjoyment can point to a solution. This brings us to the second pragmatist aspect of Selznick's value theory: their basis in problem-solving experience. Values are discovered and developed as people learn from the problems they encounter in their moral experience (1992, 37). This is the central point of Selznick's argument about the nature of values: "(...) genuine values emerge from experience; they are discovered, not imposed" (1992, 19). They are discoverable because they are latent in social reality (1961, 90).[2] Value is part of the social reality we inhabit; it is an aspect of the satisfactory arrangements and objects in the social world. At this point, the immanent character of Selznick's view of values is clear: values are inherent in reality. Exactly how to interpret the immanence of values in Selznick's theory is not quite clear. It is possible to understand his ontological views in the tradition of Aristotelian natural law thinking, but also to understand them as based in a pragmatist world view. This is part of a broader pragmatist world view, which is holistic: not only the ideal and the real, but also man and nature are part of one world we can experience.[3] Because human beings are seen as organisms within nature, their experiences are continuous with other interactions that occur. The one aspect that distinguishes human interactions from others is that human beings are capable of intelligent behaviour. Pragmatist ideas about values or ideals have to be understood in the light of these ideas about the interactions of human beings with their environment. An ideal is not thought up in isolation, it is recognized when an experience is problematic and then used to improve upon that experience. Thus, ideals are directly related to concrete experiences, and they are determined by the specific circumstances of that particular situation.

In this light we can understand Selznick's ideas on the objectivity of values. Selznick describes an objective value as follows: "It is, or is the source of, a good experience of a certain kind" (Jaeger & Selznick 1964, 667). What is a good experience depends very much on the circumstances, primarily social and cultural, of that particular kind of experience. Consider what Selznick says about monogamy and polygamy:

2 I will examine the meaning of the latency of ideals in the next section.

3 Dewey explains his metaphysics most extensively in *Experience and Nature*, emphasizing the connection between man and nature: "Yet if man is within nature, not a little god outside, and is within as a mode of energy inseparably connected with other modes, interaction is the one unescapable trait of every human concern; thinking, even philosophic thinking, is not exempt." (1925, 351).

> But if some social arrangement, such as monogamy, is objectively valuable, this does not mean that it is the exclusive source of value, even within its special sphere. Nor does it mean that monogamy always and everywhere makes the same contribution to human well-being, or has only positive attributes. That the same can be said of polygamy does not vitiate the objectivity of the values to be found in each (Jaeger & Selznick 1964, 667).

The idea that both monogamy and polygamy have objective value is not easily grasped. In a subjectivist theory of values the value of both can easily be explained: one group of persons holds that monogamy has value, while a second group is in favour of polygamy. But if we do not locate the validity of values in subjective beliefs, then how can opposing values both be objective? The pragmatist answer is that both values are answers to experienced problems that are real, but differ from place to place and time to time. An explanation of polygamy could, for instance, be related to a problematic ratio of male to female members of society. If a society is confronted with a large number of its men dying young, polygamy has value because it ensures continued existence of the society. At the same time, for a society in which men and women have comparable life expectancy, monogamy is the more likely value in this sphere. Explanations of this kind can be sought and elaborated to make clear that there are often factual conditions that explain and validate certain values. For a good assessment of the value of monogamy and polygamy serious study of their conditions is needed, but the example can serve to make certain things clear. If problems differ, values will differ as well because they are part of the problem-solving experience of people. But this variety of values does not affect their objectivity, because their objectivity is based on the connection between value and real problems and needs.

This brings us to the third pragmatist claim: the need for empirical knowledge. Locating values in problem-solving experience makes a focus on experience necessary to understand values. The way to know what problems people face and how values help to solve these, is by studying situations empirically. A second reason, at least as important, for emphasis on empirical evidence is that the pragmatist method is experimental: values have to be tested to determine their worth. These considerations make clear what Selznick's basis is for claiming that a social science approach to values and a pragmatist philosophy converge (1992, 29). Both concentrate on the way values function in everyday situations and are reluctant to make a priori claims about the nature of values.

Connected to the reluctance to make a priori claims about values is the fourth pragmatist thesis we find in Selznick's work: the denial of the eternal validity of values. As said before, the objectivity of values is grounded in the method by which they are reached. This does not entail that values have unquestionable validity. The method of intelligent inquiry looks into the conditions and consequences of values and these are not stable. Because values are seen as hypotheses that are tested, their validity is always conditional. Circumstances can arise, consequences can be discovered, that call into question continued assertion of a value. Both our knowledge of the circumstances giving rise to a value and the circumstances themselves can change; in both cases we need to revise our view of the value's validity. When we acquire better knowledge of the conditions of a value, it is our understanding of the value that must be amended to incorporate this new knowledge. When the circumstances themselves change, the value itself is called into question and we must ask ourselves whether it is still valid under new conditions. No value's validity can ever be final, eternal, or absolute.

The denial of absolute and eternal validity does not prevent Selznick from making claims about the enduring importance of certain values or about the universal reach of some values. Here he moves away from pragmatism and supplements it with ideas from the natural law tradition to form his own specific form of naturalism.[4] Selznick himself stresses the continuity between pragmatist ideas and (Aristotelian) natural law thinking, but I will argue that the combination of the two is not quite as successful as Selznick claims. My main point is that his argument for vague universal values in which he draws on the natural law tradition is not compatible with pragmatism's emphasis on change and experimental method. With the natural law tradition he shares the attention for "enduring truths" (1961, 102) and the "quest for universals" (103), which are at odds with Dewey's stress on uncertainty and change. To substantiate these claims I will turn to the discussion of the natural law strand in Selznick's work.

Selznick believes that a number of basic values are adhered to universally.

[4] As I did in Chapter 2, I reserve the term naturalism for the view that grounds ideals in human nature (and thus believes them to be universal) but leaves leeway for different interpretations. Both Selznick and Nussbaum can be seen as adherents of this view. Pragmatism moves still further away from an Aristotelian view of ideals by leaving the focus on a secure and universal basis for ideals. Selznick himself uses the term naturalism in a much broader sense, including Aristotle, Spinoza, Hume, Santayana, Dewey, and himself, referring to the view that ideal states are part of nature (1992, 24). This is the thesis I have called the immanence of ideals. Selznick calls Dewey's theory 'pragmatic naturalism', which I have simply referred to as pragmatism. In this chapter, I am challenging the idea that Selznick's combination of pragmatism and natural law thinking yields a defensible theory, denying that Selznick's own 'pragmatic naturalism' is a good alternative.

These are the values that are connected to primary human needs and functions, such as preserving human life, caring for close relatives, the need for affection (1992, 96). The values of a basic morality occur across cultures because they are based on the characteristics of human beings as such: they go together with the natural features of mankind (1961, 101-102). Because man is a social animal, the existence of societies and certain features of them are natural as well. The nature of man and, derived from that, the nature of society thus determine that there are certain universal basic values. These are very general values, of course, and Selznick does not deny that their specifications may differ hugely from one society to the other (1992, 96). In the same way as Selznick argues that man is by nature social and therefore there are natural social values, he argues that it is a universal characteristic of human beings that they need particular arrangements (1992, 102). The need for difference, for practices peculiar to a culture or group, is a universal need.

However, the recognition of the need for particularity does not undermine the importance of universals. For Selznick, the universal characteristics of humans are as important as their particular features, and, we might add, he is more interested in the first category than in the latter. At first sight, he appears to remain faithful to pragmatism in his argument because he appeals to empirical knowledge: both universal and particular characteristics can be recognized when we study different kinds of human experience empirically. But underlying this empirical recognition of universal values is a view of human nature that has an Aristotelian inspiration. If we look at Selznick's theory closely, we can see that this view on human nature carries the weight of the argument about universal values. According to Selznick, such universal values are an integral part of being human: "When we say that certain values are 'inherent' in humanity we mean (1) they are necessary elements of a certain level of existence, not of existence per se, and (2) they arise and are sustained in the normal course of human experience" (1992, 102). Values are not part of the most basic levels of subsistence, but part of human flourishing, emerging in the normal course of a human life. Universal values have a biological basis: they accompany natural phenomena such as sex and parenthood. Realization of such values is essential to human well-being. What is important to Selznick is moral well-being, which for him is essentially a social kind of well-being consisting in the enhancement of fellowship (1992, 32). Selznick's conception of human nature as essentially social again comes to the fore: moral well-being can only be achieved in the relationships with others.

Selznick's highly normative vision of well-being is problematic because it is supported by the idea of a natural development towards its realization. Selznick holds the view that there is an immanent tendency towards the ideals or values that promise well-being (1992, 192). In this way Selznick equates a tendency towards the good with the normal course of human life. He does not argue, however, why this tendency to realize values is normal. This makes his view of human nature unduly positive. To me it seems that, especially in relation to each other, human beings are as capable of violence, taking advantage, degrading others, as they are of fellowship, cooperation and love. Selznick is right to say that the latter values are good for us, that they provide moral well-being. However, it does not seem warranted to conclude that human beings are naturally inclined towards these positive values.

In defence of Selznick, one could say that he does recognize that values are precarious, that their realization is dependent on congenial conditions, that a "malignant heart" is a possibility (1992, 175). He is not blind to the widespread occurrence of delinquency and immoral behaviour (1992, 126). There is, however, a tension he does not dissolve between the recognition that moral value is precarious and the idea that moral value is realized in the normal course of experience. If we take the precariousness of values seriously, this means that it takes effort and watchfulness to ensure that these values are sustained. If they are realized in the natural run of things, this means that it is not necessary to make a conscious effort to sustain them. More is needed for a convincing naturalist view of ideals than Selznick provides; the claim that human beings are naturally inclined to realize values conducive to their well-being cannot stand on its own.

Apart from this general criticism of naturalism there is a second problem: the usefulness of universal values as standards of evaluation and criticism. This point relates to the impossibility of combining natural law ideas with pragmatism, because a pragmatist view sees this practical role of values as the key justification of inquiry into values. In short, my point is that vague universal values do not provide meaningful guidance to the solution of concrete problems and to understanding values in specific contexts.

Selznick acknowledges that the study of human nature can only yield general values that still need to acquire a specific meaning in a context, but insists that this does not make them pointless or irrelevant (1992, 103). The main use he sees for such universal values and virtues is that they point to the limits of variation: "What constitutes honesty or fidelity may differ in different situations, but the generic virtue, properly formulated, can help us distinguish the true from the false, the genuine from the fake" (101). It is doubtful, however, whether a universal value can indeed be used to point to clear limits.

Consider Selznick's example of the ideal of preserving human life (96). This indeed sounds like something every human being strives for, and as something which we can use as a standard of criticism for certain practices. But when we apply it to more concrete problems, it is not always so clear whether the ideal provides a limit. Does it outlaw assisted suicide when someone suffers from terrible pains without a prospect for recovery? Does it prohibit killing a new-born baby by a mother who knows she is too poor and weak to feed it?[5] Not everyone may agree about what is an inevitable exception to the preservation of human life. The point is that it is not clear to what costs it should be preserved. These are problems that cannot be solved with an appeal to a universal value, because it is too vague to provide direction. One needs to know the specific circumstances to understand what the value means in a particular context and to be able to use it as a standard of evaluation. The pragmatist focus on problem-solving experience is a focus on concrete problematic situations in which we can invoke value-standards that similar experiences have warranted. These are not standards that we arrive at by studying the idea of humanity itself; they require attention to the particular features of the situation and considering the consequences of acting upon a particular value. Only then do values become meaningful.

Thus, in my view the more convincing ideas of Selznick's are the ones he derives from pragmatism. His naturalist arguments do more to make his theory problematic than they add to its applicability. There is, however, a good reason for Selznick to appeal to a theory of human nature to ground his theory of values. A purely pragmatist theory of values has difficulty providing a full justification of values because it restricts justification to the direct context of problematic situations. To see what the problem is more precisely, we need to return to the pragmatist construction of good by way of the pragmatic method. A pragmatist theory claims that values are objectively valid when they have been subjected to intelligent inquiry into their conditions and consequences. When we look at that method critically, we see that its potential for generating objective standards is limited. The pragmatist claims objectivity of values because values have been tested with regard to their consequences. Racial segregation does not have value because it has pernicious effects on the well-being of people. On the other hand, friendship has value because having friends enables people to flourish and to lead a meaningful life. There is a problem with this line of argument: how do we judge the effects and

5 The example of infanticide is given by Selznick himself, who apparently does not see it as detracting from the ideal, although "the clash of values is by no means beyond sympathetic understanding" (1992, 97).

consequences of attaching value to certain states of affairs? It is necessary to have some standard of what good consequences are, if we are to judge a value by its consequences. To judge the consequences of a value we need to invoke a value standard. That means a pragmatist account of values suffers from circularity: good consequences determine the worth of a value, which is in turn the standard by which the goodness of consequences is judged. Let me explain by using one of Dewey's examples. We can say that when a fruit is edible it has value. If we want know whether a particular kind of fruit, say a mango, is edible, we test the consequences of eating it. If these are good, then mangoes are edible and have value. But how do we determine whether the consequences of eating a mango are good? Here we apply a standard of being edible that we have acquired from experience: we have established that apples and oranges are edible under certain conditions (not being rotten, for instance) and we apply that knowledge to mangoes as well. But since we derive the standard of being edible from experience with apples and oranges, we can ask the same questions: how did we determine that apples and oranges were edible? There is always the need of applying the standard that is at issue in the situation at hand. The process need not be directly circular: other values are part of the process as well, which can be used to judge the consequences. We can say that eating fruit has good consequences because it is good for one's health. In that process we do not question why we value our health, but valuation is involved: the consequences are about other things that have value. Consequences cannot be assessed neutrally, some standard of reference is needed. The pragmatist account is not specific enough about the way to find the relevant standards.

We can see clearly why Selznick invokes an account of human nature to ground moral values: in this way, he can escape the circularity of a pragmatist argument. His theory of human nature, however, is not very helpful because the link between vague universal values and specific problematic situations is not established. Moreover, his rather optimistic view of human nature is not the most plausible theory of what human beings are like. Although Selznick rightly notes the need for a theory of the good (1992, 98), his own theory based on human nature is not totally satisfactory.

## 3. THE LATENCY OF VALUES

In the last section I mentioned in passing that the immanence of ideals in reality in Selznick's view can be interpreted in different ways. In Selznick's view, the most important feature of the relationship of ideals and reality is the latency of ideals. The idea of latency is subject to the same ambiguity as the more general idea of immanence. In this section I want to discuss Selznick's reasons for emphasizing the latency of ideals and the way it should be interpreted. The most important aspect of ideals in Selznick's view is that they need to have a natural foundation, i.e. a foundation in real groups, relationships, and concerns. Ideals do not always have this intimate connection with existing arrangements. Sometimes they are highly abstract or purely imaginary, for example when they spring from utopian theory. But according to Selznick such abstract ideals suffer from defects and vulnerabilities which are avoided when ideals have a natural foundation.

The weaknesses of abstract ideals all derive from the same characteristic: abstract ideals are too far removed from the experiences of everyday life. There are five such weaknesses. First of all, abstract ideals are inflexible. They do not adapt to the changes in factual circumstances that occur continuously, which makes them vulnerable to challenges of irrelevance based on new insights or new arguments (1992, 197). Secondly, abstract ideals are barely any help for problem-solving. They are necessarily at a distance from concrete contexts, and since problems arise within a specific context, such ideals do not offer any solutions. Therefore, abstract ideals are often virtually empty concerning the issues that really count. They can only work when supplemented by theories about their meaning in context (1992, 215). The third weakness is an invitation to overreaching. Because abstract ideals state general goals without paying attention to contextual constraints, they invite wholesale realization even when more modest realization would be more appropriate. As a result, a caricature of the original ideal is likely to be achieved (174). The fourth weakness is an encouragement to opportunism. Abstract ideals state so little about what is to be done that they can be used for window dressing by people who are only interested in serving their personal objectives (249). Fifthly, abstract ideals are less stable. Because they are not rooted in ongoing daily concerns, they are easily set aside when the developing situation makes their realization more difficult (248).

According to Selznick, all of these weaknesses are lessened when ideals have a grounding in the natural world. That ideals have a natural basis means two things: that they are latent in experience and that they are viable (1992, 160). The idea of latency points to the roots that ideals have in people's concerns in everyday life. Even if there is no explicit reference to ideals or values in an existing practice and the people concerned are not conscious of being guided by ideals, such practices contain beliefs, norms, and behaviour that can be understood as oriented towards ideals. The idea of viability means that ideals should be a "live option": they must have a secure basis in people's needs and wants and be able to contribute to their lives (160). Latency and viability are two aspects of the same approach: while latency is about the origin of ideals, viability stresses the ideals' potential for a meaningful contribution to well-being. For Selznick, viability thus depends on the latency of ideals, because without roots in experience ideals cannot be a real part of people's concerns.

So far, I have only discussed Selznick's normative plea for ideals with a natural basis, but this argument about the importance of latent ideals is combined with two other, descriptive, claims. First, there is the claim that we can "perceive latent values in the world of fact" (1969, 10). Second, perceiving such latent values is necessary to understand the phenomena in which such values inhere. Therefore, only the values that are latent in experience are really important: they are of influence and without them we could not understand the social world. Let me begin with the claim that we can perceive latent values.

The naturalist argument says that seeing that values are latent in experience means recognizing that phenomena have a natural potential for being valued (1969, 10). Under normal conditions fathering a child will cause a man to value the relationship he has with his child, i.e. to value being a parent. This is a natural process because parenthood only functions well if parents value the relationship with their child. It does not mean that being a parent will have value for every mother or father, but valuation serves a biological purpose: they will be more successful as parents if they value that role. And if we recognize that latent values play such a role in any social phenomenon, we see that we need to understand what realizing the value means and how this determines the most fully developed mode of a phenomenon. Only then can we get a grip on the differences, similarities, and problems of various instances of the phenomenon.

Latency does not mean that the value in question will always be realized, even to a minimal extent. As I said before, emergence of the value is likely, not inevitable. We should think of the latency of values as the potential for value realization. Think of a talented musician: a child that has a gift for playing the cello still needs to be taught and coached and needs to practise to be a really good cellist. The ability to play the cello is latent in the child, but if the child never touches an instrument, its ability will never be discovered, let alone come to realization. Similarly, conditions have to be congenial for values to be realized. And like musical talents, the potential of values themselves is variable: in some cases more needs to be done than in others to bring out the value or talent.

The analogy with talents brings up the first problem with the argument about latency, regarding the descriptive claim that latent values are present. If it is possible that a latent value may not be realized, how do you know that it is there in a latent form? To put the point differently, there is no way to prove the latency of values because it is a characteristic that remains implicit. What Selznick tries to do, namely to give an *empirical* argument about latency — we perceive latent values in the world of fact — cannot be done. An empirical argument depends on the possibility of perceiving a phenomenon: it assumes that there is some way to observe an occurrence or situation. It is precisely this it is impossible to do regarding a latent value that has not been realized, because such a value is not observable. The argument can only work in a different way, by showing that the connection between values and the natural functioning of human beings is a necessary one. In the previous section, I argued that such a connection can in theory be established between values and the good life, but not between values and human functioning as such: values are necessary for a certain kind of life, but not for bare survival (1961, 91). Such a connection, however, does not help the descriptive claim about latency: there is still no way of knowing if any given value is latent in the world of fact, when it is in no way realized.

How does this affect the rest of the argument about latency? It means that the second step in the argumentation — the claim that we can only understand social phenomena if we perceive the latent values within them — cannot be taken directly. But there is a way around this problem. If we say that relationships and practices can only function well if they are realizing values, the study of values is necessary to understand what makes such phenomena work. And I think that this premise is sound: a friendship is only successful if friends value the relationship they have. I agree with Selznick as well that the really interesting aspects of social life have to do with reaching a certain level of achievement. We want to make our legal system a good system and we are not content with having just any legal system. To improve our legal system we must bring it closer to the ideals that point out what a good legal system needs to achieve. But such ideals cannot simply be pointed out in the reality of law.

If Selznick's argument for the latency of ideals as perceivable in reality is not convincing, a weaker form of the argument about the latency of values may be based on the claim that they are necessary for the success of a phenomenon. In this more pragmatist version, values are latent in reality because they are answers to problems that occur in the reality of human experience. This view of latency reduces it to a minimal basis in reality, but it is combined with a stronger notion of implicitness. Values are latent in a problematic situation in a minimal sense, because as standards to improve that situation their meaning is constrained by the situation. As possible solutions, values must have their roots in actual situations, and this connection is their latency in the situation. The stronger sense in which a pragmatist view can see values as present in experience, is as implicit standards that have developed in experience and are applied without articulation. They have come to arise naturally in certain situations because they have turned out to be the best way to cope with such situations. Such values have become an implicit part of a practice. The natural basis of values is now a basis in experience. Not every value that is proposed has this quality, so the normative argument that values should have a natural basis stands. Imagined utopias lack this connection with real problems, they have not been tested in everyday experience and the dangers of implementing them without regard for the real situation should be kept in mind.

The points to be gathered from this discussion are the following. The idea of latent values as present in potential cannot be supported by definite proof, but that does not mean that the idea of a real basis of values should be given up. Abstract ideals are too far removed from experience to be meaningful. Values that count find their basis in the problems to which they are solutions. The important point is that valuation is necessary to make people and their relationships, practices, and institutions flourish. To understand how social reality works, we need to see how certain levels of achievement are reached. For that we need to grasp that values have a real connection to the concerns of everyday experience and that we have to study values in that light.

## 4. MASTER IDEALS

I started this chapter with a discussion of Selznick's argument about ideals in terms of master ideals of normative systems. I then turned to the philosophical foundations of his concept of ideals in pragmatism and natural law philosophy, and highlighted the idea of latency as the core of Selznick's immanent concept of ideals. However, Selznick's most original contribution to the theory of ideals has not yet received separate attention: the concept of master ideals itself. Here, I want to address the implications of such a concept.

Master ideals are defined as ideals governing normative systems. More precisely, one master ideal is the ideal that governs one specific normative system. Thus, the first claim made on behalf of master ideals is that they express the unity of the normative system (1961, 87). The first question to be raised is what this means: in what sense does the ideal provide the unity of the normative system? Following upon the precise characterization of master ideals, one can ask whether the connection between ideal and unity is a plausible one. The second claim made about master ideals is that they are complex ideals, consisting of different standards of assessment and criticism (1961, 94). In what sense should we understand this complexity? What is the relation between the ideal and its constitutive standards? The third claim is that master ideals are only incompletely realized in actual experience (1961, 88), or that they cannot always be completely realized (1961, 107). The first aspect of that claim is unproblematic: the empirical assertion that a master ideal is not completely realized in a certain situation. The second aspect of the claim that they cannot always be completely realized is ambiguous: does it mean that ideals can sometimes be completely realized, or that they can never be completely realized? And what is a more interesting question: what makes it so difficult to realize a master ideal completely?

The idea of unity is present in Selznick's first description of master ideals. Of democracy, he says: "A democracy is a normative system in that much complex behavior, as well as many specific norms, is governed by a master ideal. Behavior, feeling, thought, and organization are all bound together by a commitment to the realization of democratic values" (1961, 87). The ideal of democracy is that which holds together certain behaviour and norms, and makes them recognizable as democratic. Selznick insists that the master ideal is part of the normative system, that is, it is a point of orientation and commitment to the people involved in the normative system. The master ideal can be identified by careful study of the normative system in question, so presumably the study of any normative system will lead to the uncovering of a corresponding master ideal. If we study democracy, we will find a master ideal of democracy; if we study friendship, we will find a master ideal of friendship. Thus, for Selznick, the master ideal does indeed provide the unity of the normative system: the ideal as part of the normative system is a common point of orientation. If it does not serve as such in any instance of the normative system, there is something wrong with that particular instance: the ideal now serves as a standard of assessment. This account is problematic in a number of respects.

If much turns on the empirical discovery of the ideal, the selection of the normative system becomes highly important: how does one recognize a normative system as such? And what determines the boundaries of such a system? Selznick points to public opinion, to democracy, to citizenship as examples, but these are not phenomena that are readily perceivable in social reality. One needs to select certain aspects as defining the normative system to delineate the field of study. We have seen that Selznick adopts the strategy of a weak definition here: an undemanding, non-normative, set of criteria. This will determine the field of study in which we are to find the master ideal, but it does not suffice to explicate the ideal itself. For that, a normative theory needs to be formulated. One could formulate a master ideal and test this formulation to see whether the proposed master ideal is equal to the ideal actually adhered to in the normative system. To see how this might work, it is best to consider an example.

Parenthood can serve to illustrate the problem: it is relatively easy to define as the relationship between an adult and the child of which he or she is a parent, either biologically or by accepting familial ties (in the case of adoption or stepparents). Relationships thus identified can then be studied to discover the ideal of parenthood to which the persons involved are (or should be) committed. A formulation of the master ideal of parenthood probably includes loving the child, caring for the child, protecting it from harm, providing its needs for food, shelter, clothing, overseeing its education, etc. This might seem straightforward, but when we consider a specific relationship that does not involve a standard nuclear family, it is not so easy to apply. For example, consider a child whose parents have divorced, living with his mother who remarried. The stepfather may see himself as the child's parent, loving and caring for it, committed to an ideal of parenthood. The child, however, has a biological father who also tries to realize the ideal of parenthood, loving and caring for the child. Are these two men committed to the same master ideal of being a good parent? To the same ideal as the child's mother? For father and stepfather, being a good parent may involve making space for the other father, accepting the other's role. It is doubtful whether they will both see it that way, but can we use the master ideal to criticize their views? The biological father is at a distance, not living with his son, which asks for different behaviour. In this case, some may argue that it is indeed the same ideal to which each is committed, but that this must be interpreted differently in different circumstances. There is a point, however, at which it becomes strained to insist that the same ideal is adhered to. When the shared meaning of an ideal is reduced to an abstract formula that is interpreted in completely different ways, it is no longer in keeping with the idea that ideals must have a real basis to insist that the abstract formula still can be seen as the unifying ideal governing a normative system. To be a governing ideal, a master ideal must be a genuine standard of evaluation, that is, one should be able to use it for meaningful criticism. If parenthood can be understood as guided by very different but equally valid interpretations of the master ideal of parenthood, it will be these more specific interpretations that provide the standards of criticism. Once that is conceded, it is more plausible to see these interpretations as governing ideals. Then there can be different ideals at work in one normative system, and the thesis of the ideal providing unity collapses.

The unity thesis can also be collapsed in a different way. Selznick himself says about rationality: "A familiar and widespread illustration is the governing ideal of rationality in economic and administrative systems" (1961, 91). Here we see that the governing ideal governs a range of economic and administrative systems. It seems unlikely that a bureaucratic government agency and a new economy business company are committed to the same master ideal, although it is likely that they are both committed to the idcal of rationality. Here we see that the role of a master ideal as providing unity can also dissolve because the ideal is relevant to a number of normative systems. An ideal such as rationality is equally relevant to many normative systems — e.g. to science, to economics, to administration — so that it is unlikely that it governs one system especially. Such ideals do not hold together one specific normative system, but cut across systems as a more pervasive ideal.

I think the conclusion is warranted that the relationship between master ideal and normative system is not quite as tight as is suggested by the thesis of unity. Both the possibility of different interpretations of a master ideal within one normative system and the relevance of a master ideal across different systems suggest that there may be many normative systems that are governed by more than one ideal. Here is a possible connection to the second claim that I want to examine: the complexity of a master ideal. One could try to salvage the unity thesis by appealing to the complexity of master ideals. The argument would then be that the master ideal consists of a number of constitutive values which are of variable importance in different circumstances. The commitment in a normative system is to the overarching complex ideal, not to a specific combination of values, which makes room for different interpretations.

In a number of passages Selznick appeals to the complexity of master ideals. Legality is said to embrace "(...) standards for assessing and criticizing decisions that purport to be legal, whether made by a legislature or a court, whether elaborating a rule or applying it to specific cases" (1961, 94). Justice is said to embrace a complex set of interacting variables; it is constituted by principles such as equality and justification (1992, 431-432).[6] Due process is a master ideal restraining government, which consists of five more specific ideals (1969, 252). Selznick makes a distinction between the ideal and the specific norms that are required to realize the ideal (1961, 87). Normative systems strive to realize ideals and specific norms regulating behaviour are necessary to accomplish the realization of an ideal. The ideal is therefore distinct from specific norms; the ideal can be used to criticize specific norms, asking whether the norm contributes to the realization of the ideal (1961, 103).[7] If we see ideals as a specific kind of standard of evaluation, it is plausible to see the standards of which a master ideal consists as value standards. In the example of parenthood, I included love, care, protection, education, in the master ideal of good parenting. All of these can be regarded as values or ideals: they indicate desirable states of affairs to be realized. Selznick uses the concept of a master ideal to refer to the governing ideal of a normative system; here, it appears as the governing idea demanding a set of constitutive values.[8] In the relation between master ideal and constitutive ideals, the latter appear as subordinate to the former. The master ideal of parenthood demands parental love and parental care, which means that ideals of love and care take on a specific form in the light of the ideal of parenthood. However, the ideals of love and care have relevance in other contexts as well, and can even be said to appear as master ideals themselves in a different normative system.[9] The ideal of love can be said to govern the relationship between romantically involved couples. It then takes on a different meaning from that in parental relationships and gives rise to different constitutive

[6] In the discussion of justice, Selznick also connects the meaning of the governing ideal with other ideals. In a communitarian theory, "(...) we enrich familiar forms of justice by infusing them with ideals of mutual trust, respect, reconciliation, and interdependence" (1992, 433).

[7] Here Selznick speaks only of norms in general. At times it seems as if the point only applies to rules. However, although Selznick does not usually make a clear-cut distinction between ideals and principles, the concept of principles has been awarded a specific meaning and role in legal theory that would be underrated if principles were reduced to the constitutive elements of ideals. For now, I will stay with the description of Alexy given in section 1.4: principles are norms prescribing the highest degree of realization of an ideal or value. I will return to the role of principles in Selznick's legal theory in the next section.

[8] Here, my interpretation echoes Radbruch's concepts of idea and constitutive value. There is an important difference, however, between Radbruch's view of values requiring each other at a conceptual level and my interpretation of Selznick basing values on empirical information.

[9] The ideal of care does not seem to be a governing ideal of a specific normative system. In this it resembles the ideal of rationality, which also appears as a pervasive ideal influential in different normative systems.

values. My point is that such ideals can take on the role both of master ideal of a normative system and of constitutive value subordinate to another master ideal. As a consequence, there is no simple hierarchy of ideals: in some contexts they are of greater importance, while in others they are of minor importance; in some contexts they are a governing ideal, while in others they are subordinate to another ideal. Thus, we return to Selznick's idea of variability and the importance of empirical study: to understand the way a master ideal works it is necessary to pay attention to the context in which it appears and to gather information from empirical study.

Thus, we can understand a master ideal as a complex ideal consisting of constitutive ideals performing a subordinate role in a particular context. Can that context now be identified as a normative system to which the master ideal gives unity? The answer must be that it cannot: the idea of a complex master ideal says something interesting of the way in which different ideals can be related to each other, but does not establish a relationship of commitment between normative system and master ideal. The unity that is established is between the values that constitute the master ideal, not between the ideal and the normative system.

The last claim I need to address is that of the unrealizability of ideals. Selznick himself is not quite clear on the matter. He suggests that ideals are usually not completely realized, but is careful in his formulation: "Legal ideals cannot always be completely realized, . . . , but they remain as living potentialities, awaiting the appearance of historical developments that will permit their application" (1961, 107). Selznick's reference to unrealizability can be described as practical unrealizability: the historical or practical circumstances can be such that it is, at a specific moment in time, in a specific context, impossible to realize an ideal to the full. The main condition for the realization of ideals is that circumstances have to be congenial to realization. I would add that the complexity of master ideals seems to be a second source for practical unrealizability: because the master ideal consists of different constitutive values, it is hard to determine to what extent these values have to be realized to advance realization of the encompassing master ideal.

In conclusion, the concept of a master ideal is, nevertheless, worthwhile because it provides us with a notion to indicate important governing ideals in value-laden phenomena of social reality. It can be used to argue why certain values are especially important in a specific field and creates a perspective to view relations between ideals. There is, however, one important aspect of Selznick's theory of master ideals that must be discarded: the suggestion that one master ideal provides the unity of a normative system. Variety of interpretation and the possibility of different master ideals being equally relevant to one normative system indicate that a truly pragmatist view of master ideals, with an eye on empirical variation, should reject the idea that there is a simple relationship between master ideal and normative system. In a different sense, the concept of master ideal is useful: it can indicate that governing ideals are complex ideals consisting of constituting values. These values can be understood as holding together in a specific way because they are related to a governing master ideal.

## 5. IDEALS AND LAW

The subject of this section is the role of ideals in the context of law. In Chapter 1 I raised the issue of a specific category of legal ideals. In the light of Selznick's concept of the master ideal, one could expect him to emphasize the specific character of the master ideal of legality. But what exactly is the character of that master ideal? In what way is it distinct from, or connected to, non-legal ideals? Such a focus on the ideals within law will also require an examination of the relations between the master ideal and other elements of the legal system. The way the connection between legality and other, non-legal, ideals is viewed also bears upon the broader issue of the relation between law and society. What role does Selznick give ideals in supporting or undermining the openness of law towards society? These are the three issues that will be discussed in this section: the master ideal of legality, the relation of that ideal to other elements of the legal system, and the role of ideals for the openness of law.

### *The Ideal of Legality*

The ideal of legality has a central place in Selznick's view of law. Seen as the master ideal of law (1961, 94) it determines, to an important extent, what is specific about law. Legality is characterized as the "progressive reduction of the arbitrary element in positive law and its administration" (1968, 52). Legality, or the rule of law, is a complex ideal consisting of standards for assessing the making and applying of rules and other decisions made in the name of law (1961, 94). It is a procedural ideal in that it concerns the restraint of power by principles of order, which enhance the conformity and predictability of decisions (1961, 95). It aims to guarantee the quality of law by setting standards of rationality, order and accountability.

At first sight the ideal of legality seems a main source of the autonomy of law: it is the ideal which holds together law as a system, it is that which governs the legal system. The standards which the ideal embraces are all internal to the legal order. This impression of legality is reinforced by the way legality is connected to justice. According to Selznick, legality is a part of justice, which is itself an ideal with a much broader scope than the law alone (1969, 12). Legality, in contrast to justice, is confined in its meaning to law. Law and legality, reality and its governing ideal, are even mutually defining: we cannot understand the one without the other. This suggests a clear division of labour between the ideals of legality and justice: legality embraces the values internal to law and is the guardian of law's autonomy, while considerations of justice connect law to broader social concerns.

As long as legality is regarded as a procedural ideal, connecting justice to openness and legality to the autonomy of law is possible. However, for Selznick there are important substantive elements in legality. Legality is an affirmative ideal with rich connotations:

> Legality begins as a principle of restraint, but it promises more than a way of moderating the uses of power. The "progressive reduction of arbitrariness" knows no near stopping-place. The closer we look at that process, the more we realize that it calls for an affirmative view of what it means to participate in a legal order, whether as a citizen, judge, or executive (1969, 18).

The ideal of legality is a main determinant of what law is about, the meaning of law is dependent on the meaning of legality. If we connect this thesis to the discussion of the three stages of legal development, we see that a commitment to legality is a feature of both autonomous and responsive law. In autonomous law legality is procedural as the dominant character of law is procedural. In responsive law, however, the meaning of legality shifts from formal to substantive justice (Nonet & Selznick 1978, 108). The character of the ideal of legality parallels the character of the type of law to which it belongs. As the law as a whole grows to be more substantive, so does the ideal of legality.

One might say that this is not surprising: if the ideal of legality and law are mutually dependent, it follows that a change of character of the one entails a change of character of the other. I believe it is not quite so simple: the changing character of legality has consequences for the importance of the ideal itself in the legal order. Responsive law is committed to a focus on outcomes and its ideal of legality is committed to substantive justice. The progressive reduction of arbitrariness is no longer interpreted as the refining of procedure and enhancement of legal security, but as the mending of social inequalities and supporting of rights. The meaning of arbitrariness is seen as injustice instead of unpredictability. But this interpretation of legality practically reduces its meaning to justice: where is the place of legality as a distinctive master ideal? A change in the character of legality makes it less important in determining the character of law: legality and law both directly serve the social ideal of justice. General social ideals gain importance while the distinctively legal ideal of legality diminishes. I think there is good reason to see justice as the master ideal of responsive law and to reserve the ideal of legality for autonomous law. Distinguishing between different ideals as belonging to different types of law makes it easier to see the prevalence of one ideal as an indication of the corresponding type of law: detection of a greater concern for (substantive) justice is one of the markers of a development towards a responsive legal order.

I have slightly exaggerated the change in the ideal of legality. In Selznick's theory the procedural element of the ideal is not completely overshadowed by the substantive element. Nor does he overlook the dangers of the emphasis on outcomes, such as opportunism (Nonet & Selznick 1978, 77). But the conclusion I want to draw from this discussion of legality is not merely that the ideal of legality should consist of the right mix of procedural and substantive values. The distinctive character of law can only be protected if its master ideal keeps its own distinctive characteristics, the internal values of the legal order.[10] The ideal of legality is indeed supportive of the autonomy of the law, and the more it incorporates general social values the more open the law becomes. Selznick's theory breathes optimism about the openness of the law, even if he warns against total reliance on the benign effects of the interaction of law and society. Maybe we need to recall Radbruch's lesson about the values of the law: the most important place is for formal justice and legal security, both necessary to curb the excesses of the sovereignty of political goals. Legality as a genuine master ideal can protect the integrity of the law, an achievement which should not be given up too quickly.

*Rules, Principles, Values*

The shift from autonomous to responsive law is not only characterized by the change of meaning of legality, but also by a shift from rule-based to principle-based reasoning. Reasoning from principles is necessary to accommodate the generalization of purpose that is characteristic of responsive law. Principles have a more general scope than rules, making them natural companions to a system of responsive law with its focus on general objectives. Nonet &

[10] Here I think of Fuller's internal morality of law (Fuller 1969, 33-94).

Selznick (1978, 81) follow Dworkin's early formulations of the character of principles: unlike rules principles do not apply in an all-or-nothing fashion, principles have a dimension of weight, and they are seen as requirements of morality (Dworkin 1978, 22-26). To my mind, the reason why principles are important to a responsive legal order is that they are one of the main sources of flexibility. Because of their dimension of weight, principles require balancing in a specific case. This balance will differ according to the circumstances of the case. Principle-based decision-making is therefore more sensitive to the peculiarities of the case and more flexible.

Principles differ from rules in many respects, but the question that needs to be answered in the context of this study is how principles differ from ideals or values. In Selznick's theory, ideals and principles are closely linked. The most extensive discussion of principles is in the chapter on law in *The Moral Commonwealth*. Principles of law are the elements of a legal system which are most directly related to legal values: "Principles of law, . . . , formulate legally recognized values rather than definite rights or obligations" (1992, 438). An important difference between principles and rules is that principles are a direct expression of legal values, while rules are the result of a balance of values which takes account of relevant facts. A difference between legal principles and values is that principles have a clearly conventional element in their authority. Legal principles derive their authority from convention or tradition itself. In part, their authority is not substantial, i.e. based on the acceptability of their content, but conventional, accepted now because they have been accepted for such a long time. But the mark of principles of justice is that the conventional element has limited meaning: such principles ideally formulate the universal values of natural law. Of course, there are also many values that have a conventional basis, but an explicit justification by appealing to convention is not acceptable there. The most probable reason for this difference is the conventional character of law. As we saw above, Selznick takes for granted that value-orientation ensures the openness of law and that this presupposes that the meaning of legally relevant values is not confined to the legal order. Then it makes sense to interpret principles as the legal embodiment of social values, and this could account for the more conventional character of principles.

As is usually the case with conceptual distinctions in Selznick's theory, the distinction between principles and ideals is not watertight. Some principles have a character that comes close to the one ascribed to values, for instance in the case of principles of justice. Selznick is more concerned to stress the difference between principles and rules, the more open character of principles, and the connection of principles and values, than to concentrate on differences between the two. The conventional authority of principles, however, is an interesting thought to use as a basis for the distinction between principles and values. So far, I have used Alexy's definition of principles as prescriptions to realize values to the highest degree. The idea of conventionality would add to this definition that principles can not simply be appealed to as norms that promote an important value, but that principles need to be justified as acceptable within the given legal order. Legal principles are norms that are recognizable as flowing from the existing legal system. This is not necessarily the case with legally relevant values. Dworkin's example, the principle that no man may profit from his own wrong, is recognizable as a fundamental norm embedded in the American legal system, but the value it promotes is a moral value of 'doing the right thing' which moves beyond the legal order. The norm is acceptable as a legal principle because it can be shown to be part of the legal system.

*The Ideals of Responsive Law*

In the discussion of the ideal of legality we saw that the meaning of legality shifts when a legal system develops from autonomous law to responsive law. In order to see how this shift in meaning takes place and what it entails for the role of ideals in the relation between law and society, we need to take a closer look at the transition from autonomous law to responsive law. In *Law and Society in Transition*, the different types of law are characterized in terms of openness and integrity (Nonet & Selznick 1978, 76). In the previous chapter we saw that responsive law is seen as a reaction to the isolation from society that occurs in autonomous law. Autonomous law is primarily concerned to protect its own integrity, emphasizing its own procedures and its independence from politics. Responsive law restores the connections between law and society by directing its attention to the general purposes of law: "sovereignty of purpose" is one of the hallmarks of responsive law (1978, 78). The sovereignty of purpose is said to ensure the openness and flexibility of law. In Selznick's view the crucial step is to discover the values implicit in legal rules and policies (1978, 79). Once the reasons for rules and policies, their point, have been articulated, it becomes possible to use these values as a standard of criticism of specific rules or particular policies, to base new rules or policies on them, and to extend their meaning to other contexts.

It is an unspoken premise that a focus on values transcends the domain of the purely legal: values are not just the values internal to the legal order, they include values law shares with politics or other social concerns. However, this is not a matter of course. Looking for values implicit in existing legal rules and policies does not ensure that the values found will be political values. It can be argued that an autonomous legal system which comes to pay attention to values will focus on different values from those of a responsive legal system, on values internal to the legal system. Autonomous law is described as preferring specific rules over general values and favouring the ideal of legality in a procedural interpretation (1978, 54). The shift from autonomous law to responsive law has three aspects that are important here — the shift to general purpose and value, the shift to a substantive interpretation of ideals such as legality, and the shift from isolation to responsiveness. It does not follow directly that a shift from specified rules to general purpose, looking for implicit values in legal rules and principles, is also a shift to more substantive political values. A legal system that moves in the direction of general purpose can interpret such purposes in accordance with the procedural values highlighted in autonomous law. It is even less likely that attention to implicit values will lead to a shift to *current* political values. If the implicit substantive values of a legal system are explicated, it is more likely that these will be the values of a past political order that has influenced the formation of the legal system than the values adhered to in present-day politics. It then seems that the shift to general values cannot ensure attention from legal officials to values of the current political order. The more plausible explanation is that it is the responsiveness of responsive law that ensures the openness towards political values.[11] By this I mean that responsive law is explicitly looking for political values by responding to social pressures and needs. The responsive element is what makes the "sovereignty of purpose" the sovereignty of political purpose because it involves social and political actors in the formulation of political values. It incorporates knowledge of the values adhered to by these actors in the formulation of legal purpose.

The question that occupies us here is the role of ideals in the shift from autonomy to openness. We saw that legality itself is interpreted more generally in responsive law, moving beyond procedural fairness to substantive justice (1978, 108). Where autonomous law makes a clear distinction between justice and legality and concentrates on the latter, responsive law interprets legality

11 This is a point inspired by Gunther Teubner's criticism of Nonet and Selznick's theory of responsive law: "(...) their analysis confounds two related but distinct trends in post-modern law, namely, the move towards greater substantive rationality and the emergence of reflexive rationality" (1983, 245). Teubner argues that the reflexive dimension is dominant in post-modern law. Although I do not share his view, I think the distinction between the two elements is helpful.

to accord with substantive justice. I believe that this move to substantive interpretations of legal ideals is the key to the openness of law towards society. Selznick's characterization of autonomous law as concerned with procedure is right, but this includes a concern for procedural values such as clarity and predictability. Law loses its distinctive character when this concern with procedural values is traded for a focus on substantive values such as justice, liberty, or mutual respect. A main reason for this is that formal procedures are precisely what distinguishes a legal system from other forms of social regulation: law is not distinctive because of the content of its rules — criminal law is the best example — but because of the way these rules are formed and administered. This means that a concern for procedural values ensures law's distinctive character. As I indicated in the discussion of the ideal of legality, my opinion is that it is important to retain what is distinctively legal. Underrating procedural values is dangerous because judgments on substantive values alone are extremely difficult to give. To know what is just is indeed a legal actor's unrealizable ideal.

## 6. CONCLUSIONS

As I did in the conclusion to Chapter 4 regarding Radbruch, I want to review Selznick's answers to the main questions of this study. That means first of all, his views on the ontology and epistemology of values, and the relation between value and reality. Second, it means relating these ideas to law, considering his views on the characterization of legal ideals and on the role of ideals in law and society. I will start by giving a systematic overview of his position on these matters and then turn to the problematic aspects of that position.

As I have shown in section 6.2, Selznick's views on the ontology and epistemology of ideals is a mix of pragmatist and naturalist theses. Selznick's basic thesis on the nature of ideals is that they are the governing standards of social phenomena that have natural roots in social reality. From this statement his theory of ideals can be built up. First of all, the idea of ideals having natural roots in social reality is further developed. Selznick invokes human nature to argue that certain key ideals are necessary for human flourishing, for the achievement of a satisfactory human life. These ideals are rooted in basic biological phenomena such as sex and parenthood. Selznick extends this argument to social phenomena of which one can give a parallel argument: ideals are necessary to achieve a satisfactory functioning of a social institution, such as law or democracy. The ideal has roots in the social phenomenon because it is a standard based on the functioning of the phenomenon. The link between the natural and social basis of ideals is achieved by a sociological theory connecting life in society to the basic needs of human beings.

The idea of ideals having roots in reality needs to be further developed to make clear how the ideal as a standard of evaluation arises from its basis in that reality. To do this, Selznick appeals to pragmatism's idea that values are part of people's problem-solving experience. Looking at Dewey's argument about values we find that a value standard can be articulated when an inquiry is made into the conditions and consequences of a problematic situation. A value is what gives rise to positive consequence and contributes to improvement of the situation. Values are developed as the result of reflection upon their conditions or roots in a factual situation and realized when action is taken to bring the situation in accordance with them. This means that in a pragmatist view, values are only partly inherent in reality when they are used as the standard to evaluate a problematic situation, only to the extent of their factual roots. When they are realized, however, they do inhere in reality: objects then have value. We now see that the pragmatist view of values is dynamic. Because values are part of the interactions that make up experience, they move from being standards to guide the changes to be made, to being aspects of satisfactory arrangements.

Saying that values are developed on the basis of inquiry into problematic situations also entails a claim about our knowledge of values. This is an important aspect of Selznick's theory in which he adopts the pragmatist method. His main epistemological claim about values is that they are discovered by empirical study. This means inquiry into the particulars of situations where values are at issue and finding out what circumstances give rise to a value. Knowledge of values can be achieved by studying the interrelations between fact and value in social phenomena. Connected to the empirical knowledge of values as used in experience is the denial that we can ever have absolute certainty about values. Because our knowledge of values is connected to empirical situations, improved understanding of such situations can cause us to amend our understanding of the connected values. Dewey even makes the stronger claim that reality is continually changing: the world is not a static environment. This means that the conditions giving rise to values change, and that these values themselves need to be adapted to new circumstances. Then we do not only have provisional knowledge of values, the values themselves come to have provisional validity. I am not sure whether Selznick follows this reasoning to the full. He certainly believes that our knowledge of values is never more than provisional, but because of the basis of values in human nature and the nature of society, values themselves are connected to the more enduring aspects of our existence.

Selznick distinguishes vaguely between different kinds of ideals. He does not distinguish between ideals and values; he uses both those terms to refer to the whole set. The first important distinction is made between the universal values following from human nature and the values that are relative to particular cultural arrangements. The second distinction is between master ideals and, what I have called, their constitutive values. The first distinction is not categorical: there is a gradual transition from universal to culturally determined values. Moreover, there is usually a connection because vague universal values are given different interpretations in different cultures. The distinction between master ideal and constitutive values can be made because Selznick refers to master ideals as complex ideals that govern normative systems. They are complex because they consist of a set of subordinate standards making different demands. Master ideals are important in Selznick's theory because they are the governing ideals of normative systems: the behaviour of the persons involved, the specific norms of the system and the values making up the ideal all need to be interpreted in the light of the governing master ideal. As I pointed out, it is more fruitful to see the master ideal as a role that can be performed by an ideal than as a separate type of ideal. Ideals can both appear as the governing ideal in a normative system, and can then be called a master ideal, or as a constitutive ideal of another master ideal.

The concept of a master ideal is central to Selznick's understanding of law, so I can now turn to the second theme: the role of ideals in law. Let me first discuss the issue of legal ideals. In Radbruch's theory we saw a fairly clear distinction between specifically legal values and other social values. Selznick uses the master ideal of legality to point to what is distinctively legal. Thus, it seems that legality can be also be seen to be a specifically legal ideal. Selznick is interested in the relationship between legality and broader social ideals, primarily justice. However, the distinction between the ideal of legality and justice cannot be neatly maintained because of the dynamic character of legal systems. Selznick sees legality as guarding the integrity of law in autonomous law, while legality provides the opening to social ideals in the stage of responsive law. In the course of changing from an autonomous legal system to a responsive legal system, legality changes its character fairly radically. The question can indeed be raised if it is still the same master ideal of legality that governs both autonomous and responsive law. Legality is defined as the progressive reduction of arbitrariness, but the interpretation of arbitrariness in responsive law makes it much more substantive than it is in autonomous law. Arbitrary leans towards the unjust in responsive law, and because of this the distinction between legality and justice fades. Justice comes close to being the master ideal of responsive law.

Apart from the change in the ideal of legality, Selznick also connects the shift from autonomy to openness to principles and the generalization of purpose. Thus, Selznick sees the attention to values as such as an important determinant of the openness of law towards society. Principle-based reasoning is less strict than rule-based reasoning and can therefore more easily accommodate legal decisions that serve general social purposes. The idea that attention to values as such makes law open to societal influence reveals that Selznick has a bias towards substantive values. Procedural values that are central to the autonomy of law, such as certainty and clarity, are subordinated to substantive moral values such as justice and equality.

The problems to which Selznick's theory gives rise are to a large part caused by his tendency to combine theoretical insights that are valuable without considering whether this will still yield a coherent theory. One of the consequences is that Selznick's theory is not very helpful to develop conceptual distinctions. I found that for a good understanding of his theory of ideals it was necessary to return to Dewey's ideas, but in my effort to reconstruct a theory of ideals I did not succeed in blending the different components into a coherent whole. I think this is to a large extent the consequence of Selznick's combination of pragmatist and natural law ideas. The uneasy combination of the two is my first point of criticism. Related are my second and third point, regarding Selznick's conception of human nature and the vagueness of the values following from it. Unfortunately, rejecting that conception of human nature leaves pragmatism with a circular argument to justify ideals. Apart from these points concerning the combination of pragmatism and natural law thinking, there is a problem with Selznick's concept of a master ideal, which makes the relationship between ideal and normative system too close. More specifically, Selznick's conception of the master ideal of legality is too inclusive; he does not acknowledge that there might be a change of master ideal due to the development of law.

The main problem with the combination of pragmatism and natural law thinking is that arguments that certain ideals necessarily accompany human nature are combined with an adaptive, concrete and provisional concept of ideals. In a pragmatist conception the emphasis is on the relevance of ideals in concrete problematic situations, while a natural law view concentrates on universal and enduring ideals. This causes a strain because such universal and enduring ideals can only be established at a highly general level and only give vague directions. This detracts from their ability for guidance in concrete problematic situations, which is the important role of ideals in a pragmatist view. Connected is my criticism of Selznick's conception of human nature, or more precisely, of his claim that value-realization comes naturally to human beings. Selznick too easily concludes that, because ideals have roots in human experience, human beings are naturally inclined to realize those values. His point that ideals are necessary for human flourishing is convincing, but the idea that realization of these ideals is natural depends on the presupposition that people are naturally seeking to flourish. Since Selznick's vision of well-being includes the enhancement of fellowship as moral well-being, this constitutes a view of human nature that is overly optimistic. To convince, Selznick needs to argue why human tendencies towards vice and harmful behaviour are less natural. I have already touched upon my third point about the vagueness of universal ideals. Even if Selznick's view of human nature is accepted, the ideals connected to human nature are too vague to give direction in concrete situations. To function as a standard of evaluation, an ideal needs critical potential: it needs to specify what a valuable state of affairs is. Such standards do not have universal reach because what is good depends to a large extent on circumstances. Against these two critical points regarding Selznick's natural law leanings, a wholly pragmatist theory also has a problem. Because the validity of ideals is made dependent on the improvement they can make in practical situations, on the consequences they have in concrete experience, they are justified in terms of the good end to which they contribute. However, they also determine what that good end is: the ideal sets the standard to which the situation ought to be brought. Thus, the justification of the ideal is circular. If we want to use a pragmatist theory of ideals, this problem needs to be addressed.

Selznick's concept of the master ideal is valuable because it enables one to indicate ideals that are especially important in a specific field and to argue that these have a closer relation to that field than other ideals. The problem with Selznick's view on master ideals, however, is that the relation with the normative system they govern is so close that the normative system and the ideal are virtually defined in terms of each other and the ideal provides the unity of the system. This is at odds with Selznick's belief in empirical variation: there is no good reason to exclude orientation towards the master ideal from the range of empirical variations. By this I mean that it is very well possible that a normative system is governed not by one master ideal, but by more than one, or that it comes to be governed by an entirely new ideal over time. The latter possibility would fit in Selznick's own theory of legality. Selznick sees the development of law from autonomous to responsive law as a change in the meaning of legality as the master ideal of law. However, because legality in responsive law is interpreted as the banishing of injustice, it seems more in keeping with his ideas to see the development as a change in governing ideal as well, from legality to justice. An argument can also be made that the change from autonomous law to responsive law is not complete and that both legality and justice are the governing ideals of law at the moment. I will argue for the latter position in section 7.4. In this revised form, the concept of a master ideal is a valuable tool.

# CHAPTER 7
# DEVELOPING A CONCEPT OF IDEALS FOR LEGAL THEORY

## 1. DIFFERENT CONCEPTS

In the previous four chapters I have examined the views of two theorists about the nature of ideals and their role in the field of law. In this chapter I want to compare my conclusions regarding these theories and, on the basis of that comparison, work on the further development of a plausible concept of ideals. Because I primarily want to use such a concept to assess the role of ideals in law, I will apply the concept in the context of law and propose an account of legal ideals.

From my discussion of the views of Radbruch and Selznick on the nature of ideals it will have become apparent that the two theorists hold different views on the ontological basis of values. Whereas Radbruch starts from a dualistic point of view, Selznick is committed to a monistic point of view. At first sight, it seems that one could attribute to Radbruch a transcendent concept of ideals and to Selznick an immanent concept. However, exactly in what way and to what extent their views correspond to the two types of concepts developed in Chapter 2 needs to be examined. First, I want to show which specific versions of the transcendent concept and the immanent concept are endorsed by Radbruch and Selznick, respectively, and what this entails for their conception of the specific features of ideals. In section 7.2, I will examine whether Radbruch and Selznick have an answer to the problems related to the two concepts of ideals, which were pointed out in section 2.4. I will then concentrate on the pragmatist view of ideals as the most plausible theory, and try to improve its weaker points (7.3). In section 7.4, I will connect the discussion of concepts of ideals to law and, building on insights gathered from Radbruch and Selznick, give a pragmatist account of the ideals of law.

*Radbruch's Transcendence*

To see which concept of ideals Radbruch endorses and to what extent it can be characterized as a transcendent concept, we need to recall Radbruch's characterization of values. In Chapter 4 we saw that Radbruch conceives of values as retraceable to self-evident, absolute axioms. Radbruch follows a

Kantian mode of argumentation for his concept of ideals. He shares the view of ideals as necessary elements of human thinking which order the world as we know it. Although the basis of Radbruch's view is generally Kantian, there are many specifically neo-Kantian elements in his view of ideals. First of all, Radbruch is neo-Kantian in identifying ideals with values (*Werte*) and in seeing the category of values as the central ordering force of the cultural world. In this neo-Kantianism differs importantly from other types of Kantianism and the theory of Kant himself.[1] The central feature of a neo-Kantian ontology of values is that values are seen not as existing in reality, but merely as having validity. Thus, by attributing different modes of existence to facts and values, neo-Kantianism is a prime example of a dualistic world view.

These characteristics of Radbruch's theory of Kantian and neo-Kantian origin enable me to show in what manner and to what extent Radbruch's concept of values is in accordance with the transcendent concept of ideals presented in Chapter 2. The central features of that concept are that ideals are perfect, abstract, inherently unrealizable, and not susceptible to complete formulation. Although Radbruch does not speak of values in these terms, his endorsement or non-endorsement of these features can be inferred from other claims he makes. The absolute values serving as axioms of value systems can be described as highly abstract: they are the fundamental concepts of goodness, truth, beauty, justice. Evidence that these values are in themselves seen as abstract can also be gathered from the attention Radbruch pays to ways of giving these values more specific content. A noteworthy example is the formal value of justice which needs to be supplemented with specific interpretations of the good (1932, 278-279).

The issue of the unrealizability of values is complicated in relation to Radbruch's theory. At first sight inherent unrealizability seems easy to attribute to Radbruch: because he characterizes values as *überwirklich*, as beyond reality, the ideal and the real are by definition never joined completely. If his dualism is thus taken to be synonymous with the inherent unrealizability of values, Radbruch does indeed defend it, but this does not quite do justice to his position. If unrealizability is taken to mean that there is no way in which the demands made by values can be completely satisfied in real situations,

[1] The central place of values and the connection to culture is specific to the neo-Kantianism of Windelband, Rickert and Lask. Other modern theories with a Kantian inspiration (Rescher 1987, Emmet 1994) are working with the term ideal instead of value, focusing on the appeal exerted by the unrealizable. The concept of value cannot be found in Kant's own theory because it was then only current in a restricted sense, meaning economic value. Its modern use (as broader than economic value) dates from the late nineteenth century.

inherent unrealizability is harder to attribute to Radbruch. He says that cultural realities have the meaning to realize values without implying that such realization is impossible. However, even if Radbruch should be interpreted as saying that cultural realities mean to realize values and therefore in some sense must be able to realize them, it can be argued that he subscribes to the view that values can never be *completely* realized in reality. This is because values make such strong demands that a complete fulfilment is impossible, and because values necessarily conflict. The claim to unrealizability of Radbruch's legal values is rather strong because the different values require each other and conflict with each other out of necessity: the one cannot be realized without, but at the same time is impeded by, the other values. This is not the inherent unrealizability that is directly implied by a dualistic method, but unrealizability following from the difficulty to satisfy the demands made by conflicting values.

Unrealizability because of the strict demands values make is connected to the issue of perfection. I identified perfection as a central feature of a Platonic view of ideals, which carried over to Kantianism. It is not clear whether Radbruch sees values as necessarily displaying perfection. In favour of the idea of perfection the axiomatic values are seen as the epitome of what ought to be: their absolute validity fits well with the idea of perfection. The idea of perfection, of flawlessness, is an excellent reason for supposing absolute axioms: perfection is exactly what makes the unqualified validity of axiomatic values plausible and it can explain why these values can serve as the basis for other values. It is, however, not the perfection of a perfect world: each value in itself is flawless, but in Radbruch's theory the absolute values conflict, so that there can be no harmonious realm of perfect values. Values are formal ideas we construct, they do not inhabit their own realm of perfection. In this, his theory differs essentially from the Platonic view of ideals. It seems that Radbruch could accept the feature of perfection, in the sense of the flawlessness of an idea, regarding absolute values. We should keep in mind, however, that in Radbruch's system this abstract account of values as ideas is combined with a relativistic account of how values work in cultural realities: then they do not appear as abstract ideas but as part of the value systems to which people are committed. The concrete value judgments people make can eventually be traced back to an absolute ultimate value, but the derivative values that form the bulk of value systems cannot be seen as perfect value ideas.

The last of the proposed features of the transcendent concept of ideals, impossibility of formulation, cannot be attributed to Radbruch. Radbruch does not appear to support the idea that values might be essentially impossible to formulate completely. The value that takes centre stage in his theory, *Gerechtigkeit*, is given a very precise formulation: it is the formal equality of treating like cases alike. As Radbruch of course acknowledges, formal equality has only part of its meaning specified, namely that of the relationship it constructs. But for him this does not mean that the value cannot be completely formulated, only that it needs supplementation from other values. For Radbruch, the key issue is that the value of justice cannot stand on its own, which is connected to the issue of abstractness, not to that of formulation.

*Selznick's Immanence*

In a manner reminiscent of Radbruch's combination of necessary absolutes and relativistic elements, Selznick combines two strands of the immanent concept of ideals: the moral universals of natural law and the provisional values of pragmatism. Of course, Selznick does not see these two as opposites — because of his integrative theory one could hardly expect that — but as continuous (1992, 24). In his focus on universals, values that are valid for every human being because they are grounded in human nature, Selznick can be associated with an Aristotelian variety of natural law theory.[2] He is a pragmatist in his emphasis of the provisional character of our knowledge of ideals, of a scientific approach, and of the continuities between, not only fact and value, but also theory and practice, means and ends. Selznick combines the Aristotelian concern for values in connection to human flourishing (1992, 102) with the pragmatist view of values as of variable importance grounded in experienced problems (60).[3]

Selznick's commitment to pragmatist naturalism leads to a mixed conception of the features of ideals. In Chapter 2's discussion of the features of the immanent concept of ideals, I mentioned the following features: ideals are identical to values, they are inherent in social reality, they are latent or implicit in practice, and they are essentially realizable. Naturalism was seen to differ from pragmatism in seeing values as universal and enduring. About

[2] Selznick explicitly acknowledges the natural law connection in 'Sociology and Natural Law' (1961, 85) and the Aristotelian connection in *The Moral Commonwealth* (e.g. 1992, 59, 209).

[3] Selznick calls the combination of the two 'naturalism'. In my discussion of Selznick's theory I try to separate the Aristotelian/natural-law influences from the pragmatist influence as much as possible. This is complicated by the fact that a form of naturalism is also an aspect of the pragmatist theory of John Dewey; when referring to pragmatism and Dewey I focus on the parts of the theory that are distinctive, i.e. the provisional validity of values, the emphasis on problem-solving and on consequences.

the identity of ideal and value I can be brief: in Chapter 6 we have seen that Selznick uses the terms ideal and value as interchangeable concepts and that he emphasizes similar characteristics in regard to both. However, Selznick's position on the other proposed features of ideals merits more extensive discussion.

The inherence of ideals in reality is as central to the immanent concept of ideals as the inherent unrealizability is to the transcendent concept: it follows directly from a monistic ontology, from the unity of fact and value. For Selznick, the importance of the inherence of ideals lies in the basis of ideals in nature and experience. On this point, the contrast with Radbruch is at its greatest: whereas Radbruch is concerned to retrace values to an absolute foundation of indubitable validity, Selznick finds the validity of values in their experienced worth for human life. The factual basis of values ranges from clearly biological to inherently social phenomena, unified in being found in human experience. Because of this view of the natural basis of values his theory can be characterized as naturalistic, meaning that values are seen as based in human nature.

Selznick's theory of human nature is supported by his pragmatist emphasis on empirical knowledge: what human nature is has to be determined by empirical research, the results of which are always subject to further inquiry and therefore never completely certain. Similarly, knowledge of values has to be acquired by studying them as aspects of empirical phenomena. But Selznick does not see values merely as answers to contingent problem situations — which is the view of Dewey on values; instead, he shares the natural law quest for enduring universal ideals. Selznick proposes to combine the view that values answer concrete problematic situations with the idea that there are a number of universal, nature-based values. Thus, his views on the universal and enduring character of values are related to the different kinds of ideals that can be distinguished. Ideals that have a basis in human nature are universal and enduring, while the more concrete and local values need not be.

For Selznick, the inherence of ideals in reality is very closely connected to the latency of ideals. I identified latency as the idea that ideals are present in natural or social phenomena in a rudimentary form, even if they are not recognized. In Selznick's theory the latency of ideals follows from their having natural roots. It is because of the connection to a natural phenomenon that ideals have a role to play even when they are not explicitly recognized by the people involved. The social scientist studying the phenomenon can articulate the ideal latent in it to understand and evaluate the phenomenon. Again, his argument is a naturalist one: it is because of the connection to the functioning of natural and social phenomena that ideals should be understood as latent in these phenomena. Selznick does not say much about the role of implicit ideals as such, that is, about ideals without their being articulated either by a participant or by an observer. He is concerned to connect the articulation of an ideal by a scientist to the real roots of the ideal; implicit ideals only work for the people within the practice itself. The idea of ideals remaining implicit but being effective standards is compatible with his views, but not his prime concern.

Concerning the essential realizability of ideals, Selznick's view is not immediately clear. As in many other aspects of his theory, he is concerned to emphasize the variability in the realization of ideals.[4] Demanding and far-reaching ideals may be unrealizable, but for modest ideals it is very well possible that they can be realized. Selznick does not give criteria for assessing the degree of realizability of an ideal except the rather vague idea that demanding ideals are less easily realized than modest ideals. What makes an ideal demanding? Part of Selznick's answer would be that this is a matter that can be solved by examining ideals in the context of the empirical phenomena in which they are at work. Here we can appeal to the idea of a master ideal and its constitutive values. A master ideal consists of different standards, which makes it more difficult to realize the encompassing ideal because different values have to be realized all at once. Selznick himself suggests as much when he points out that the attainment of complex ideals depends on a precarious set of congenial circumstances (Nonet & Selznick 1978, 26). Additionally, it is probable that the constitutive values of a master ideal often make competing demands.[5]

Selznick is thus seen to defend an immanent concept of ideals that combines aspects of the naturalist and the pragmatist versions of an immanent concept. By distinguishing different kinds of ideals, ranging from universal moral ideals to specific, problem-oriented values, he sees ideals as having particular features to varying degrees. The problems to which this combination gives rise are the subject of the next section.

## 2. EVALUATING RADBRUCH AND SELZNICK

The characterization of Radbruch's and Selznick's concept of ideals as

4 Personal communication, 8-2-1997.

5 This would mean incorporating some of Radbruch's ideas about conflict. I will present an argument concerning the complexity of ideals in section 4 on ideals and law.

transcendent and immanent, respectively, does not yet reveal much about the merits of their theories of ideals. Here, I want to evaluate the different strands I distinguished in those theories and the connections that are made between them. Both theorists combine different versions of the transcendent and immanent concepts; I will examine how convincing those different versions are and how successful the combinations between them are.

I will look at Radbruch's theory first. In Chapter 4, I have already indicated that, in Radbruch's combination of absolute values and limited relativism, there is a problem in keeping that relativism contained. There appears to be no good reason to limit the reach of relativism to interpretations of the good, assuming that it does not affect interpretations of other absolute values. Thus, the first point to be taken is that Radbruch's theory needs to be reinterpreted to make a plausible, non-arbitrary division between absolute and relative elements. The second point to be addressed is the plausibility of values as constitutive principles of cultural realities. I argued that a convincing account of values as constitutive for reality necessitates a formal interpretation of such values, which impairs their ability to function as evaluative standards. That leads to the third point: if the constitutive and evaluative functions are separated and only constitutive formal values can be derived by a priori argument, the question becomes urgent where to find evaluative standards. Relativism is an answer to that, but it does not seem a very satisfactory one because it does not provide objective standards of evaluation. The second and third points against Radbruch's theory are forms of more general objections to the transcendent concept of ideals. If the argument from a priori necessity can only ground formal ideals, stripped of content, the bulk of evaluative standards have to be found elsewhere. It is only by giving up the strict necessity of ideals that the transcendent concept can keep form and matter of ideals together, but as we saw this makes the foundation of ideals less secure.[6]

To return to the first point: a plausible reinterpretation of Radbruch's value theory, in my view, would combine a set of absolute formal values with a relativism of interpretation of all those values. Radbruch's relativism, we saw, is particular in its idea that the choice of a highest value is limited to a choice among strictly limited varieties. This limitation was based on the idea that only what derives from human beings can be awarded true value — Radbruch's anthropocentric principle. Now this principle, which can already be questioned in regard to the ethical value of the good, becomes more problematic if it is right to say all the absolute values are formal and need be given content on a

6 This is the move made by the constructivist theory of ideals, which distinguishes it from Kantianism (see section 2.2).

relativistic basis. Possible interpretations of the values of truth and beauty, and maybe also of justice, cannot plausibly be limited to versions of man-based value. In regard to all of these values, it seems arbitrary to exclude possible interpretations because they do not rank man-related objects highest. If Radbruch's aim of a typology of value systems is taken seriously, other possible interpretations of truth, beauty, the good, and justice should also be considered. It seems that, for instance, the beauty of nature could plausibly be regarded as a higher form of beauty than the beauty of a painting. Radbruch's thesis that only a small part of reality (connected to man) can be the substratum of highest values is unduly restrictive. Radbruch's idea that relativism concerns interpretation and choice of highest values in no way seems to bar a broader range of alternatives of interpretation than he himself offers. But what then remains of Radbruch's ambition of giving a typology of values, a system of value systems? This could still be done, although it would have to be done differently: taking as a starting point the formal absolute values, possible interpretations will be constrained by the form of those values and the range of choices would therefore not be unlimited.

Again, we have returned to the starting point of formal absolute values, so it seems right to address the issue directly and move on to the second point of criticism. In Radbruch's case, the argument of the a priori necessity of values is made in relation to cultural realities. Cultural realities can only be understood as having the meaning (*Sinn*) to realize values, and this necessary relation between reality and value is how a value is constitutive of that reality. Being oriented towards a specific value makes a cultural reality what it is, which means that the value is necessary to distinguish a part of reality as a specific cultural reality. The value must be presupposed if one is to make sense of the cultural reality. To repeat Radbruch's example: the cultural phenomenon of science only has a point, is only recognizable as a particular part of reality, if it is supposed to be oriented towards truth. Therefore, there is a necessary relation between truth and science. But, as Radbruch recognizes, practising science and recognizing science as science is compatible with variation in the achievement of truth, and also, I would add, with a range of different interpretations of what truth is. If the unity of such a part of reality is connected to the notion of truth, it does not depend upon a unified striving for a full-blown ideal of truth. For instance, both a traditional biologist who believes truth is what correctly maps physical reality and a pragmatic physicist who believes truth is what works are intelligibly at work in the field of science. The value that makes up the field of science must be on a more abstract level transcending these differences in order to define that reality, which makes it a very formal value.

At such a level of abstraction, values are virtually devoid of content, and by that token, unable to function as independent standards of evaluation. There is a rift between the constitutive and evaluative functions of values, which we have already encountered when discussing Radbruch's ambiguities in the use of justice (*Gerechtigkeit*). To function as an evaluative standard a value needs a degree of substance that is not compatible with the abstraction needed to form a cultural reality. In order to evaluate to what extent a value is realized in a certain field or situation, it is not enough to have a merely formal idea of that value, it is necessary to have a full picture of what ought to be realized. The example of justice can again be instructive. The formal interpretation of justice serves well to identify what counts as law: rules or court proceedings are recognizable as legal because they purport to treat like cases alike, that is, to serve justice in the formal sense. However, if one wants to evaluate the justice of a certain rule or decision — the extent to which it realizes the value of justice — it is not enough to assess whether like cases are treated alike: one needs to turn directly to the merit of the decision of what counts as like or unlike. In order to use the value of justice as an evaluative standard, one always needs to go into the adequacy of the criterion employed to determine what is equal or unequal. The outrage of punishing a redhead more severely than a blonde is not in their being treated as unlike while they are alike: they are unlike in this respect. The outrage is in employing the wrong criterion, a trivial difference in hair colour, for inflicting punishment. Evaluating the realization of justice can only be done by including the worth of the criterion to distinguish equal from unequal.

The tension between the two roles of values in Radbruch's theory brings us to the third difficulty: where to find evaluative standards. In their constitutive role, as formal prerequisites, values have a secure basis: they can be shown to be necessary for recognizing cultural realities. In their evaluative role, such a secure basis is lacking. In my discussion of the relation between the absolute and relative elements of Radbruch's theory, I have shown that a coherent reconstruction of his theory would yield a formal core of all absolute values and a relativistic interpretation of these values. Consequently, the substantive values needed as evaluative standards will have to be relativistic, that is, depending on the personal choice for a value system. For Radbruch, this is the way values acquire content: the substantive side to the *Rechtsidee* was the element relativistically determined. There is, however, a major problem in determining evaluative standards by a relativistic method: the problem of justification. If the substance of a value is simply dependent on the choice of a person or group believing in it, how can the use of that value as a standard of evaluation, of criticism, be justified? In Radbruch's theory, the interpretation of a value is a matter of personal choice or allegiance; no reasons can be given for preferring the individual over the collective as the highest good. If his relativism must be extended to other values than the good, this becomes an even bigger problem. That this generates difficulties is apparent from Radbruch's own post-war writings: there, Radbruch gives justice a more substantive interpretation, because the value of *Zweckmäßigkeit* does not yield an objective standard — it is this element of the *Rechtsidee* that is relativistic. Radbruch himself saw the need for an indubitable foundation for values. Unfortunately, his theory can only provide it to a small extent: only the absolute values have a solid foundation as necessary preconditions of the cultural world, and then only as formal values.

Selznick's theory promises us objectivity by locating values in the reality of social life instead of in subjective consciousness. His theory does indeed steer clear of most problems of Radbruch's neo-Kantianism, but it is not without failings of its own. Because Selznick's theory connects values to human nature and social practices, the way to establish the objectivity of values is by reference to factual findings. In the place of the a priori argument for absolute values, which is strong but hard to satisfy, there is the more contingent empirical argument for values following from human nature. Such an argument gives values an objective basis, but it is more contingent than the argument from necessity in two ways: because knowledge about values and human nature is provisional, and because human nature itself and its accompanying values may change. This small set of values with a basis in human nature is accompanied by other values with an even more contingent basis in social practices. The merit of this kind of theory is in the combination of an empirically grounded objectivity with an open and dynamic character of values. This is predominantly achieved because of the pragmatist theory of knowledge that underlies it: because true knowledge is defined in terms of what solves specific problems, it is liable to change in altered circumstances. The claim to objectivity is preserved, but the conditions to be satisfied have been made more dynamic. This has the advantage that values are not necessarily all-encompassing, relevant to all situations, but neither are they the whims of particular persons. However, although the theory provides an attractive model of values, there are a number of problematic aspects to its argument.

The difficulties arising from Selznick's theory parallel those of Radbruch's theory to a certain extent. One could say that both combine a secure basis of universal values with an account of local values as more shifting or provisional. Both also claim rather more for their secure basis than is warranted. In Selznick's case, because of his strain against dichotomies, the difference between the two parts of the theory is obscured by the stress on gradual difference and variation, but there is a break between the basis in human biology and the varieties of social practice. Selznick bridges the two via the social nature of human beings, but the role of the natural side of his theory is rather different from the mainly social. The first and major difficulty regards the ease with which Selznick draws unequivocal conclusions from human nature. His argument is much weakened if his conception of human nature is questionable. The second point of criticism also concerns the universal values with a natural basis. Even if we accept Selznick's theory of human nature, the vague values following from it do not give us much direction. As with Radbruch's abstract absolutes, Selznick's vague universals have little power as evaluative standards. Thus, more emphasis needs to be put on the pragmatist element of the theory. The third difficulty concerns the pragmatist conception of values: because of the connection between values and consequences, the justification of values is directly circular. This is problematic if values need to function as standards of criticism and directions for change.

Selznick's view of the nature of human beings is distinctly teleological, meaning that it includes a vision on human flourishing, the fulfilment of a human life. Of major importance for human flourishing is the realization of the values that are inherent to human life. What human flourishing is, however, is hard to define. Selznick would agree that there are a multitude of ways in which human beings can bloom, but there are certain natural paths along which human development goes well (1992, 150). The main problem that I discern is that Selznick identifies the values of human life as natural, as arising "(...) in the normal course of human experience" (102). This creates the impression that the positive aspects of human existence are somehow more normal, or more natural, than its negative aspects. Of course, the positive things are important for human flourishing as the negative are not, but that does not make the negative less natural. The picture Selznick sketches of human development as naturally geared towards flourishing gives the impression that the negative things in human life are external impediments to the inner drive of the human being towards the good. Let me illustrate this argument. Selznick gives examples of the natural basis of values that purport to show how values arise as a matter of course from completely natural phenomena: the value of love naturally accompanies sex, giving birth gives rise to the ideal of motherhood. Something is wrong, unforeseen, unnatural, if these values do not arise. But is it not as natural that sex and love generate jealousy, or that a crying child causes its mother frustration? Such negative emotions can be seen as disvalues, if value is seen as what contributes to flourishing. These things generally do not contribute to human flourishing, but they do not seem to be less normal. It follows, if disvalue is as natural as value is, that we cannot conclude that there is a tendency of development towards a rewarding life as is suggested by the idea of natural human flourishing.

Selznick does acknowledge that there are also negative human tendencies (1992, 171). He also believes effort is needed to counteract natural tendencies towards evil (175). However, if this is the case, if humans always need to work to overcome their natural dispositions towards wrongdoing, how can it be that there is a "latent promise of growth and interaction" (171) or "*a strain toward* an ideal pattern of interaction, obligation, or belonging" (192)? Selznick is very careful not to overstate his case for the natural basis of ideals, but at bottom there is always the presumption that there is an inherent human urge to strive towards the good.

One might also advance as an argument in favour of Selznick's view that he does not defend the view that values are an integral part of any kind of life, but only part of life with a certain level of well-being. This, however, would miss my point. I completely agree that the realization of values is necessarily part of a satisfactory kind of life. My argument is against the idea that it is natural, a matter of course, for human beings to achieve such a life: there is no good reason to suppose that such a life of flourishing is more natural, or less for that matter, than a life of frustration or misery. If a conception of human nature is formed accordingly, it will be more neutral about the realization of value; it will say that human beings are neither destined to promote nor to frustrate value-realization. I must emphasize here that I agree with Selznick that it is necessary to pay attention to values or ideals in order to distinguish the good life from the bad. Saying that human nature does not lead us in either direction is not saying that there is no such thing as a good life, only that our nature does not provide the basis for concluding what is good.

I find a more agnostic view of human nature more convincing than Selznick's view of the latent promise of humanity, but it too is only a theory of human nature, and therefore not necessarily better than Selznick's theory. Suppose conclusive evidence can be produced in favour of Selznick's view of natural values: what does that tell us about the role and character of such values? Here we arrive at the second point of criticism. In *The Moral*

*Commonwealth* Selznick defends the idea of moral universals, general moral values that are common to all human beings by virtue of their humanity. Included in the morality of all societies are values such as, for instance, the preservation of human life, affection and companionship, prohibition of murder and theft, hospitality (1992, 96). These values follow from human nature and the requirements of group life (97), which through the social nature of mankind can also be seen as natural. If this is all that the study of human nature has to offer, the role of enduring universal values seems very limited. Moreover, Selznick himself acknowledges that these general values are worked out differently in particular groups and societies, so that the concrete values held by a person or group are much more specific and widely variable. Thus a serious question keeps presenting itself: what do these universal values have to offer, how do they function as standards of evaluation, as tools for understanding and explanation? I think the answer must be that they offer very little. Take the value of hospitality. In some cultural settings it is of paramount importance to open your door to any passing stranger, while in others this is done only for your neighbours, or not even that, only for friends and family. This means, first of all, that the value of hospitality as such does not explain much about the way a certain practice works. Apart from that, the general value of hospitality is of no use as a standard to criticize behaviour or a practice. One can hardly condemn a citizen of New York for not being hospitable because she only receives close friends and relations as guests. Both to enhance our understanding and to function as an evaluative standard, the formulation of a value at least needs to take certain circumstances and conditions into account. Both points of criticism give reason to turn to the pragmatist parts of Selznick's theory instead of the naturalist part for a satisfactory account of ideals, and to take more seriously the emphasis of "the primacy of the particular" (1992, 193) than the search for "enduring truths regarding the morally relevant nature of man" (1961, 102).

The pragmatist inspiration of Selznick's conception of values, which is the subject of my third point of criticism, is best recognizable in Selznick's ideas about knowledge of values and in his emphasis of the factual context of values. I will not repeat all the particularities of a pragmatist theory of values,[7] but some central ideas need to be recalled to make clear what are the positive and negative points of Selznick's pragmatism. The strength of the pragmatist view is in its down-to-earth view of values, which is visible in the direct connection between values and concrete problems and the interest taken in

7 See section 5.2 for a general discussion of Dewey's pragmatism, and the relevant parts of sections 2.3 and 6.2 for more specific treatment of his theory of value.

what is empirically known and learnt from experience. Such a view makes the relevance of values to practical concerns immediately clear. That values are embedded in the context of experienced problems makes knowledge of facts and values interdependent: trying to grasp the meaning of values in the abstract is as little use as trying to understand and solve factual problems without taking values into account. However, at one crucial point pragmatism fails to take this interdependency seriously: in the definition and perception of problems and consequently also in the evaluation of the solution of problems. What is seen as a problem goes unquestioned in pragmatist theory, while a serious consideration of the continuity and interdependence of fact and value (and of means and ends) should also involve the reasons for something being problematic in the process of reflection. To grasp what is problematic about a situation, why something needs to be done about it, standards are also invoked: the situation is not the way it should be. Because a pragmatist theory does not relate values to the origin of the problem, but only to the solution, its justification of values is directly circular: what has value is what works as the solution to a problem, but what counts as a solution depends on the value standard that gave rise to problem. At times Selznick seems to recognize this problem of pragmatist theory, for instance, when he says that a theory of the good is needed (1992, 98). Such a theory is one of the mechanisms which help to avoid circularity. Selznick's specification of such a theory is only a vague notion of human well-being, which should be empirically informed. It does not give enough support to strengthen the pragmatist theory of values.

Let's pause and take stock. We are confronted with two theories of values, both making an uneasy combination between two parts and both with some strengths and some weaknesses. There are two dimensions along which the two theories can be compared. The first is the dimension of absolute versus relative elements in the concept of values. The second is the dimension of the objectivity versus the subjectivity of values. The first dimension is about the validity of values, about the extent to which they can be proven to be valid. The second dimension is about value ontology, about the way in which values can be said to exist. Radbruch concentrates on the first question and denies an objective ontological status of values. Selznick concentrates on the second question and denies that values can have absolute validity. The absolute and the relative have a fixed place and a clear meaning in Radbruch's theory. In his concept, values are of an absolute nature, or can be retraced to an absolute value. These absolute values are subject to relativistic interpretation: their concrete meaning and hierarchy are subject to personal choice. The strong point of Radbruch's theory is its argument for the foundational, abstract, absolute values. The existence of such values is necessarily presupposed by our understanding of the cultural world. However, it only convinces if these values are conceived as more formal than they appear in his own theory. And it has the important drawback that the content of values has to be found elsewhere. Radbruch's relativism does give values specific content but it is more problematic, because it consists of a subjectivism of personal choice combined with a very strict meta-theory of possible value systems.[8] Radbruch's concept of values is derived from the Kantian strand in his theory, but in effect his relativism dominates because it is the choice and interpretation of value that determines the concrete constellation of values influencing the cultural realities. Selznick rejects an a priori and absolute character of ideals as having an indubitable foundation. In his theory the division is not between absolute and relative elements, because he does not accept the possibility of the first. He makes a division between universal, enduring elements and concrete, changeable elements in his value theory. In his case, there is a division between general values derived from the naturalist part of his theory which has universal implications but has little relevance for concrete practices, and a more adaptive, context-bound theory with a pragmatist basis which is dominant in the determination of specific values. In his case, however, it is the pragmatist theory that is most important for the concept of values: it is the continuity between fact and value that forms the basis for Selznick's immanent concept of values as latent in the world of fact, and the pragmatist theory of knowledge that makes the validity of values provisional and based on their practical worth. It is precisely these aspects of the immanent concept of ideals that award ideals the combination of objectivity and a dynamic quality that can make them into relevant standards of evaluation.

In regard to the objectivity and subjectivity of values, it is Selznick who argues for an objective ontology. Because Radbruch constructs his concept of values from within the subject — it is the human mind that chooses to take the value-relating attitude — the necessity of values is always in relation to that subjective mind, which means that values cannot be objective in the sense that they are a part of reality. Values do not exist, they are valid, so for Radbruch the questions about values concern their validity. The objectivity of values in

[8] As I pointed out in 1.2, a non-cognitivist form of relativism (as which we can describe Radbruch's relativism, because of the emphasis on the unarguable choice of ultimate values) often shades into subjectivism, the idea that values are no more than personal preferences. In Radbruch's case this has a limited role: only regarding the choice of ultimate values.

Selznick's theory is achieved by a grounding of values in factual situations. Values are objective because they follow from and answer to empirical situations. This does not directly yield certainty about values: in a pragmatist theory facts are also fluctuating events. The validity of values is based, not on rational necessity, but on practical success: values are valid insofar as they successfully answer the problems posed by empirical situations. Radbruch rejects the objectivity of values in an ontological sense because of the gap between reality and value, while Selznick defends value objectivity in this sense because his conception of what belongs to reality is broader, including value.

Thus, from the comparisons along these two dimensions we can gather three main differences between Radbruch's and Selznick's theory of values. First of all, there is a difference regarding the core features of values: absolute and abstract versus provisional and concrete. Second, there is the difference in justification: rational necessity versus practical success as the basis for the validity of values. And most importantly, there is the difference in regard to ontology: dualism versus monism. These fundamental differences in their theories make it impossible to combine aspects of both into a coherent theory about the nature of values or ideals. The dichotomies that are central to Radbruch's neo-Kantianism are precisely what is unacceptable in Selznick's pragmatism. Moreover, it is not only in their views on values that the two theories differ but also in their manner of reasoning. The points on which the theories are convincing are such that trying to combine them would create serious inconsistencies: justifying values by means of rational necessity is a foundationalist strategy that is diametrically opposed to the contextual basis of values that are latent in practice.

In my view, a theory of ideals that can work for law should be coherent and convincing. To achieve coherence the theory must be based on one (coherent) philosophical position. For a theory of ideals, this means that it cannot be based on both a transcendent and an immanent ontology of ideals. This means that a choice has to be made: either to use a transcendent basis, embracing Radbruch's starting point, or to use an immanent basis, following Selznick. Consequently, I should either find a way to build a theory about the substance of values around the core of empty value forms of Kantianism, or strengthen the justification of values to lessen the circularity of pragmatism. The main problem with the first alternative is that the dualistic ontology of Kantianism bars a role for facts in the justification of values: factual matters can never be conclusive because the argument for values is always in relation to ultimate starting points and their acceptability for the subject that has to give a final judgment. When the road of rational acceptance ends, nothing more than personal convictions remain as a ground for the choice of a certain value. By rejecting the fact-value dichotomy, pragmatism opens up the possibility to explain the content of values from factual circumstances. The constraints on values that derive from their being embedded in practice provide a basis in reality, which is absent in the Kantian view which stresses the acceptance by the subject. In the pragmatist view of values, there is no beginning or end to the justification of values, which in the Kantian view is formed by the absolute necessity of formal values. This yields a profound difference in outlook because the pragmatist view eschews a deductive model of justification: values are always in the middle of practical concerns — they arise out of them and propose answers to them. It means that the objective basis is concrete and contextual, that the justification of values has to start with the specific situation in which they are embedded. The main shortcoming of the pragmatist theory of values is that the circle of relevant considerations to a specific value is drawn too narrowly. By widening the range of considerations, including other values, the justification of values can be improved. On balance the pragmatist theory of ideals is preferable because of its focus on the practical importance of ideals, highlighting their relevance to concrete problems and its modest conception of value objectivity. So, now that the reasons for preferring the pragmatist concept have been laid out, the task of improvement of that concept needs to be taken up.

## 3. IMPROVING THE PRAGMATIST THEORY OF VALUES

As I have argued, a Deweyan pragmatist theory of values, despite its flaws, appears as the better option to conceptualize ideals.[9] However, some additions and modifications need to be made to make the problem of circularity less acute. There are two starting points in Selznick's theory that can be extended with the help of other theories to improve the pragmatist theory. I already touched upon the first idea in my criticism of Selznick's theory: the need to have a theory of the good. This can be given more body with a constructivist approach, for which Dewey's theory itself provides a point of departure. The second idea that can give a pragmatist theory of values a more secure basis starts from Selznick's idea of the necessity of values for normative systems. This can be improved by merging it with a theory of practices.

9 Following Selznick, I will continue to use the terms 'value' and 'ideal' as identical.

I have said before that the circularity of the pragmatist theory can be lessened by paying explicit attention to a theory of the good. The naturalist basis of Selznick's theory is a step in that direction, but we saw that it only gives a very general idea. Moreover, not all the conclusions drawn from human nature about values are convincing, and a modified, more plausible account of human nature yields even less material to base values on. The largest problem is that, because of the general character of theories of human nature, these do not give enough grip to come to a full understanding of the role of values for specific problems. To grasp the role of values in determining problematic situations it seems more promising to look for more detailed, specified theories. Although development of such theories goes beyond my conceptual inquiry into values, I should say something more about the way such theories might function.

For a pragmatist framework, we can build on ideas of Dewey about the construction of good and the importance of context.[10] In the idea that the good or value must be constructed, and cannot simply be found, we first of all recognize Dewey's idea that a critical method must be applied to ascertain what has value. We can extend this idea of construction by reflecting upon the model of science which Dewey proposes to use in the assessment of value. Science proceeds by formulating hypotheses and testing these in experiments. Such a hypothesis is not formulated as a proposal *ex nihilo*, but is related to two things: the context of the problem at hand and the theory which can explain it. Pragmatism emphasizes the first, the context of the problematic situation, but is by no means blind to the second, the theory that supports the proposed hypothesis. For a satisfactory account of values, theories that can justify them are a necessary component.

The importance of context, however, is a reason to limit the scope of such theories. Dewey points out that attention to context cannot mean attention to all that is possibly relevant to the problem we are considering. In a fruitful investigation, most of the environment that surrounds a situation will remain unquestioned. Attention to context means differentiating between what is immediately relevant and what remains in the background; a selective interest in certain aspects of the context is unavoidable (Dewey 1931, 98). In the context of the search for a theory of values that is useful for legal theory, this means making explicit what theories are necessary to support an account of values that can be applied to law.

It is difficult to indicate such theories in the abstract, because of the

[10] I refer to Dewey's title of the chapter on values in *The Quest for Certainty*: 'The Construction of Good' (1929), and to the essay 'Context and Thought' (1931).

importance of context. In general, I can say that at least a theoretical argument for the specific values relevant in a legal context is needed. Arguments need to be given that can justify the values in question and establish a relationship between the particular legal field and the value in question. The hypothesis that a certain value is relevant to that legal field needs to be backed by theoretical considerations justifying the connection. Let me explain by returning to the example of private property I gave in Chapter 1.

I used a case about the abuse of ownership rights to indicate the importance of the ideal of freedom in relation to the right to private property. The case of the water tower raised the problem of the scope of such a right: how far can the owner of property go in the exercise of his rights? To answer such a question, the values underlying the right to private property need to be examined. The ideal of personal freedom can be advanced to justify the right, but the scope of that ideal is limited by other value considerations. In relation to property, these considerations will often be other values important to society as a whole, e.g. environmental concerns. Freedom is also limited by the rights of others, bringing in considerations of equality: in the case of the water tower, two owners have similar rights which clash and thus limit each other's exercise of rights. However, arguing that these are the values at stake is not enough to determine the scope of an owner's freedom: simply stating that freedom is apparently a value supported by the institution of property is inadequate. The mere identification of values needs to be backed by a justification of the importance of private property for personal freedom. A good argument can be made that some form of property is necessary for a person's autonomy: the moral development of a person requires independence as an important source of self-respect.[11] Such a justification favours the power of control over property, not the least because this can enhance moral responsibility. Hence, one can argue that the free exercise of property rights is needed to stimulate self-restraint. However, when someone fails to show such self-restraint, legal measures are taken.[12] There is a basic sphere of freedom of ownership, but misuse of that freedom is not tolerated. A court decision, as in the water tower case, restraining the abusive exercise of

11 See Waldron 1988 and Munzer 1990 for full arguments. Waldron discusses the Hegelian inspiration for this kind of argument extensively. This justification has drawbacks. It cannot be applied to all property: growth of wealth no longer enhances self-respect after a certain point, and the argument only applies to personal property. It also has strongly egalitarian implications (if property is necessary for moral development, everyone has a right to it).

12 In current Dutch law, the basis for a legal reaction is the rule prohibiting the abuse of rights: article 3:13 Burgerlijk Wetboek (Civil Code).

property rights can be seen as a reaction to a lack of responsibility on the part of the owner. In the case of the water tower this took the form of prohibiting a use of ownership rights purely to spite one's neighbour.

I believe such an example illustrates how an account of values in a legal context can be worked out. Considering a specific legal problem or a set of rules can lead to relevant ideals. The theoretical background of such an ideal can then be used to construct a more specific interpretation of the ideal. Relating that interpretation to the details of a case or rule then gives an idea of the meaning of the ideal in a particular legal context. The most important role of background theories is to explain the relation between ideals and a field of law.

A more ambitious project, but one popular with legal theorists such as Radbruch and Selznick, is the attempt to identify values relevant to the whole of law and to relate these both to more specific legal provisions and to theories about the function of law in society. I will try to sketch my own ideas on this subject, leaning on Selznick and Radbruch, in the next section. An additional reason to focus on the broader context of law as a whole is found in the second addition to pragmatism I propose: linking ideals to practices. The values relevant to law as a whole can be seen as core ideals of the practice of law, and as such they also form the background to more specific problems.

The idea of practices builds on Selznick's view of the link between ideals and normative systems (1961, 86-91), and, less directly, on Dewey's emphasis on the practical use of knowledge (1929, 82-83). Contemporary theories that use ideas similar to Selznick's notion of a normative system usually employ the notion of a practice. At times in this book I have also used the notion of a practice to refer to parts of social reality, of group interaction, without specifying clearly what the term means or arguing for what it is needed. Speaking of 'practices' makes explicit that practices are part of everyday life and everyone's experience. Adding the idea of practices to a pragmatic theory of values gives the pragmatic focus on problematic situations, to which values answer, a background of functional domains with certain central values. In the context of this study, this view of the background to specific problems is important because it is exactly such a functional domain that is waiting to take centre stage: law. But before we turn to the specific discussion of law, I need to explain my understanding of practices, the role of values in them, and the connection to pragmatism.

Practices can be seen as complex forms of socially established cooperative human activity.[13] A practice is a medium for people's actions in a social setting, a way of acting that makes smooth cooperation possible. A practice is a way of acting that needs to be learnt. This learning is to a large part by experience, not primarily by one's own experience, but from the experience of others who are also participating in the practice. Although existing traditions are important to the functioning of a practice because they provide a framework of reference, participants have the freedom to use the practice in certain ways and to innovate it: each can use it for his own purposes and add new ways of expression to it. For example, consider the practice of portrait painting. This can be seen as a gradually developing tradition of painting that started with figurative work that was continually refined, but under the influence of individual artists the practice was extended to include new forms of painting, such as the cubistic portraits by Picasso.[14]

Value-realization is an essential part of every practice. Learning to participate in a practice also means learning what the point of that practice is and what can be achieved through it. Learning to be an architect involves learning about both the technical and the aesthetic aspects of designing a good building. For this, the values that come with such practice need to be understood. However, once our young architect knows what it takes to design a good building, she can give her own interpretation to the technical and aesthetic values and maybe modify the practice. Because the practice itself is a medium that is continually evolving both in reaction to changes made by participants and to changing circumstances, so are the values that accompany it. Anyone subscribing to a practice has to commit himself to realizing the values that are inherent to that practice in order to use the practice well. Let me use the example of friendship to illustrate the role of values in practices. We can regard friendship as a practice that is a specific kind of relationship between two people. In a concrete friendship, two persons conduct themselves according to norms and values that come with this kind of practice. The particular actions they undertake together are not usually central to a friendship: what is important is being able to share interests or opinions, to be in each other's company and above all being able to trust each other. A good

13 In this account I combine aspects of MacIntyre's and Oakeshott's theories of practices (MacIntyre 1984, 187-196; Oakeshott 1975, 54-60). MacIntyre's conception of practices is problematic because it makes practices appear too homogeneous and coherent (compare Tamanaha 1997, 170). Oakeshott pays adequate attention to the input of individuals and their contributions to innovation of practices, but he fails to address the issue of the values of a practice.

14 I borrow the example of portrait painting from MacIntyre, who does not however extend it to include Picasso (1984, 189).

friendship is characterized by the realization of values of trust, generosity and commitment. However, how such core values of friendship are developed in a concrete relationship depends on the interpretation these two friends give them. The norms following from such values differ, depending on a number of variables: in a friendship between two little girls letting one's friend borrow a favourite toy may be the supreme form of generosity, while to a friendship between adult women generosity may take the form of lending a willing ear to the other's problems. Taking such variation into account is important to understand the concrete shape of values, but it should be accompanied by an effort to identify the core values of a practice because these are central to its functioning well. Thus, understanding core values of a practice is necessary in order to evaluate the way a concrete activity makes use of a practice. Focusing on core values is not tantamount to saying that these are inherent to a practice in any inescapable way. Because practices are open to whomsoever learns to use them, and can be modified by their users, participants also have a voice in criticizing and adapting core values. Both practices and their core values are subject to change by innovative users. However, such changes are gradual and slow: the core values of a practice have most often proven to be highly important to run a practice well. Justice has been a core value of law for many an age, and although its meaning has shifted in some respects, its focal points are remarkably stable.[15] Care should be taken neither to overemphasize nor to understate the evolving character of such values.

Let me then sketch the pragmatist value theory as it might look when such a view of practices is incorporated. Values are an integral part of the practices that qualify human behaviour. Such practices are needed to perform and coordinate activities in a satisfactory way. Values play the important role of inherent standards of evaluation that indicate the optimal way to conduct the practice. Thus, values are developed in a practice and they are tested by their success in guiding the activities performed by means of that practice. This means that the evaluation of values themselves is done by relating them to concrete activities — their capacity to guide, to suggest possibilities — and, following from that relation, to a wider web of other values and practices, of past experience and normative and descriptive theories. Values are flexible, liable to change, to expand and to decay. They are learnt in the course of participation in a practice and therefore largely acquired through experience. They are latent in practices, which means, as Selznick says, that they are not always realized but that they need to be if the practice is to function well. They

[15] I will discuss justice more elaborately in the next section.

often remain implicit but can to a large extent be constructed and articulated on the basis of practical use and norms that support them. Such an explication of values should be seen as a proposition, a hypothesis about the meaning of the ideal. This is a moment in which the subjective interpretation of the person who does the explicating looms, so care needs to be taken that the articulation of the ideal is not accepted as definitive. Possibilities should be kept open for improving on the articulation of ideals, both because better interpretations are possible and because ideals evolve in reaction to changing circumstances.

Combining a pragmatist theory of ideals with constructivism and the idea of practices as the framework for concrete actions and problems alleviates the problem of circularity of justification. That an ideal itself is part of the reason for having the very problem the ideal is supposed to solve is a kind of circularity that is to an extent caused by neglect of the broader context of both the problematic situation and the ideal. The limited focus on the concrete context of a problematic situation can be overcome by adding a constructivist appeal to relevant theories and an incorporation of practices. Constructivism brings in relevant theoretical considerations, which go beyond the mere consideration of the consequences for a problem; orientation on practices indicates how ideals have roots in ongoing traditions — they are not merely hypotheses formulated in reaction to a problem, they are standards that have been developed as a part of an existing practice. This both enhances their stability and it improves justification because reasons supporting ideals are found in the way they improve the functioning of practices.

Both additions fit a pragmatist theory well because they tie in with tendencies recognizable in pragmatism itself. The constructivist element is an extension of the pragmatist idea that there is a moment of construction involved in the discovery of ideals: they have to be formulated as hypotheses before they are put to the test. It means paying attention to the theoretical reasons for formulating a hypothesis. Emphasizing the connection between ideals and practices is close to pragmatist philosophy because it connects ideals to practical experience. As long as care is taken to avoid an absolutist interpretation of the ideals of a practice — a danger that is imminent when the relation between a particular ideal and a practice is seen as necessary — connecting ideals to patterns resulting from practical experience builds on the pragmatist idea that ideals prove themselves in their everyday use.

This easy fit with pragmatism does have one important drawback: these amendments lessen but do not solve the problem of circularity. Linking ideals to practices gives a context to specific problems but this relocates the problem of justifying ideals: if an ideal can be assessed by its guiding power for a practice, how is the functioning of a practice evaluated other than by reference to the ideal? The constructivist strategy of considering relevant theories involves a moment of selection by the person concerned. This has the consequence that there is always an arbitrary element: there are no hard and fast rules for selecting theoretical considerations. Thus, although the method puts the pragmatist focus on problematic situations in a broader perspective, it does not provide an independent source of justification. This is the price to be paid for having an adaptive theory of ideals without absolute and eternal claims: ideals become flexible and sensitive to context, but thereby lose a secure grounding.

To conclude this section I will trace the implications of this discussion for the pragmatist concept of ideals. Many of the features distinguished in Chapter 2 have again come to the fore here. The inherence of ideals in experience, in practice, is the key feature of the pragmatist concept. The starting point of every inquiry into ideals is how they arise out of existing arrangements and people's experience. They are inherent to societal practices, meaning not that they are necessarily part of such practices but they are indispensable for the good functioning of a practice. Any ideal is open to improvement in the form of a proposition by those using it as a standard, but such propositions have to be sensitive to, and be seen as interpretations of, the ideal's roots in experience. Ideals are flexible and liable to change along with changing circumstances, but some ideals continue to be meaningful over time. Such ideals are most often core ideals of a practice, which consist of an intricate set of constituting values which make competing claims. Because of their complex nature these ideals continue to point to possibilities of improvement. They are usually not completely realizable because they both consist of and are related to other values, making it difficult to satisfy all its demands. The exact meaning of the notion of complex core ideals can best be explained by looking at the ideals of a specific practice, and I will turn to that task in the next section when discussing ideals in connection to law.

## 4. DEVELOPING A THEORY OF LEGAL IDEALS

Having established that the pragmatist conception of ideals, despite some shortcomings, is the most convincing conception, the task remains to specify its meaning for legal theory. In addition, I want to examine if valuable elements from Radbruch's philosophy of law can be incorporated in a theory with a pragmatist basis. Especially Radbruch's ideas about the conflicts between law's values can serve to remedy some of the blind spots in Selznick's pragmatism. I will reinterpret Radbruch's ideas to fit a pragmatist philosophy, being aware that this moves far from Radbruch's own philosophical and methodological views. I will organize the discussion around three topics on which Radbruch and Selznick both have valuable ideas: the central ideals of the law, the autonomy of law, and the meaning of justice.

*The Central Ideals of the Law*

If the pragmatist conception is used as a basis for an examination of ideals and law, the first theory presenting itself which connects that conception to law is Selznick's doctrine of the master ideal. What insights does it give us and where can we use Radbruch's ideas to improve it? Before I start the discussion, I should strike one cautionary note. Both Radbruch's *Gerechtigkeit* and Selznick's legality can be regarded as the ideal specific for law, but they have a different basis and to a large extent a different function. The major difference in the theoretical function of the two ideals is that *Gerechtigkeit* is constitutive of the domain of law, whereas the master ideal of legality arises out of the domain of law; the idea of *Gerechtigkeit* is necessary for the existence of law, while the ideal of legality is only necessary for a good understanding of law. In the context of a pragmatist theory, the constitutive role of Radbruch's *Gerechtigkeit* cannot have a place, so that the use made of Radbruch's theory of legal values is not a full incorporation of his ideas.

We saw that Selznick takes master ideals to be the unifying values of normative systems or practices (1961, 87). The understanding of a practice and of an ideal is seen as continuous: we can only understand a practice in terms of its master ideal and a master ideal in terms of its practice. There are drawbacks as well as advantages to viewing law in such a way. As I argued in section 6.4, defining law in terms of one master ideal of legality is liable to create the false impression that the field of law can simply be explained in terms of orientation towards one value. There is the suggestion that we only need to search for the ideal governing the field to understand what is characteristic of that field. On the positive side, thinking of law in terms of a master ideal does draw attention to the possibility that the values that law tries to realize express to an important extent what is distinctive about law. Therefore, when the idea of a master ideal is used with caution it is helpful to express the thought that our understanding of law is improved by thinking of law as governed by certain core values. Care needs to be taken not to overstate the case: whether law is guided by a master ideal should be seen as an open question, and if law is guided by a master ideal, the question remains what that ideal might be.

One of the problematic tendencies created by the concept of a master ideal is that a relationship is taken to exist between practice and ideal that is a union: the ideal is relevant to all of the practice, both in the sense that it governs the whole practice and that it can be recognized in the whole practice. Such a view creates the danger of defining either practice or ideal merely in terms of its counterpart: because there exists a practice such as marriage, the values attached to the practice must be aspects of a master ideal of marriage. In that case, the answer to the question whether the presence of a master ideal is plausible in any given practice, is taken for granted. However, when that question is taken seriously, an important issue arising is under what conditions one can meaningfully speak of one governing master ideal; more specifically, it is a question of how to appreciate a plurality of opinion about governing ideals. If the relation between master ideal and practice is viewed as mutually determining, it approaches the constitutive role of values found in Radbruch's theory: understanding the practice as necessarily oriented towards the ideal makes value-orientation a defining criterion of the practice. We saw how this creates a tension between the constitutive and evaluative roles of values.

However, in Selznick's view of law, the relationship between the master ideal and law is not quite so strong. Because he does not define law in terms of orientation towards legality, the relation between the master ideal of legality and the practice of law is more contingent. Law is defined weakly, following Hart, as a system of primary and secondary rules, without reference to values. It is only when expounding his strong theory of law that Selznick refers to law as governed by a master ideal.[16] This means that, in Selznick's view, it is possible to study legal phenomena without taking the values involved into account, but that this can only generate a meagre account of what law is about. A weak definition of law serves to identify what is to count as legal, but it cannot provide a complete account of the meaning of law. Only when the values of law are studied as well does one gain a full understanding. So, although the master ideal is not a defining criterion to recognize law as such, it is necessary to understand law completely. Master ideals, by indicating the direction of activity and effort in a practice, provide a handle to understand what unites a practice. Selznick keeps open the possibility that ideals may not arise because circumstances prevent them, all the while implying that a practice without a mature ideal is lacking in quality. Although we have established that the concept of a master ideal does not necessarily mean that

16 The distinction between weak definition and strong theory is discussed in section 5.2.

ideal and practice are defined in terms of each other, there is still a problem with seeing the master ideal as the source of unity for the practice. The problem is the idea of a unifying value. Seeing law as oriented towards the ideal of legality suggests that realization of this one value makes a good legal system: if arbitrariness is successfully reduced, the legal system is doing well. Although Selznick distinguishes different types of law, e.g. autonomous and responsive law, these are explained in terms of different interpretations of the ideal of legality and different mechanisms to realize legality (Nonet & Selznick 1978, 107-108). The continuity between the different types of law is found in the ideal. Disagreement and differences are only admitted regarding the meaning of the ideal of legality, not about the reign of the ideal as such.

I detect three problems in this conception of a master ideal: (1) it excludes the possibility of conflict between law's own internal ideals, (2) it downplays changes in the governance of an ideal, and (3) it denies that other ideals than legality may be of equal relevance to law. Because the theory ignores these sources of change and conflict, it makes the values of law appear unduly unproblematic. Legality is a complex ideal comprising many different standards (Selznick 1961, 94), but eventually these are all seen as serving to reduce arbitrariness. This creates the impression that the standards which are part of legality will make concurrent demands, which is unlikely. To see why, it is illustrative to look at Fuller's discussion of the principles of legality, which, as he shows, make conflicting demands (Fuller 1969, 45). Take, for example, two of Fuller's principles of legality: avoiding contradictions between rules and constancy through time (1969, 39).[17] When a new rule is made, this often requires adjustment of other rules to avoid contradictions between the new rule and the existing body of rules, but too frequent adjustment of existing rules detracts from the value of constancy through time. These principles can both be seen as demands following from the ideal of legality, but they do not form a harmonious set of standards.[18]

That Selznick's master ideal of legality offers an overly harmonious conception of the ideals of law can also be gathered from the relationship between legality and justice. Selznick pays attention to the way these two become more closely connected in responsive law (Nonet & Selznick 1978, 108), but does not acknowledge the possibility that legality can make demands

[17] All principles are quoted with approval by Selznick (1992, 438).

[18] I have used Fuller's principles of legality as constitutive values of the ideal of legality, sidestepping the discussion on the relation between principles and values. Again, Alexy's idea of principles as *Optimierungsgebote* (see 1.4) is useful: Fuller's principles can be seen as aspirational norms prescribing optimal realization of aspects of legality.

that are diametrically opposed to justice. In his view, legality has the law as its specific domain of application but legality is subservient to, and does not compete with, the broader ideal of justice.[19] By virtually ignoring the conflicts that can arise between legal values,[20] Selznick circumvents the need to account for and to deal with such conflicts. In this respect, much can be learnt from Radbruch's theory.

Radbruch's threefold idea of law exemplifies an argument about the way values are both mutually dependent and conflicting. The complexity of the idea of law is caused by the limited scope of each of the values that it consists of. These values therefore require supplementation by other values but this opens the door to possible conflict: the values are relevant to the same subject matter but make different demands. Radbruch only used the argument of antinomies in regard to the idea of law, but a similar argument can be made about other complex ideals. Whenever a set of values can be discerned which are all necessary to form an ideal complex enough to govern a practice meaningfully, there is the likelihood of a conflict between the values making up the ideal. To salvage the idea of a harmonious ideal, two possibilities for solving such value conflicts present themselves: one is by denying the conflicts by saying that the complex ideal really consists of a balanced mix of values, the other by locating solutions in the context of concrete cases. The first option, establishing the weight of values is not really plausible. Let's take up the example of the ideal of legality again, assuming for the moment that it simply consists of Fuller's eight principles of legality: it is extremely hard to determine before a concrete case arises how the conflicting demands of those values are to be resolved.[21] It is only when assessing a specific rule that one can say that in this set of circumstances the constancy of a rule has to be given up and the rule changed because a contradiction has come to light. Thus, the idea that conflicts can be solved in concrete circumstances stands a better chance. In a specific context, the complex master ideal can even be helpful to

19 In *The Moral Commonwealth* justice and legality seem virtually synonymous when he refers to the progressive reduction of arbitrariness as 'the moral objective' of the science of justice (1992, 445). In earlier work the scope of legality is seen as narrower than that of justice (1961, 95; 1969, 12).

20 The only conflicts between legally relevant values Selznick explicitly recognizes are those between the different demands of justice: "(...) within a given community, accepted principles of justice are often in conflict and require trade-offs" (1992, 433). However, this recognition is made about accepted principles of justice, not about fundamental values.

21 Fuller himself indicates that there is variability in the ranking of the principles and the stringency with which they should be applied, depending on the branch of law and the type of legal rule (1969, 93).

determine which value needs to prevail in the case at hand. When confronted with values giving contrary directions, it is often easier to decide in the light of an overarching ideal. In terms of the example: in a specific case, it may be relatively clear that repairing a contradiction is more important to reduce arbitrariness than keeping the rule constant. However, the possibility of resolving conflicts between the elements of the ideal in concrete cases does not bring true harmony to the complex ideal. Knowing which of the elements should prevail in the given situation does not always detract from the importance of the elements which are not realized in this case. Solving a concrete value conflict is often accompanied by a sense of loss regarding the unrealized values.[22] This constitutes the important sense in which a complex ideal is unrealizable: the demands it makes can never all be realized to the full. Although we may desire complete realization of an ideal, this cannot be achieved because the ideal consists of conflicting elements. The elements of a complex ideal form antinomies in Radbruch's sense: they require each other to form a rich ideal but they make demands that cannot all be realized.

The second and third problem about master ideals are closely related and best discussed together. The possibility of change in the governance of legality and the possible relevance of other ideals are both connected to the following question: if the ideal and the practice of law are not defined in terms of each other, how can the master ideal be determined? Selznick's argument about master ideals is based on the idea that there is an inclination in a practice such as law towards value realization. From this premise it is easy to move on to the idea that a certain practice inclines towards a specific ideal. This is part of the argument in 'Sociology and Natural Law', where Selznick pairs normative systems with accompanying master ideals, which more often than not are even named after the normative system. The ideal of friendship governs the normative system of friendship, as the ideal of democracy governs a democracy (1961, 86). This makes it seem as if the master ideal of such a practice is simply a name for the set of values that guide the practice at a given moment. This impression is strengthened when the place of legality in the argument about the development of law is considered (Nonet & Selznick 1978). One of the differences between the stage of repressive law, on the one hand, and the stages of autonomous and responsive law on the other is that it is not governed by the ideal of legality. Repressive law is not governed by legal ideals, it is an instrument of power to those in charge and only serves

22 Thus, the conflicts between the elements of complex ideals are potentially tragic conflicts as described by Van den Brink (2000, 27-38): realizing the one necessarily frustrates the others.

dominant social values. In the stages where law does serve a legal ideal, it serves the same ideal: "The 'master ideal' of responsive law, as of autonomous law, is legality" (1978, 107). However, the ideal of legality changes from a formalistic to a purposeful ideal; the emphasis on security and procedure is traded for a focus on adaptation and moral aims. If both are interpretations of the ideal of progressively reducing arbitrariness, what does that mean for the continuity of that ideal? It seems that the interpretation of what is seen as arbitrary and needing elimination is radically different. As I have indicated before, legality in a responsive legal order comes so close to justice that it is hardly distinguishable. In the context of Selznick's model of legal development, it is possible to see justice as the master ideal of responsive law and to reserve the ideal of legality for autonomous law. Distinguishing between different ideals as belonging to different types of law makes it easier to see the prevalence of one ideal as an indication of the corresponding type of law: detection of a greater concern for (substantive) justice is one of the markers of a development towards a responsive legal order. This does not mean that legality and justice must be seen as exclusive ideals: we can also think of legal systems which are plausibly viewed as guided by both legality and justice, without one or the other being the dominant master ideal.

Once the argument is accepted that a certain master ideal can lose its predominance over law, the question can immediately be raised what other ideal might take its place and how such master ideals might be related. In the context of Selznick's theory, the argument can be made that there is a shift from legality to justice as the dominant ideal of law, because of the changing character of law and its changing place in society. Here, I want to make a different argument, not on the basis of Selznick's developmental model, but by looking more concretely at parts of positive law that display the orientation towards ideals and at theories about the function of law in society. Positive law provides a specific context needed in a pragmatist theory, and a theory on law's functions can provide some of the necessary theoretical background. I hope this may give some indications of which ideals can plausibly be regarded as central ideals of law. Theories about law and society that are coherent with the pragmatist theory of ideals, apart from Selznick's ideas, are other theories with a pragmatist leaning such as the legal realism of Llewellyn and Fuller's interactionism (Llewellyn 1940; Fuller 1969; 1981). Both theories distinguish certain purposes or social functions that law serves, recognizing that these involve an ideal aspect.[23] From the combination of positive law, legal ideals and these theories, an argument can be constructed for certain central legal ideals. A note of caution, however: the following is no more than an indication of how such an argument can be built up. For a full argument, more detailed information is necessary which would require a study of more specific legal practices which are outside the scope of this work.

To derive the content of general legal ideals from positive law, one would need to look at a shared orientation of the body of rules of a legal system. To see how this can be done, Radbruch can be taken as an example. In the second part of his *Rechtsphilosophie*, Radbruch connects his legal philosophy to specific parts of legal doctrine and examines the way values appear in these fields of law. What is most striking about these discussions is that the influence of substantive political values, instead of specifically legal values, is paramount in most fields, except in procedural law. For instance, in the main branches of private law, property law and contract law, an ideal of personal autonomy is in tension with the value of social utility (Radbruch 1932, 375, 380). The specifically legal values of *Rechtssicherheit* and *Gerechtigkeit* can be recognized primarily in the formal aspects of law, in its structure and its procedures (e.g. 416-417). Radbruch's examination is not comprehensive and it is inspired by the German legal system of his day; but, taking the limiting factors of its historical and local character into account, there are some general points that can be gathered from Radbruch's work. The influence of general social or political ideals on the content of law is dominant, but specifically legal ideals exert their influence by way of the structural and procedural aspects of law. However, the question remains whether Radbruch's identification of justice and legal security as the two legal ideals can also be generalized. To see whether it can it is helpful to look at the rules and principles of an existing legal system. To that end, I will proceed by examining examples from Dutch law as additional material about positive law before moving on to background theories.

I have chosen examples from three fields in Dutch law: constitutional law, administrative law and private law. In each of these examples the orientation of rules and principles towards legal ideals can be recognized. The clearest example can be found in the Dutch constitution, which starts with an article

[23] Llewellyn's theory of the 'law-jobs' contains reference to both the 'bare-bones' and the 'questing' aspects of the law-jobs (1940, 1375). These resemble Selznick's combination of baseline and flourishing. Fuller's theory contains a comparable combination of the morality of duty and the morality of aspiration, which are both present in the morality of law (1969, 5).

formulating a principle of equality — like cases are treated alike — and forbidding discrimination on a number of grounds such as sex and race. This article, which was included when the constitution was revised in 1983, can be regarded as the codification of a fundamental value that is generally accepted as a part of Western political thought.[24] Thus, the most fundamental constitutional principle in Dutch law is the recognition of an ideal in a formulation that closely resembles Radbruch's conception of justice as formal equality. Although it is less formal than Radbruch's value of justice because it identifies certain unacceptable criteria for unequal treatment, it is a clear formulation of an ideal of justice as equality.

My second example is taken from Dutch administrative law: decisions by administrative bodies have to conform to 'general principles of good administration' (*algemene beginselen van behoorlijk bestuur*).[25] These principles, which are used by courts to assess such decisions, concern, for instance, the care with which decisions are prepared and taken, the way decisions are argued, and the way powers are used. They can be described as a combination of fairness and legality: they are meant to reduce the arbitrariness of decisions and to make sure all the interests involved are given due consideration. These principles can thus be described as formulations of the meaning of the ideals of legality and justice in the context of government administration. The principles give indications that Radbruch's strict formulations of justice and legal security are too narrow — at any rate, to understand the ideals of Dutch law. For instance, there is a principle expressing the command to observe proportionality between the purpose of the decision and the burdens put on those involved.[26] It is a consideration demanded by the ideal of justice, but it does not follow directly from justice as formal equality; thus, it gives an indication that the ideals of law need to be seen as having a broader meaning.

The third example is taken from Dutch private law and concerns the importance of the doctrine of reasonableness and fairness (*redelijkheid en billijkheid*). In the Dutch Civil Code, there are a number of instances in which legal subjects are enjoined to conduct themselves reasonably towards each other, even setting aside legal rules when such a rule would have unacceptably

[24] Compare Maris 1988, 41. He also points out that the precise meaning of the ideal of equality is contested. See also Van der Burg 1991, 201-207.

[25] Van Wijk and Konijnenbelt identify twelve principles, most of which have been codified in the Algemene Wet Bestuursrecht (Awb) of 1994 (the general statute on administrative law) (1997, 308-417).

[26] This principle is laid down in article 3:4 Awb.

unreasonable or unfair results. What defines reasonableness and fairness is kept open: it is an appeal to unwritten legal principles, to shared legal opinion and the recognition of individual and social interests.[27] The open character of the doctrine of reasonableness creates the possibility of a direct appeal to legal principles and a sense of fairness in a specific situation. It calls for consideration of what is fair in the circumstances of a concrete case, and because of this it can be interpreted as a reference to an ideal of justice. Because of the open character of reasonableness and fairness, such an ideal of justice is in tension with demands of legality: the precise norms laid down in the Code, serving the predictability of the law, can be set aside to give way to fairness in the specific instance.

On the basis of this discussion of positive law the tentative conclusion can be drawn that there are indications of an orientation towards ideals of justice and legality in existing legal rules and principles. I will now turn to the background theories and see if similar indications can be gathered from these. I will be brief about these theories here, because I will return to the issue of theories of law in the next chapter. Here I want to consider specifically if and how legal ideals can be based on the specific social functions law needs to perform. In order to examine those functions I will consider Karl Llewellyn's theory on 'law-jobs'. Llewellyn distinguishes different law-jobs that "(...) can all be summed up in a single formulation: such arrangement and adjustment of people's behaviour that the society (or the group) remains a society (or a group) and gets enough energy unleashed and coordinated to keep on with its job as a society (or a group)" (1940, 1373). The law-jobs are seen as the tasks that need to be performed by a legal system to ensure the continued existence of a society. Llewellyn recognizes that law-jobs can be performed at different levels related to the extent that they enhance the quality of the society: they can serve to ensure bare survival — the "bare-bones" aspect, or serve to ensure efficient running or realize ideals leading to a fuller life — the "questing" aspect (1940, 1375). The law-jobs include the disposition of trouble-cases, the preventive channelling of conduct, the allocation of authority, and the net organization of society as a whole.[28] In their questing aspect, these four functions of law can all be seen as in some way linked to ideals of justice and legality. Disposing trouble-cases at its best serves the ideal of justice: it is

[27] *Redelijkheid en billijkheid* is defined in article 3:12 of the Burgerlijk Wetboek (BW, Dutch Civil Code) and it is invoked explicitly in the articles 6:2, 6:248 and 2:258 BW. It is widely used in Dutch case law.

[28] I will not discuss the fifth law job here because that law job (juristic method) is an aspect of the four other jobs and not an independent function (1940, 1392).

aimed at reaching a decision that is fair to all concerned (1376). By channelling conduct, law makes life more predictable and less arbitrary: these are aspects of the ideal of legality. The allocation of authority is a matter of determining who makes decisions in a society and of legitimizing that authority by subjecting it to procedural constraints (1386). The latter aspect also reduces arbitrariness because it limits the power of those with authority and because it formalizes the ways in which that authority is exercised. The fourth law-job, net organization or drive, is the integrative function of law: organizing the legal system as a whole and thereby giving the society direction. It is in this function that the ideals of law and society are primarily joined: there is a mutual influence of legal and cultural ideals. It is here that the elements of justice that connect it to broad social ideals come to the fore: justice as an integrative ideal (Selznick 1992, 431). As Llewellyn puts it: "(...) it is under this Net Drive focus that one can most readily pick out that phase of the Justice ideal which looks to long-range welfare of the Entirety" (1940, 1391). Thus, this example of a focus on the social function of law also points in the direction of justice and legality as leading ideals specific to law; they are by no means the only ideals influencing law but can be seen as ideals which in part give law its specific character.

In conclusion, it seems warranted to advance the idea that a constructivist strategy might lead to two central ideals of law: justice and legality. These two leading ideals need to be interpreted broadly: justice moves beyond formal equality, and legality is not restricted to the non-arbitrariness of determinate rules.[29] It seems best to abandon the idea that there is one master ideal of law. Instead, we can distinguish a number of complex ideals that govern law in variable measures, of which justice and legality are the central and most encompassing ideals specific to law. Not only is there variation in the prominence these ideals take in the practice of law, they themselves can be seen to consist of a number of values that also have variable importance according to context. Legality can fruitfully be seen to consist of the values that Fuller takes as the internal morality of law; justice encompasses, among other things, standards of desert, need, equal concern and respect. Neither the complex ideals nor their constituting values can be said to have an a priori higher standing: the importance of one ideal over the other depends on the specific legal context, on the place of law in society at a given moment and the tasks law needs to fulfil. The subject of law in society, however, brings me to the next theme I wanted to discuss: how to regard the autonomy of law.

[29] Thus, they incorporate but are not restricted to Radbruch's ideas of justice as formal equality and legal security (which is here seen as part of the core meaning of legality).

*Law's Limited Autonomy*

To describe my idea of the relative autonomy of law in respect of other societal domains, I want to use Radbruch's idea of the threefold idea of law as a handle once more. Radbruch identified two of law's central values as specifically legal, namely justice and legal security, while seeing the third value of *Zweckmäßigkeit* as the introduction of ethical and political considerations in the domain of law. This conception indicates how to see the two roles that values can take in the relations between law and connected societal practices. I think Radbruch's idea can be expanded to form a more general argument about the different values influencing legal practice. It then reads as the thesis that in every concrete determination of what law means there is an interplay between ideals specific to law and ideals from the other practices involved in the case at hand. If there is a need for legal regulation of a practice in which there is a set of clear and strong core values, such regulation will take these values as a starting point and try to find a balance between the values of law and those of such a practice. For example, in health law one can recognize the ideals of a good doctor and of patient autonomy in its rules and principles. But in the same set of legal rules the observance of values of legality can also be recognized. The balance struck between the different ideals and values depends on the content of these ideals, on how well the different demands can be reconciled in concrete regulation. At times, the core values of a practice may harmonize perfectly with certain legal standards, but there are also cases where the demands of such a practice clash with important legal values. There is always the need for adjustment in order to realize the ideals involved to the largest extent.

If this picture of legal activity as involving the search for the right mix of values is correct — it is rather crude now but I will refine it later on — it means that the autonomy of law is both limited and variable. Autonomy is limited because law always concerns other practices; it is never completely separate and closed but is related to something else, be it the economy, politics, art or medicine. Since all of these are practices that come with their own core values, law has to take these values into account even if it decides to disregard them. The possibility of disregarding the values of another practice also indicates in what sense the autonomy of law is variable. The more the core values of law are upheld, the more autonomous law will appear. Selznick is right in relating the responsiveness of a legal order to the degree in which it takes societal purpose seriously: a legal system is more responsive and less autonomous to the extent that it serves the values of other societal practices. The autonomy of law is not only variable over time, although this is an important aspect because shifts in the relative autonomy or openness of law change the character of the legal order. It is also variable in regard to subject matter, constituting the degree to which law can uphold its own values while considering the values of the practice involved. So even if there is a general responsiveness in a legal order, there is still room for variation in the weight given to law's core values in the regulation of specific subjects.

Until now, I have spoken of the legal order as a whole as a practice concerned with value realization. This image needs refinement in two respects. First, my picture of the legal order creates the false impression that value-realization is the main purpose of law. The point of this study is indeed to show how paying attention to ideals or values can enrich our understanding of law, but this should certainly not be read as a plea that law should only serve to promote ideals. The fact that the concerns of law lie elsewhere as well, has consequences for the issue of autonomy: the specific character of law is not only found in the values that are distinctively legal but also in mechanisms and institutions that are particular to the legal order. Legal language and reasoning, the form of statutes and rules, courts and lawyers, all of these are elements that contribute to the specific character of law. However, the interesting issue in this context is how and to what extent that specific character is expressed in law's central ideals, so I will not discuss the other features relating to autonomy here.

Second, value-realization is not of equal importance in every part of the legal order nor are the same values equally prominent. The most important distinction here is between legislation and adjudication. If these are described simply as primarily concerned with the making of rules and the resolution of conflicts on the basis of rules, respectively, the first is directly concerned with ideals and the second only indirectly. The making of laws is preeminently an activity in which a balance has to be found between legal ideals of justice and legality and the ideals of other practices. An obvious need for balancing ideals in legislation occurs because both legal ideals and political ideals are always involved in the process of law-making. This is different in adjudication: judging takes place in an institution (the courts) which is designed to keep political ideals at a distance. A judge has the task of interpreting and developing existing legal rules and principles, only taking political ideals into account to acquire a better understanding of the law. That, however, is an important qualification: even though adjudication is concerned with the right application of the law, doing this can involve taking the values of other practices into account. This is why the difference in value-orientation between legislation and adjudication can be understood as a difference between a direct and an indirect concern for values that are not incorporated in law. Similarly, there is a difference in the focus on particular values, stemming to a large part from the distinct primary functions of legislation and adjudication: determining general policies versus deciding individual cases. The principles of legality, distinguished by Fuller, are all relevant to the making of laws, but they are not all applicable to the deciding of conflicts. For instance, a judge has no need to worry about the generality of his ruling because his concern is with the fair decision of a particular case, but he does need to make sure that his decision does not require the impossible. In a similar fashion, ideals can consist of a different constellation of constitutive values according to context. In the context of judging, the central point of the ideal of justice lies in fairness to the specific interests of the parties involved, not in the right criteria for unequal treatment. For the legislator, considering and deciding on the criteria for unequal treatment is a key demand made by justice. These are only rough contours of the differences in value-orientation between different parts of legal practice, but I hope the main idea is clear. The role of the central values of law is of variable importance in different legal contexts and so is that of the ideals of other practices. The specific functions of legal institutions entail prominence of particular values as well as a specific interpretation of general legal values, which is something to be kept in mind when assessing a general argument about legal values.

*Justice*

The relationship between ideals and law's autonomy is most acutely felt in one of law's central ideals that has long been a focal point in jurisprudence: the ideal of justice. Justice is not only recognized as a central ideal in legal theories, it is also the subject of moral and political philosophy. Because it is claimed as a key value both for law and for morality, especially political morality,[30] the question arises how to view the place of justice in both: is there a special bond between law and justice or is justice primarily relevant in the broader context of political morality? On this question both Selznick and Radbruch provide useful ideas. As I indicated in my discussion of the central ideals of law, justice is best seen as a complex ideal consisting of a number of values which are more or less specific to law. In Selznick's terms, justice is an integrative ideal, combining different principles (1992, 431). Selznick does

[30] The broad, political and moral, scope of justice is advanced in the well-known work of Rawls, who begins *A Theory of Justice* with the description of justice as 'the first virtue of social institutions' (1971, 3). Rawls also refers to the political and moral aspects of justice in *Political Liberalism* (1993, 11).

not, however, specifically identify elements of justice that are responsible for its relevance to law, nor does he formulate a core meaning of the ideal of justice itself; two things that are necessary to get a grip on the role of justice in regard to the autonomy of law. How then to describe the ideal of justice and its constituting values?

At the core of the ideal are two related notions: the idea of giving each his due — the value of fairness, and that of treating like cases alike — the value of equality.[31] The notion of justice as equality can be recognized in many more specific legal values, such as the procedural equality before the laws and judicial impartiality, in prohibitions of discrimination based on race or sex, etc. That law aims to serve the value of fairness can also be seen in a number of more concrete values, e.g. in the proportionality of punishment in relation to a crime, and in the weight given to a victim's own fault in tort cases. This core meaning of justice as a combination of equality and fairness is rather formal, but underlying it are a number of more substantive values giving the ideal body. Among these, a key value is that of moral equality: each person is entitled to equal concern and respect.[32] The value of moral equality, expressing that each individual is of equal worth as a person by virtue of being a person, underpins the formal equality of justice, making it more robust because it creates a presumption of equality in all cases: good reasons have to be given to treat persons differently instead of equally. Other important substantive values concern criteria of distribution, giving content to the value of fairness by specifying the basis of what each is due. Among these, the key criteria are need, desert, and again, equality. The criterion of desert calls for distribution according to past performance, while the criterion of need centres on a person's needs. The criterion of equality calls for equal distribution on the basis of moral equality.

Two things should be noted about these more substantive values that are part of justice: it is about these that opinions start to diverge, and to these substantive values law has a less direct connection than to the formal core of justice. On both points, Radbruch's theory provides valuable insights: he argued that the formal value of *Gerechtigkeit* is specific to law and that the substantive value of *Zweckmäßigkeit* invites differences of opinion. When

[31] The combination of fairness and equality as the core of the concept of justice is also propagated by Neil MacCormick (1978, 73). Fairness as the core of justice is proposed by, e.g., David Miller (1976). Justice as equal treatment can also be found in — apart from Radbruch (1932, 278) — Hart (1994, 159), Harris (1996, 171), and Aristotle (1934, Nicomachean Ethics, V. iii).

[32] Developed by Ronald Dworkin (1978, 182) as an interpretation of Rawls' and Kant's idea that each person should be treated as an end in itself, never as a means only.

these thoughts are incorporated in an argument about justice as a complex ideal, they acquire a slightly different character because the all-encompassing notion of the idea of law has been abandoned. On the one hand, seeing justice as a complex ideal abandons the complete reach of the idea of law over the realm of law, because it is not the only ideal that is a guide to law; on the other hand, justice reaches beyond the boundaries of law, because it is also a key value in morality and politics. These modifications do not alter the importance of recognizing that the more formal and procedural aspects of justice are the ones that give it a special relevance to law.

Distinctive of law is a far-reaching concern for procedural values, which is most recognizable in the ideal of justice according to the law: it is the ideal of doing justice in a case by administering the law correctly while observing such values as impartiality and justification.[33] But the meaning of justice is not exhausted by such procedural considerations: even when the primary concern is the correct administration of the law, the ideal of justice always impinges upon deeper questions of substantive justice, which in the context of administration means that applying the law involves considering the justice of the laws themselves, trying to interpret them in a way that best serves justice. Here, again, conflicts between the different constitutive values of the ideal appear: it is often impossible to give all values belonging to justice the weight they ought to be given because they make conflicting demands. Such conflicts, however, are even more apparent between the substantive values underlying fairness: giving each person what he needs clashes with giving each what he deserves or giving each an equal share. Therefore, it is not surprising that theories of justice differ precisely over these substantive issues of distribution: according to some, need should be given priority over desert, while some claim the opposite, and still others advocate radical equality. The differences between conceptions of justice are thus found in the interpretations of fairness and equality, the core of the concept of justice. Different conceptions of justice attach varying importance to the ideal's different constitutive values, in part depending also on whether the focus is on justice in the context of law or in another context. The substantive aspects of justice are more prominent in the context of politics, for instance, than in the context of law; and within law, they are more prominent in the context of legislation than in that of adjudication. This means that the substantive aspects of justice have a more

[33] Impartiality, i.e. excluding bias and self-interest, and justification, i.e. giving reasons when imposing burdens, are two of the principles of justice recognized by Selznick (1992, 431-32). Like the substantive values I distinguished, these procedural values are also part of the complex ideal of justice.

subdued role in law than the formal aspects. The shifting importance of the different constituting values of justice can be differentiated further if more specific situations and practices are examined: although fairness and equality are central to both legislation and adjudication, the distributional criteria are not usually at issue before the court. Similarly, when one considers criminal law and civil law different considerations of justice gain prominence in each field: in a criminal case, doing justice is closely connected to truth-finding, making sure that an innocent person is not convicted, but truth is a value that is less relevant in a civil suit, where uncontested facts are not further investigated. The meaning of the ideal of justice is thus in part determined by the context in which it operates. Apart from formulating core values, giving precise indications of its meaning is not possible without considering a specific context as well.

## 5. CONCLUSIONS

This chapter provided a direct comparison between the theories of Radbruch and Selznick, in order to establish which of the two provides a more convincing theory about the nature of ideals. Both Radbruch and Selznick make combinations of more universal and more contingent elements in their theory, although these are more sharply separated in Radbruch's theory. For both the combination is troublesome. Radbruch's abstract ultimate values work well as formal prerequisites of our cultural world, but fail as standards of evaluation because the relativistic determination of their content prevents their functioning as objective standards. Selznick's universal values depend on a robust conception of human nature that remains unargued and which is in tension with the adaptive, problem-solving view of ideals of pragmatism.

A more plausible theory of ideals in law can be built up from the best elements of these two theories. The basis is a pragmatist theory of ideals. Ideals are seen as arising in the course of people's problem-solving experience, which means that their meaning is to a large extent determined by context and that they are relatively concrete. Because of its empirical orientation and its adaptive view of ideals, a pragmatist conception of ideals is able to give ideals an objective basis without depending on absolutes and rational necessities. However, by basing the justification of ideals solely on their direct practical consequences, pragmatism overlooks the role of ideals in determining what good consequences are. Thus, the theory results in a direct circularity of justification. In order to alleviate the limitations of such a justification, the pragmatist view needs to be enhanced by extending two lines of argument implicit in it: a constructivist methodology and an account of practices. Combining it with a constructivist method allows for a more explicit role of background theories without turning these into an absolute basis. An emphasis on practices provides a focus on ideals that are complex guides to a field and are not as changeable as ideals tend to be in a purely pragmatist view. These two additions, although not quite solving the problem of circularity, do make it less acute.

With these additions the pragmatist concept of ideals takes the following form. The key feature of the pragmatist concept remains the inherence of ideals in experience. They are standards of evaluation inherent in societal practices, meaning that they are indispensable for the good functioning of a practice. Propositions concerning the interpretation of these ideals can be used as hypotheses for their improvement. Ideals are flexible and liable to change along with changing circumstances, but some ideals continue to be meaningful over time. Such ideals are most often core ideals of a practice, which consist of an intricate set of constituting values which make competing claims. Because of their complex nature these ideals are not usually completely realizable: they continue to point to possibilities of improvement.

Such a pragmatist theory of ideals still has one major drawback that is not solved by improving the method of justification or by a more robust account of the practices to which ideals are connected. Ideals appear as leading values that evolve to suit a practice at any given moment, as guiding standards that make practices successful. This optimistic view overlooks the important role of conflict in the shaping of ideals. Following Radbruch, I argue that both in the relationship between different ideals and within one complex ideal itself, value conflicts are inescapable. This is mainly caused by the limitations of single value elements; these are one-dimensional and therefore insufficient to provide complete guidance to a practice. A central ideal of a practice will consist of different constitutive values, which are necessary to give the ideal substantial meaning but which also make contrary demands. These tensions within complex ideals make them dynamic: the exact mix of values will depend on the concrete situation for which the ideal is employed as a standard. It also makes the exact articulation of an ideal's meaning difficult: highlighting certain value elements will obscure others. Furthermore, the complexity of the ideal is a bar on complete realization — it is practically impossible to satisfy all of its, conflicting, demands at once.

Such a complex ideal can serve as the master ideal of a practice, but again we should guard against an overly harmonious view. In extensive practices, such as law or education or medicine, leading ideals are not always reducible to a single guiding ideal. When more than one central ideal can be recognized, for instance justice and legality in law, the most conspicuous value conflicts are between the different guiding ideals of a practice.

The central ideals of a practice are important determinants of the specific character of that practice: the concern for these particular ideals give a practice autonomy. In regard to law, we saw that the focus on ideals of justice and legality is reflected in procedural concerns. However, the autonomy of a practice is limited. A practice may sometimes appear to be a closed circuit, but that appearance is false. Distinct practices are in contact, if only because people are involved in more than one practice. Values form a point of contact between practices in a special way. When exploring the meaning of a particular ideal, one finds that a reference to other values is necessary to reach a genuine understanding of that ideal. Not all of these values are internal to the practice to which the particular ideal is connected. This can be seen clearly in the case of justice. The special relation to law is caused by the formal core of justice which is best described as a combination of fairness and equality. This core meaning brings it close to the central functions of law. However, the core of fairness and equality is intimately bound up with substantive moral values such as the moral equality of persons and distributional criteria of merit and need. Because of this, justice not only serves as one of the guardians of law's autonomy, but also as a link to moral and political domains. The ideals of a practice thus provide connections to other practices. Even though an activity may appear to take place solely within the context of a specific practice, trying to articulate the meaning of the ideals involved takes one beyond the boundaries of that practice. This is even more strongly the case with the practice of law, because law concerns itself with other practices as the subject matter of its regulations. To achieve regulation of other domains, law cannot ignore the values that come with them.

# CHAPTER 8

# RECOGNIZING THE IDEALS OF LAW
*Beyond Legal Positivism and Natural Law Theory*

## 1. THE AIMS OF THIS CHAPTER

In this chapter I want to link the ideal-oriented theories studied and developed in the previous chapters to the main currents of legal theory today. Much of the discussion in legal theory is still cast in the mode of a debate between legal positivist and natural law theories, in which sophisticated theories are presented as improvements of the one or the other. Examples that come to mind are MacCormick and Weinberger who present their institutional theory of law (1986) as a sophistication of legal positivism, and the theory of John Finnis (1980) as a rediscovery of the natural law theory of Aquinas.

In this chapter I will present ideal-oriented theories such as those of Radbruch and Selznick as taking a position avoiding the pitfalls of both positivism and natural law, especially because they give a good explanation both of law's own central ideals and of the continuities between law and other social practices. As an extensive preliminary step in the argument I will give a description of the debate between legal positivism and natural law as a discussion on the separation of law and morals. After describing that debate I will evaluate both theories and argue that the difficulties of each position can be explained in terms of a concern about the proper role of values. Legal positivism is concerned to limit the role of values in its description of law. Natural law theory, on the other hand, seeks to identify the values that law necessarily incorporates. Therefore, a fruitful way of understanding the opposition between the two is as a debate over the nature and role of values.

In the next section I will review the current debate by considering a number of interpretations of legal positivism and natural law theory. My discussion of the debate will not be comprehensive; I will discuss key elements of both theories to highlight the main points of disagreement. I will go on to trace the value theories implicit in both theories in the third section, pointing out their limits, and consider alternatives. In the third section, I will bring in the ideal-oriented theories of Radbruch and Selznick as an alternative and relate these to the questions dividing natural law theorists and legal positivists. Finally, I will present some of the possibilities that a non-positivist and pragmatist theory offers.

## 2. THE DEBATE BETWEEN LEGAL POSITIVISM AND NATURAL LAW THEORY

To locate the core of the contemporary debate between legal positivism and natural law theory, a good place to start is with H.L.A. Hart's thesis on the separation between law and morals. In the 1958 article on the subject, Hart formulates the *Separation Thesis* as follows: "(...) the contention that there is no necessary connection between law and morals, or law as it is and ought to be" (18, note 1). Hart advances the *Separation Thesis* as one of the central tenets of legal positivism. The thesis has retained that position ever since, although there has been extensive debate over its meaning both between legal positivists and natural law theorists and among legal positivists themselves.[1] In this section I will similarly take the *Separation Thesis* as a starting point, and sketch the interpretations it has been given and their implications. In addition, I will raise the question what endorsement or rejection of the *Separation Thesis* means regarding the characterization of a theory as positivism or natural law. Does acceptance of the *Separation Thesis* automatically entail that a theory is positivistic? And conversely, does rejection of the *Separation Thesis* automatically make a theory a natural law theory? If not, what features are necessary for these characterizations?

In the past, legal positivists have ascribed to natural law theory the position that, because the separation of law and morals is rejected, an immoral law is not really law (e.g. Hart 1958, 31). Legal positivism can then be presented as the superior position because it separates the question of legal validity from the moral evaluation of laws. According to Hart, this has the advantages of clarity, of reflecting the common sense understanding of law, and of allowing a critical attitude towards law (1958, 34). The responses of natural law theorists differ. Finnis denies that any natural law theorist has ever held that immoral laws are not truly laws (1980, 26). On the other hand, Moore concedes the rejection of the separation between law and morals, although not every clash with substantive morality robs a rule of its legal character (1992, 198). Before these positions can be characterized or evaluated, I should make clear what the separation between law and morals, or law as it is and ought to

[1] See e.g. Fuller 1958, Raz 1979, Finnis 1980, Coleman 1982, Lyons 1982, Shiner 1992, Waluchow 1994.

be, can be taken to mean.

Primarily, the denial of a necessary relation between law and morals has been developed in two directions by positivist theorists. First, it is understood as the thesis that law can and ought to be described or identified with reference to social facts and without resorting to moral argument. For short, I will refer to this thesis as the *Neutrality Thesis*.[2] Secondly, it is taken as meaning that there is only a contingent relationship between the content of law and that of morality. I will refer to this thesis as the *Contingency Thesis*. The *Neutrality Thesis* is an epistemological thesis about the concept of law and answers negatively the question whether a reference to morality is necessarily involved in the identification of law. The *Contingency Thesis* is an ontological thesis about the moral content of law and answers negatively the question whether law necessarily satisfies certain moral demands.

The *Contingency Thesis* is ambiguous: the assertion that there is only a contingent relationship between the content of law and morality can be interpreted in two ways. Either it says that it is an open question whether law satisfies moral demands, claiming that law is morally fallible, or to put it differently, that law does not necessarily have positive moral value. This is the *Moral Fallibility Thesis*.[3] Or it can mean that law can but need not make the same substantive demands as (part of) morality. The second interpretation can simply mean that any overlap between the content of morality and that of law is accidental, but it is often put more strongly: law only has moral content when moral demands are explicitly laid down by law. In this form, it can be referred to as the *Explicit Moral Content Thesis*.[4]

Thus, to sum up the distinctions made above, there are four theses to be recognized, which can be seen as interpretations of the original *Separation Thesis* formulated by Hart, which says that there is no necessary connection between law and morals.

2 This term is used by Klaus Füßer, who contrasts it with the *Moral Fallibility Thesis* (1996, 122). The thesis is defended, among others, by Joseph Raz (1979, 39), Hans Kelsen (1934, 38) and Norbert Hoerster (1989, 10). Füßer indicates that this is the prevailing interpretation of the *Separation Thesis* in Germany (121).

3 Term used by Füßer (1996, 122). David Lyons refers to the thesis of moral fallibility as the Minimal Separation Thesis (1982, 68). I prefer to call it the *Moral Fallibility Thesis*, because all the theses here distinguished are weaker or stronger versions of the *Separation Thesis*, so referring to their content gives more information.

4 Term coined by Lyons (1982, 83). Lyons rightly notes that this thesis is logically independent from the *Moral Fallibility Thesis*. Believing that law is morally fallible does not commit one to believing that the moral content of law must be explicitly laid down.

I. *Neutrality Thesis*:
Law can be identified with reference to social facts, without resorting to moral argument.

II. *Contingency Thesis*:
There is only a contingent relation between law and morals. (Connections depend on changeable factors.)

II.a. *Moral Fallibility Thesis*:
Law may, but does not necessarily have positive moral value. (Law can be wrong from a moral point of view.)

II.b. *Explicit Moral Content Thesis*:
Only when moral demands are explicitly laid down by law does law have moral content.
(Moral demands have to be explicitly acknowledged by legal officials.)

The *Separation Thesis* can be analysed as comprising two independent components: Theses I and II. It is possible to hold either one without the other, or to hold both. In its turn, Thesis II can have two distinct meanings: Theses II.a. and II.b. Thus, the *Neutrality Thesis*, the *Moral Fallibility Thesis*, and the *Explicit Moral Content Thesis* are the three different interpretations of the separation between law and morals over which positions differ.

The *Neutrality Thesis* builds on the idea that straightforward factual criteria suffice to find out what is a valid legal rule — criteria such as the passing of a bill by parliament or the pronouncement of a rule by a supreme court. In this explanation, an ambiguity in the formulation of the *Neutrality Thesis* is overlooked: what level of generality is meant of the "law" that is to be identified? As I have presented it now, law is understood as a specific legal provision, e.g. the rule that one must drive on the right side of the road. "Law" can, however, also mean law in general, at the level of the legal system, or even more generally, the phenomenon of law as such. In the debate, positivists and anti-positivists sometimes seem to be at cross-purposes because of a different understanding of the appropriate level of discussion.

Similarly, the *Moral Fallibility Thesis* is slightly ambiguous in the form presented here: that law does not necessarily have positive moral value can refer to two levels of law, to individual legal propositions and to the legal system as a whole. The different levels of moral fallibility of law are often confused in the debate between positivism and anti-positivism. The *Moral Fallibility Thesis* is independent of the *Neutrality Thesis*: belief in (both levels of) law's fallibility is compatible with either acceptance or rejection of law's neutrality.

Positions regarding the *Explicit Moral Content Thesis*, on the other hand, usually combine with a specific position on the *Neutrality Thesis*: the more the scope of the moral content of law is limited, the easier it is to accept both theses. Wholesale acceptance of the idea that law incorporates moral standards is incompatible with morally neutral identification of the law, when the first means that a reference to moral standards enters into the question of *what the law is* on a given matter. However, some forms of the *Explicit Moral Content Thesis*, which limit the extent to which moral standards can be made part of law, combine very well with the *Neutrality Thesis*. As long as moral considerations do not affect the identification of law, the combination enables a positivist to explain the moral content of law without making law's existence dependent upon morality. Whether or not the *Explicit Moral Content Thesis* is compatible with the *Neutrality Thesis*, therefore depends on the scope allowed the moral elements. An example given by Philip Soper can clarify the point (1977, 18). Soper asks us to imagine a king Rex, in whose kingdom law is identified by the social rule "Whatever Rex enacts is law". Rex only enacts one rule: "All disputes are to be settled as justice requires". The identification of law seems to be a morally neutral matter, because all it is dependent on is the fact of Rex's enactment. However, because the content of this enactment makes legal decisions all-dependent on moral considerations, there is no way of determining what the law requires without resorting to moral argument.

There is one other important reason for the ambiguity of the *Separation Thesis*: there is more than one way to understand the meaning of morality. Hart made a distinction between positive or conventional morality and critical morality; positive morality being the accepted moral code of a society and critical morality the principles by which positive morality and law can be evaluated (1994, 169-184). Positive and critical morality are closely connected: the latter builds on the former and can be understood as an elaboration of underlying principles and values of positive morality (Den Hartogh 1995, 69). However, in relation to the *Separation Thesis* it is illuminating to distinguish between the two kinds of morality because they are connected to different forms of the *Separation Thesis*. The clearest case is the *Moral Fallibility Thesis*: in asserting that law does not necessarily satisfy moral demands, the type of morality that is meant is critical morality (Lyons 1982, 65). Positive law can be criticized with the help of critical moral principles in the same manner as positive morality; both positive law and positive morality are fallible in the light of critical morality. It is different with the *Neutrality Thesis* and the *Explicit Moral Content Thesis*. In connection to explicit moral content, it is more plausible to regard the reference to morality as a reference to morality as a whole. If the relevance of morality to law is made dependent upon explicit acknowledgment of moral demands, such moral demands are most plausibly conceived as the accepted moral demands of the community (compare Waluchow 1994, 232). Defenders of the *Neutrality Thesis* have less need to specify the type of morality they are referring to, because the assertion that law must be described in non-moral terms effectively rules out both types of morality. Because of this feature, however, anti-positivists can attack the *Neutrality Thesis* both from the point of view of positive morality and of critical morality.

Before I go into the subject of adherence or rejection of these theses, there is one point that should be kept in mind regarding the distinction between positive and critical morality. The distinction is clearest from an external perspective; from an internal point of view the distinction is less clear. For instance, an observer who stands outside the legal system he is observing can argue for the *Explicit Moral Content Thesis* by pointing to the way a legal system makes reference to the positive morality of the society to which it belongs. Such an observer can also evaluate that legal system, and the accompanying positive morality, with an appeal to critical morality. These are distinct activities. From an internal point of view, positive and critical morality are not so clearly distinguishable. Although a participant in a society can distinguish the society's morality from his own, he is part of that society and will usually accept parts of societal morality as his own. To the extent that he does, he cannot see the accepted morality of his society as merely positive. And similarly, critical morality is an integral part of that person's morality, not an external standard to apply to one's own morality: criticism becomes internal criticism. For a participant, moral evaluation of the law will involve the whole of morality, without a distinction between positive and critical morality.

### *Legal Positivism*

Part of the confusion regarding the meaning of the *Separation Thesis* is caused by Hart, who has described the *Separation Thesis* both in terms reminding of the *Neutrality Thesis* and of the *Moral Fallibility Thesis* (1994, 184-85). Thus, it is not surprising that Hart's ideas have given rise to many different interpretations of the *Separation Thesis* as the core of legal positivism. In later work, however, Hart clarified his own position: in his reply to Dworkin in the Postscript to the second edition of *The Concept of Law*, Hart denies that he subscribes to the thesis that the identification of law must depend on social facts only (1994, 247). There he also endorses the *Explicit Moral Content Thesis* (269), in the sense that he acknowledges that law can make moral demands if there is an explicit link to morality to be found in the sources of law. Thus, most of the possible interpretations of the *Separation Thesis* can be linked to different aspects of Hart's position. Over some thirty years, a number of legal positivist theories have been developed, differing primarily in the version of the *Separation Thesis* they defend.

An important distinction can be made between positivists who defend the *Neutrality Thesis* as the core of legal positivism and those who only defend some version of the *Contingency Thesis*. The first position, exclusive legal positivism, rejects any role of morality in the identification of law. Usually, such authors also hold that law is morally fallible and that overlap between the content of law and morality is a contingent matter. However, variations are possible. It is possible to stress the need for a neutral method of identifying law, while at the same time holding that law and morality are not merely contingently related. Nevertheless, the combination of the *Neutrality Thesis* with at least some form of the *Contingency Thesis* is a common characteristic of exclusive legal positivism. The second position, inclusive legal positivism,[5] rejects the thesis of the neutral, non-moral identification of law. Adherents of this position recognize the importance of morality for the determination of law but their adherence to positivism is shown in their insistence that such a role for morality is a contingent feature of existing legal systems. For instance, Waluchow argues that legal systems which include human rights charters have created an opening for rights-based moral arguments and thus have given morality a central place in their law (1994, 115). The positivist character of the theory lies in the demand that the community must explicitly recognize moral considerations as part of the legal system for such considerations to carry (legal) weight. Waluchow can thus be said to defend a version of the *Explicit Moral Content Thesis*. Such inclusive legal positivism can be contrasted with exclusive legal positivism as defended by Joseph Raz, who insists that the concept of law can be identified exclusively by reference to social facts that can be described in a morally neutral way (1979, 39).

Inclusive forms of legal positivism have arisen as a reaction to, and to a large extent an incorporation of, Ronald Dworkin's criticism of the theory of

5 A term I borrow from the title of Waluchow's book: *Inclusive Legal Positivism* (1994). It nicely indicates that this type of positivism aims to include moral considerations in its account of law. Among those holding such a position are Coleman (1982), Lyons (1982), Soper (1977), and Waluchow himself.

H.L.A. Hart.[6] In his early work Dworkin argues for the inadequacy of a rule-based model of law in which all rules are identified by a test of pedigree, that is, a test on the basis of social facts in the form of neutral formal criteria (1978, 43). He argued that principles with an inescapably moral dimension play a vital role in legal argumentation and interpretation, because hard cases are resolved by an appeal to such principles. This caused legal positivists to re-examine their claim of the separation of law and morals and led those who advocate inclusive legal positivism to argue that they could incorporate the role of moral principles without giving up their positivist position. Dworkin primarily attacked the positivist denial of the role of morality in legal interpretation, but the inclusive positivist has partly conceded his point by recognizing a moral component in the identification of law as well as in its interpretation and content. However, inclusive positivism still differs from Dworkin in its insistence that such moral components are part of law only contingently.

Thus, the *Separation Thesis* only has limited meaning in inclusive forms of legal positivism, which defend no more than the contingency of all connections between law and morality. By no longer claiming a non-moral test for law's existence, inclusive legal positivism can be said to lose one of the main advantages of a positivist theory: indicating a clear factual method to identify law by relating the identification of law to its social sources.[7] On the other hand, by incorporating the possibility of a reference to morality, inclusive legal positivism provides a better description of existing legal systems, which do contain moral argument and references to moral demands. This raises one major question about legal positivism: does it still have the advantages that were claimed for it by Hart, i.e. clarity, reflecting common sense understanding, and a critical attitude? Before I answer that question, I should pay attention to the opponents of legal positivism.

### *Anti-Positivism*

With the rise of inclusive legal positivism the differences between proponents

[6] Hart is now usually seen as an inclusive legal positivist, owing to his Postscript in the second edition of *The Concept of Law*. His earlier work, including the first edition of *The Concept of Law*, predates the distinction between the two types of positivism, and can be read in both ways. Hart holds that law contains a necessary core of moral rules ( "the minimum content of natural law"), while he can plausibly be interpreted as accepting the *Neutrality Thesis* as well. For example, Raz reads him as an exclusive legal positivist (1979, 53) and Waluchow as an inclusive legal positivist (1994, 84).

[7] Dworkin makes this point in his 'Reply to Critics' when he discusses the inclusive positivism of Soper and Lyons (1978, 347-48).

and opponents of the *Separation Thesis* have become minimal. What distinguishes the opponents of the *Separation Thesis* other than their rejection of the separation between law and morals? Are they all natural law theorists? Here, matters become even more complicated than in the discussion of the legal positivist position, because advocating a necessary connection between law and morality is not a thesis defended by all natural law theorists, nor are all those who do defend it rightly characterized as adherents of natural law theory. For instance, John Finnis, the foremost defender of natural law theory, accepts (a form of) the *Separation Thesis*. Ronald Dworkin, on the other hand, does not accept the *Separation Thesis* but is hardly a natural law theorist on other counts. To gain some clarity about such anti-positivist positions the following issues need to be resolved: we need an account of the forms of the *Separation Thesis* that are rejected, and we need to relate this to an account of what exactly constitutes a natural law theory.

At the beginning of this section I noted that legal positivists have ascribed to natural law theorists the claim that immoral laws are not truly law. Natural law theorists are thus supposed to reject the *Moral Fallibility Thesis*. "Lex injusta non est lex", the slogan that an unjust law is not law, is often attributed to natural law theory (see Bix 1996, 226). However, most modern natural law theorists and other anti-positivists only defend the moral infallibility of law at the level of the legal system as a whole, not at the level of individual legal rules.[8] Although it is true that no natural law theorists accept the *Separation Thesis* in all its forms, the idea of the moral fallibility of law is precisely the one interpretation of the separation between law and morals that they do accept in some form. It is too easy to equate rejection of the *Separation Thesis* with rejection of the *Moral Fallibility Thesis* and then condemn those denying the validity of the *Separation Thesis* as holding that evil law is not law. Because anti-positivists accept forms of the *Moral Fallibility Thesis*, the thesis as such is insufficient to distinguish between legal positivists and their opponents (Lyons 1982, 70).

In the brief discussion of Dworkin's objections to legal positivism we already saw that one form of anti-positivism is the view that moral argument is inescapable in legal interpretation. Dworkin was concerned to attack the

[8] Fuller, for instance, defends the position that a legal system always has some moral value, because a system needs to conform to the internal morality of law to be a legal system. In the debate with Hart, Fuller argued that an evil legal system cannot easily incorporate the internal morality; the procedural principles of internal morality constrain the substantive norms of a system (1958, 661). This position has been hotly debated, primarily by Hart (1965, 1287).

*Neutrality Thesis*, and show that it is impossible to identify law merely by reference to formal factual criteria. In addition, he rejects the *Explicit Moral Content Thesis* because the appeal to moral principles that judges make in their justification of hard case decisions is not dependent upon any explicit recognition of such principles in acknowledged sources: such principles are part of law because they are part of the best justification of the law. By looking at Dworkin's position, we see that the difference between inclusive legal positivism and anti-positivism turns on the explicitness of the moral content of law. Inclusive legal positivists are in agreement with anti-positivists that law in the legal systems we know cannot be identified in a morally neutral way. However, inclusive legal positivists insist that a legal system's connection to moral argument is contingent, while anti-positivists argue that the connection between law and moral argument is necessary.

Anti-positivists differ in the kind of arguments they advance for a necessary connection between law and morality, the three main positions being advanced by Dworkin, Fuller and Finnis.[9] Dworkin focuses on a theory of adjudication: he aims to refute the *Separation Thesis* by showing that it does not adequately describe the activity and argumentation of judges (1978). Fuller seeks to show that there are necessary moral dimensions to the making of legal rules; law has its own internal morality (1969). Finnis examines the moral quality of law from the standpoint of a specific moral theory (1980).

Sometimes, all theories that defend some kind of necessary relation between law and morality are labelled natural law theories.[10] In that case, theorists such as Fuller and Dworkin appear as natural law theorists as well.[11] However, a distinction can be made within the larger group of anti-positivist theories between natural law theory and other forms of anti-positivism: natural law theories include a specific, objectivist, account of morality as the basis of their theory of law. This is not a feature of all anti-positivists: neither Fuller nor Dworkin claim a set of universal, objective moral values as the basis for

9 Later in this chapter, I will argue that Selznick and Radbruch are also best understood as anti-positivists, but here it is useful to limit the discussion to other anti-positivists because I want to take some more time for the argument about Selznick and Radbruch than is suitable in this section.

10 See e.g. Brian Bix who distinguishes between traditional natural law theory, including Cicero, Aquinas and Finnis, and modern natural law theory, including Fuller and Dworkin (1996, 223-239). See also Charles Covell, who groups Fuller, Oakeshott, Hayek, Dworkin and Finnis together as natural law theorists (1992, 27-28), or Lloyd Weinreb who considers Fuller, Dworkin and Finnis to be natural law theorists (1987, 98-125).

11 Fuller himself contributed to this characterization by describing his theory as "procedural natural law" (1969, 96).

law. Fuller only claims a necessary connection between the principles of legality and law, which are given because of the character of law as a purposive order; he does not base it on an objectivist ethics (1969, 96-97). Dworkin connects law and morality in the interpretation of the law by judges: a judge has to make the best construction of the law both in the light of past decisions and existing rules and in the light of political morality (1985, 160). He does not claim universal truth for specific principles or values (1978, 160). However, precisely such claims are made by other theorists, which I will now discuss under the heading of natural law theory.

*Natural Law Theory*

As I explained above, natural law theories are best seen as a specific type of anti-positivism because they combine the idea of a necessary relation between law and morals with a specific theory about the nature of morality. Characteristic of natural law theory is a specific, objectivist, position in the meta-ethical debate about the status of moral judgments: the position that there are objective criteria making moral judgments true or false. In terms of the distinctions made in Chapter 1, modern natural law theories typically defend moral realist or rationalist meta-ethical positions.[12] A rationalist theory argues that a moral judgment can be justified with a deductive argument based on ultimate moral principles which are rationally validated (Arrington 1989, 75). The natural law theorist John Finnis defends such a rationalist theory of moral judgment: he uses a deductive argument proceeding from rationally acceptable first principles.[13] Finnis argues that basic values and basic practical principles are self-evident: they are obviously valid to reasonable persons (1980, 64-69). We then base our moral judgments on these basic values and principles. Other natural law theorists, such as Michael Moore, defend moral realism, the view that "the truth of any moral proposition lies in its correspondence with a mind- and convention-independent moral reality" (1992, 190). What they have in common is the idea of universal and objective moral truths that can form the basis for a critical theory of the nature of law.

In that connection, between objective moral truths and a theory of law, lies

[12] See Arrington 1989 for an overview of meta-ethical theories. The positions discussed here in relation to natural law theory are all cognitivist positions, meaning that they believe moral judgments are capable of being true or false. By contrast, non-cognitivist positions believe moral judgments are a matter of emotion or prescription (Arrington 1989, 1-3). See also section 1.2.

[13] Such a theory is also defended by Beyleveld and Brownsword (1986), whose theory I will not discuss in detail here. They use the meta-ethical theory of Gewirth to argue for a supreme moral principle of generic consistency (1986, 119) to be used in a critique of law.

the second defining element of natural law theory: the assertion of a necessary connection between law and morality. However, in what sense this is meant, or in other words, which of the theses connected to the *Separation Thesis* are rejected, differs. An extreme version of natural law theory would reject all of the theses connected to positivism's separation of law and morals, which could indeed yield a view that all law is (always) morally right because law is defined as the rules that satisfy moral demands. Such a stringent interpretation of the necessary relation between law and morality is not advanced by anyone. All natural law theorists acknowledge that positive law at least does not coincide with universal and objective morality. Both the *Neutrality Thesis* and the *Explicit Moral Content Thesis* are rejected by natural law theorists as they are by anti-positivists in general. There are variations in the extent to which they accept the *Moral Fallibility Thesis*. The strongest version of natural law theory defended today is that of Michael Moore, who sees it as a necessary condition for its being law that a legal proposition is just, but acknowledges that additional institutional criteria are necessary as well (1992, 198). What is more often defended, however, is the idea that morally right law is in some sense more truly law than bad law (Bix 1996, 226). Just law is the central case of what law is, while bad law only partly satisfies the criteria of what law is. The least ambitious of the natural law theorists in respect of the necessary moral quality of law is Finnis. Finnis uses his list of basic human goods to outlaw decisions that deliberately harm these basic goods, and thereby formulates moral absolutes to be respected by law (1992, 148). He claims objectivity for his criticism of law — it is bad if it does not respect moral absolutes — but does not see unjust law as *legally* deficient. Positive law is morally fallible because it can fail in the protection of basic goods and the observance of basic practical principles. With Finnis, the necessary moral quality of law seems to be reduced to the main quality of the central case of law: morally good law is what one has to look at to gain a true understanding of what law is about. This perspective does give quite a different edge against positivism's focus on neutral description, but it is a meagre version of natural law's traditional necessity claim. However, his ambitious theory of moral value does warrant a characterization of Finnis as a natural law theorist.

As it is customary to locate the basis of natural law theory in arguments about human (or divine) nature, it may seem curious to characterize natural law theory merely in terms of objectivist meta-ethics as the basis for criticism of law. Is there still a connection between modern natural law theories and human nature? John Finnis makes much of the self-evidence of the basic goods, because he is wary of an invalid derivation of an 'ought' from an 'is'.

If the basic goods were to be derived from human nature, that would be a violation of Hume's principle. However, Finnis does acknowledge that human nature is relevant for the composition of the basic goods. If we were different animals, we would hold other goods to be self-evident: the basic goods are self-evident to us because of our human characteristics (1980, 34). Leaving out any reference to human nature in the description of natural law theory creates the false impression that any objectivist ethics is to count as a natural law theory.[14] Even though human nature is not the foundation of ethics for all proponents of natural law theories, they do share a commitment to universal moral values or principles that are connected to characteristic features of human beings and human society.[15] Whether it is in the context of Moore's functional analysis or of the self-evidence proposed by Finnis, they all give an irreducible place to human nature in the broader justification of moral values.

Human nature does play a role in modern natural law theories, although it is more subdued than it was in traditional theories. It is important mainly because the connection to human nature determines the form of argumentation in the theory. The link to human nature provides a main reason to focus on universal, objective moral values and principles. Because human beings share the same features, the basic goods are of value to everyone and the same kind of reasoning holds for everyone. Therefore, natural law theory tends to focus on the basic features of the law and how these are related to the objective moral values. More particular judgments about law are deduced from this universal core. Natural law theory operates on the most general level of legal theory (Moore 1992,194). Because of this role of human nature, the objectivist ethics of natural law theory is best seen as backed by an argument about human nature and reasoning based on universal values.[16]

14 For instance, the moral realism of John McDowell is particularist or situational. He claims objectivity of particular moral judgments but does not deduce these from highest principles, basic goods, or human nature (Arrington 1989, 119-191). Such theories cannot be brought under the heading of natural law theory.

15 Moore uses the theory of Finnis as the plausible theory of the good with a similar connection to human nature (1992, 215); Beyleveld & Brownsword present a theory of human interests as representing essential human nature (1986, 148).

16 Pauline Westerman proposes four assumptions as the key to natural law theory: "1) there are universal and eternally valid criteria and principles on the basis of which positive law can be justified and/or criticised; 2) these criteria and principles are grounded in nature, either physical nature, or more specifically, human nature; 3) human beings can discover those principles by the use of reason; 4) for positive law to be morally obligatory, it should be justified in terms of these principles and criteria" (1997, 12). She uses these to study both traditional and modern (Finnis') natural law theory. She indicates that the assumptions do (continued...)

## 3. EVALUATING THE DIFFERENT POSITIONS

To summarize, the main distinction to be made in the debate over the separation of law and morals is that between legal positivism and anti-positivism (compare Shiner 1992). The dividing line is over the possibility of describing law without necessarily referring to morality. Within the group of anti-positivist positions there is a second distinction between natural law theorists and other anti-positivists. Here the major difference is between those who give a specific objectivist interpretation to the morality that is relevant to law, and those who interpret that morality differently. Within legal positivism there is a distinction between those defending the possibility of the neutral description of law — exclusive positivism — and those who merely assert that there must be explicit reference to morality for it to be relevant — inclusive positivism. If this is the range of positions concerning the debate about law and morality, we should now consider which of these four is preferable and for what reasons.

*Legal Positivism versus Natural Law Theory*

A significant difference between legal positivists and natural law theorists can be found in the way they view the moral fallibility of law. Positivism discerns the discrepancy between positive law and moral value, but remains agnostic about the kind of criticism that should follow. This is because legal positivism as such does not say anything about the moral demands to which law should conform. Because natural law theory does propose an account of these moral demands, it indicates in which way law can fail. It is a more comprehensive theory about law because it includes an account of critical standards.

Both legal positivism and natural law theory have serious failings. Legal positivism, in its exclusive form, makes the distinction between the legal and the moral too rigid. As a consequence, it is committed to an implausible separation between two types of judicial argument, which both have a place in the practice of judging but are to be seen as separated from each other from the perspective of that practice. Because morality is as pervasive as law, a "foreign law model" of the place of morality in judicial argument is implausible. Such a model makes it appear as if morality can be conceived of

[16](...continued)
not hold equally for all natural law theorists, but they can all be understood as more or less relating to them (13). I have focused on the first assumption because that is the one modern natural law theorists support in its entirety, but the others do have a supporting role.

as a second normative system beside the legal system, which can be called on when the legal system leaves a gap (Raz 1979, 50). Just as a reference to French law is needed when the validity of a French will or testament is at issue in Dutch proceedings, there can be the need to advance a moral argument when the legal system does not provide an answer. Unlike a foreign system of law, however, morality does not have a delineated scope and it overlaps (even if, according to a positivist, only contingently) with the content of law. This makes the line between legal and moral considerations a blurred one. If judges need to make use of both moral and legal arguments, both will have to be justified to be acceptable. The role of judges in the legal system is no different when they are reasoning on moral grounds, because they still have to find the best solution in the context of the legal system, and they still have to motivate their decision adequately. This makes the distinction practically irrelevant.

In addition, exclusive legal positivism, when it only provides a theory of law, is incomplete. Giving an non-moral account of what law is, but asserting that moral evaluation of law must determine whether there is an obligation to obey it (Hart 1958, 34), strengthens the need for an account of morality. Positivism needs a moral theory to account for the important moral components of practices connected to law. Moral considerations influence the decisions of legislators, the reasoning of judges, and the implementation of rules by administrators. To understand these practices it is necessary to account not only for the legal components, but also for the moral components determining these decisions. When such a moral theory is provided, exclusive positivism is most often combined with subjectivism or non-cognitivism.[17] There is a good reason for this connection: believing that moral values are no more than subjective preferences provides a strong reason to insist upon neutral identification of the law. It is a normative claim to accept positivism as the right theory of law.[18] On this view, allowing moral argument into the

17 E.g. Kelsen (1934, 15-16) and Hoerster (1989, 10). The important exception is Joseph Raz, whose liberal-perfectionist theory of morality presupposes a cognitivist position on values; his stress on the availability of 'adequate options' depends on the ability to know what is good or bad (1986, 425-26). According to Samuel Shuman, a non-cognitivist ethical theory is an essential element of legal positivism (1963, 15). However, in the recent debate on exclusive and inclusive positivism, most authors remain agnostic on the subject of the status of morality.

18 Waldron, following Postema 1986, stresses the importance of normative positivism, which he describes as follows: "It identifies the contamination of legal decision by moral judgment as a moral disadvantage; it says that we lose something of value thereby. It is by far the most interesting form of legal positivism (and indeed it is hard to imagine how a positivist definition of the concept of law could be sustained, without eventually having resort to some (continued...)

legal domain would introduce subjective elements into the law, which would undermine the authoritative position of law in society. Such a subjectivist theory of values is problematic because it cannot allow for moral argument and meaningful discussion about values.[19] A consequence of this view is that judicial moral reasoning, in the case of legal indeterminacy, is no more than the judge's moral preference, which makes such judicial decisions highly problematic. Law appears as the form of neutral order needed to keep subjective moral views in check; the combination of positivism and subjectivism has no way of acknowledging a positive role of values in legal discourse nor of criticizing value judgments made in a legal context. This does not do justice to the arguments that are made about the values involved in law. Discussion proceeds by appealing to values that can be discerned as underlying the legal order, values that can be recognized although they are not explicitly part of the system of rules. About such values meaningful discussion is possible: they are not the preferences of legal actors, but they are latent in the legal order. Judicial reasoning can appeal to such values.

The inclusive form of legal positivism seems to escape the criticism raised against exclusive positivism because it acknowledges a role for morality within the legal domain. There are difficulties, however. As Roger Shiner argues, inclusive legal positivism defends an inconsistent position. Either the emphasis is laid on the contingency of moral elements in the law, or the emphasis is on the inclusion of moral elements as such (1992, 296). In the first case, the identification of law turns on legal sources, which can also point to moral principles, but which themselves have to be neutral social sources. Otherwise morality is already part of law's sources, making it impossible to determine whether the moral content of law is contingent. On the other hand, when some source includes moral principles there is no near stopping place. When some moral principle is identified by a legal source as part of law, its interpretation and understanding are connected to a whole range of moral considerations. Are these then suddenly outside the law? If they are also part of the law, there is no distinction between inclusive legal positivism and anti-positivism. In order to remain a positivist theory, inclusive positivism has to limit the relevance of moral considerations, but to do so it also needs the *Neutrality Thesis* it is concerned to reject.

Consider a constitutional clause, for instance, the right to freedom of expression. An inclusive positivist grants that such a clause makes reference

[18](...continued)
normative thesis)" (Waldron 1992, 167).

[19] See also the discussion of subjectivism in section 2.2.

to a moral right: the meaning of the clause and the extent to which it reaches depend upon the meaning of the moral right to freedom of expression. However, he will say that this is only the case because a qualified institution such as the legislature has laid down such a constitutional rule. This means that there is a reference to (morally neutral) social facts to make the rule, including moral elements, part of the law. However, complete identification of the meaning of the rule cannot be established without reference to its moral components, and these cannot be identified by considering social facts alone. Either the moral component of such a constitutional clause is seen as in part determining the law, in which case the relation to morality is not contingent, or the moral component is seen as reducible to social facts, in which case the moral component of a constitutional clause is not relevant to identification of the law, and the *Neutrality Thesis* holds. Since one cannot hold both, inclusive positivism is an inconsistent position.

Natural law theory rejects a source-based model of law, and includes in its theory of law the moral principles used to criticize positive law. It thereby makes a distinction between fallible positive law and the eternal principles of natural law. Although natural law theory gives a more complete account of the relevance of moral considerations to the understanding of the law, its claims on behalf of morality are too ambitious.[20] Finnis seeks to show the validity of a set of objective and universal moral values and principles but fails to provide a convincing argument for that set of values and principles and also fails to show that this set can serve to give meaningful criticism of the law (Westerman 1997, 282-85). In the past, natural law theory has been accused both of being a plea for anarchism and a plea for conservatism, that is, as being too critical of positive law and as being too apologetic of positive law. Although they are exaggerations, such accusations do point to the indeterminacy of natural law's abstract principles: these can be used to defend divergent concrete proposals (see Horwitz 1992, 271). The idea that such universal objective values can generate meaningful criticism of concrete legal rules is thus effectively undermined.

There is an additional problem with natural law's objective ethics: the way to cope with conflict. Jeremy Waldron argues that the objective truth of moral values leads nowhere, unless people can be brought to agree on those values. When there is serious disagreement over the content of objective morality, there is no discernable difference between opinions about objective moral

[20] I focus on Finnis in my criticism, so it may not be valid for other natural law theorists in all respects. However, the general strategy of natural law theorists is similar to that of Finnis, so in broad terms the criticism probably holds for other modern natural law theorists as well.

principles and subjective moral beliefs: both are equally arbitrary (Waldron 1992, 182). I am inclined to disagree with Waldron that there is no difference between advancing beliefs in objective values and advancing subjective opinions: in the first case there is a basis for arguments supporting your beliefs — there are reasons that can validate your beliefs, while subjective opinions depend on the choice you make. Especially in the context of legal argument, this is an important difference, because lawyers are required to justify their opinions about the law. However, he does raise a valid point against natural law theory in that the theory needs to, but does not, indicate a way to handle disagreement over beliefs. By making a strong claim about the right ethical propositions, natural law theory takes on the burden to prove that these propositions are right. The fact of disagreement creates the need to advance something more than the self-evidence of basic values: if there is no agreement on such values, a better argument is needed than that every rational creature should be able to recognize the validity of the basic values. If there are rational creatures which disagree and doubt the validity of basic values, additional argument is needed to convince them that these basic values are valid.

As inclusive legal positivism proved to be an inconsistent position, the two theories to be seriously addressed are exclusive legal positivism and natural law theory. The two main objections against exclusive positivism are, first, that it makes an artificial and practically irrelevant distinction between legal and moral argument and, second, that it is either agnostic or too subjectivist about the moral element of legal practices. Natural law theory does provide a theory covering both, but the theory it advances on moral values has defects. First, it only gives an argument about values on a level that is too abstract to yield meaningful critical power. Second, the kind of argument advanced is insufficient because it relies heavily on the problematic concept of self-evidence which does not suffice in the face of disagreement. Because of these objections against positivism and natural law theory, I now want to consider anti-positivist theories that do not share natural law's theory of values in order to see whether there are plausible alternatives among them.

*Forms of Anti-Positivism: Dworkin and Fuller*

Forms of anti-positivism have in common that both the *Neutrality Thesis* and the *Explicit Moral Content Thesis* are rejected: anti-positivism claims that the involvement of moral elements in law is a matter of necessity and, to some extent, that the content of law necessarily has moral elements. Of the two well-known anti-positivists referred to earlier, Dworkin is mostly concerned to argue the first point, while Fuller is mostly interested in the second point.

Dworkin argues that legal argument cannot escape referring to moral principles, while Fuller argues that law always incorporates certain principles of a procedural morality. Both deny that choice has a large role to play in the incorporation of moral standards in the legal domain, although they do allow for a substantial amount of contingency in the content of the morality relevant to law. This provides an important difference with natural law theorists, who deny morality's contingency. More needs to be said about the theories of Dworkin and Fuller. Do they provide viable alternative theories to exclusive legal positivism and natural law theory?

Ronald Dworkin's theory about the important role played by principles as the overlapping element in law and morality is the most forceful criticism of positivism ever made. Dworkin has shown how argumentation in judicial reasoning makes no clear distinction between legal and moral elements because the principles underlying such reasoning do not admit of categorization as the one or the other. The background of this idea is formed by Dworkin's constructivism, saying that it is the task of a judge faced with a case to give the best possible interpretation of the law both with regard to the institutional history of the legal system and in the light of the political morality underlying that system. On the basis of the combination of a dimension of institutional fit and a dimension of political morality, Dworkin argues that every case has a right answer, which an ideal judge with full information on both dimensions could give.

Dworkin's coherence method of judicial interpretation is appealing: it gives a plausible account of the way judges argue for a decision by showing how it accords with the body of statute and precedent and is in line with the law's principles of justice. There are, however, some aspects of the theory that make it less convincing. One of the main problems is Dworkin's exclusive focus on the practice of judging. Although his account of judicial argument is convincing, it is also limited to one specific perspective: he only accounts for the internal point of view of a judge. Dworkin considers the practice of a judge to be the central legal practice (1986, 14-15). There are, however, a number of other practices connected to law, which bring their own perspectives: that of the legislator, the lawyer, the administrator, or the citizen. To these Dworkin pays no attention. Although this is more understandable in a jurisprudence focusing on the United States, in a broader context the other perspectives are as important as that of the judge. Apart from these other internal points of view in the legal field, the other important perspective ignored by Dworkin is the external perspective of the observer. That Dworkin leaves out the external perspective is no accident: according to Dworkin, the only way to really understand the practice of law is by its own internal standards (1986, 54). In this, I think, Dworkin goes too far. By taking the judge's point of view as the paradigm for a theory of law, Dworkin reduces legal theory to a study of judicial argument, as the judge sees it (Tamanaha 1997, 184). Dworkin does not acknowledge that a more external view of law, for instance, a broader view connecting law to other societal practices, can yield insights that are as valuable as his own.

The second criticism that can be made of Dworkin's ideas stays within the boundaries he sets on valid legal theory. It concerns the relation between the two dimensions central to judicial argument, the dimension of fit and the dimension of political morality. It is very hard to argue whether one or the other should take precedence when the two dimensions make conflicting demands. It is possible to imagine a system where one first checks institutional fit completely, and only then turns to the question of what is best in the light of political morality. Dworkin himself sometimes seems to regard the dimension of institutional fit as establishing a threshold; once the point of institutional adequacy has been reached, political morality is decisive. However, what is institutionally adequate is obscure. The dimension of fit is inconclusive in the same way as positivism's social sources are, so the dimension of political morality is already needed to determine what is adequate. That dimension, in its turn, is subject to similar objections as natural law theory.

A third point of criticism is closely connected to the second point; it concerns the idea of every case having a right answer. The idea of an ideal judge always able to find a right answer is useful to understand the aspiration of real judges to find the best answer. It is, however, an unrealizable ideal, which, in my opinion, entails that real cases do not necessarily have one right answer. The reason is the uncertain relationship between the dimensions of fit and of morality which creates leeway in the kinds of answers that are possible and defensible. If there is no hard and fast rule to decide how the two dimensions should be reconciled, the possibility of different answers being equally defensible becomes very real.

The two dimensions also give an indication of the way in which Dworkin balances between Hartian positivism and full-blown natural law theory. The first dimension is a (necessary) remnant of the relevance of social fact central to positivism; the second dimension is an appeal to morality with objectivist echoes akin to natural law theory.[21] The mix is both an asset and a defect. By providing a mix that combines good elements of positivistic and natural law theories Dworkin avoids their blind spots and extremes. However, as we saw, it is difficult to give a convincing account of how these two elements hang together. Especially, it remains obscure how conflicts of institutional fit and moral demands can be resolved.

Similarly to Dworkin, Lon Fuller developed an important part of his theory in discussion with H.L.A. Hart. We have already seen that they disagreed on the interpretation of Radbruch's post-war ideas, but there are more fundamental points concerning the nature of law that have been the subject of their debate. One of the most interesting themes concerns Fuller's internal morality of law. This is the subject which generated the strongest criticism by Hart. To my mind, it is one of the most inspiring and confusing parts of Fuller's theory.

In *The Morality of Law*, Fuller develops the idea that there are two kinds of morality relevant to law: an external morality, consisting of a general code of conduct, and an internal morality, consisting of principles of legality. The principles of legality impose procedural demands on the making of rules: rules ought not to be retro-active, they ought to be promulgated, they ought to be general, etc. Fuller argues that observance of these principles is necessary to good law-making, which he illustrates with the eight ways in which the imaginary King Rex fails in his law-making efforts (1969, 33-39). Fuller's argument is that significant failure to observe the internal morality of law will result in a failure to make law: the principles of legality are necessary to the existence of law. Hence, there is a necessary connection between law and procedural moral principles. One might expect a positivist to object to the *necessity* of the connection between law and these procedural principles. That point, however, is conceded by Hart. He objects to the characterization of these principles as *moral* principles. According to Hart, these are principles of functional necessity without a moral character; Hart simply sees them as requirements for the smooth and efficient operation of the law (1965, 1286). Hart's objection raises an important point about Fuller's theory: how should we understand the special character of the internal morality of law? I agree with Hart that it seems wrong to characterize the principles of legality as straightforwardly moral. Hart rightly points out that observance of these principles is independent from observing the demands of external morality.

21 Dworkin elucidated his position on moral truth in a recent article (1996). He advances a negative argument for objectivism: since it is impossible to remain sceptical about objective moral truth we have no choice but to accept value objectivity (89).

Unlike Fuller, Hart believes that it is very well possible for a legal system which is wicked in terms of (external) morality to apply the principles of legality faithfully. This seems right: there is no reason why observing certain procedures would be at odds with an evil purpose. However, Hart overlooks the fact that observance of principles of legality does enhance the value of a legal system. The principles of legality do represent genuine values, which concern the quality of a legal system. That a rule should be as clearly formulated as possible is an appeal to the value of clarity, and realizing that value makes the legal system a better system. The discussion whether these values should be seen as moral obscures the relevant point that they are internal to the legal order, and not external social values, whether these are political, economic, or a social value in a more general sense which we might call moral.

The characterization of the principles of legality as having value is important in relation to another of Fuller's theses which he discusses in terms of morality: the distinction between a morality of duty and a morality of aspiration. The morality of duty lays down the basic rules for an orderly society; the morality of aspiration formulates standards of excellence (1969, 5). This is parallelled by the typical reactions to transgressions of duty or aspiration: a breach of duty is considered blameworthy, while a neglect of aspiration is merely frowned upon. Although law can be seen as an instrument to regulate only the morality of duty, the morality of aspiration is relevant to certain aspects of law. Most importantly, the internal principles of legality need to be understood as a matter of both duty and aspiration. For instance, the principle of generality lays down a duty for the legislator to make rules sufficiently general, that is, at least, not for one case only. On the other hand, generality is an open requirement: it is a matter of excellence to be able to design the right level of generality for a given rule. Again, Hart is critical. He reproaches Fuller for misapplying the concept of a morality of aspiration to the principles of legality, claiming that it is absurd to think of such principles as matters of praise or disdain. The root of the problem, according to Hart, lies with the identification of principles guiding purposive activity in general with principles of morality (1965, 1286). I cannot follow Hart to his conclusion that the distinction between duty and aspiration has no place in the discussion of law. In a broader sense, such a distinction is helpful to indicate ways in which law is not simply a matter of all-or-nothing answers, but is open-ended. The behaviour of the participants in legal processes cannot be understood as simply doing their duty. A judge tries to live up to an ideal; it is not his duty to be the best judge he can be, but it is a motivating ideal. The idea of aspiration is especially helpful to understand the roles of key actors in the legal process: Fuller shows how aspiration is relevant to understand the role of the legislator, but it can be used similarly for a judge or a lawyer.

There is one important point to make on behalf of Fuller, and against Hart, which concerns the more general moral value of law. One idea of Fuller's which Hart glosses over too quickly, is that law — the enterprise of subjecting human conduct to the governance of rules — has considerable value for the organization of society (Fuller 1969, 96). This means that, although the supporting value of the internal principles of legality for the substantive moral quality of the legal system is doubtful, there is a connection between the principles of legality and the value of the legal system for society. When the principles of legality are faithfully observed, they enhance the quality of the legal system in terms of the value of legality and contribute to, at least, a procedurally fair system. Such a system supports the social order (whatever its substantive aims) and in that sense also serves a specific social value: that of order.[22] I do not wish to suggest that this is any more than a supportive and subordinate value, but I think we can grant that a society, however noble its purposes, needs procedure and order to put those purposes into practice. As I understand order, it is a value-laden concept: if procedural principles are taken seriously, order has a certain quality. The law's realization of procedural values provides the order needed to realize substantive moral values, and as a necessary ordering structure, law has value itself.[23]

The complications involved in the distinction between moral and non-moral elements have been somewhat obscured by Fuller himself by his referring to his own theory as 'procedural natural law' (1969, 96). The label creates the impression that Fuller accepts the main tenets of natural law theory with a procedural twist, but when we examine his theory it turns out that he solves the tensions between law and morality in a way that only remotely resembles traditional natural law theory. We have already touched upon the most important point: by focusing on the internal principles of legality, Fuller gives quite a different interpretation of the necessary connection between law and

22 In his review of *The Morality of Law*, Hart appears to hold a strict view of what counts as moral: only substantive and ultimate principles count as moral (1965, 1291). Hart withholds the name of 'morality' from principles with instrumental value, while Fuller has a much broader view of morality. I side with Fuller in thinking that order, although it primarily has instrumental value, is such an important supportive value that it should count as moral.

23 To what extent order contributes to the overall (procedural and substantive) moral value of a legal system is an extremely difficult question. In some cases of a wicked system, it seems that observing procedure might make the system more wicked because it is such a perverted combination. I do not think any judgment on this issue can be made in the abstract.

morality. He expands the domain of morality to include law's internal values and thereby looks for a different necessary connection from that of natural law theorists. That there is an intrinsic connection between the principles of legality and law is much easier to argue than that law necessarily serves substantive moral values. In the case of internal principles it is also more plausible to use the same criteria for law's existence and its quality: non-observance of the principles of legality precludes the existence of law, while the degree of observance is also a measure of the quality of the system — in terms of internal values, of course. Such claims are harder to substantiate in the case of natural law's connection between law and substantive morality. We have seen the problems involved in the argument for objective moral values, and the difficulties in establishing the link between those values and concrete legal rules. These differences lead me to conclude that the label 'natural law' is misleading in Fuller's case.

Both Dworkin and Fuller are best viewed as anti-positivists having sympathies for natural law thinking; they depart so much from natural law theory's tenets that they are best seen as advancing a different kind of anti-positivism. In Dworkin's case, taking a strictly internal perspective leads to a continuum of legal and moral considerations in legal argumentation. Although this is plausible from that perspective, Dworkin leaves too little room for other ways of viewing law in which a distinction between legal and moral considerations is valuable. Fuller's view is not limited to an internal perspective and it gives a plausible sketch of the role of internal legal values. He claims too much, however, when characterizing the internal principles of legality as a morality. His point is clearer when the principles of legality are seen as specific legal values, which support substantive morality by providing order. Internal legal values are in many ways connected to moral values, but they are specific to law, a point which is obscured in Fuller's account of the morality of law.[24]

## 4. RADBRUCH AND SELZNICK AS NON-POSITIVISTS

Until now, I have considered well-known voices in the contemporary debate between natural law theory and legal positivism: Hart, Raz, Finnis, Dworkin, Fuller. Here, I want to consider the way Radbruch and Selznick can be related to that debate. Neither Radbruch nor Selznick can easily be characterized as

[24] See also section 7.4, where the idea of specifically legal values was explored.

positivist or natural law theorist: they both propose interesting forms of anti-positivism. There is, however, an important preliminary point concerning their theories, which causes me to prefer to call Radbruch and Selznick non-positivists. Both hold positions which have much in common with anti-positivism, but neither defines his position against positivism. Unlike Fuller and Dworkin who take position in relation to the legal positivism of Hart, Radbruch and Selznick oppose positivism for a different reason: their starting-point is the value-oriented character of law.

*Radbruch*

One thing to be kept in mind when considering Radbruch's theory is that his ideas predate the discussion between positivism and natural law theory in terms of Hart's separation thesis. Radbruch discussed positivism and natural law theory in the *Rechtsphilosophie*, but these were not the sophisticated positions that have been developed since. If we do look at his position in terms of the current debate over the *Separation Thesis*, anachronistic though this is, the most striking feature is that Radbruch's way of defining law is a method diametrically opposed to the method of identification advanced in the *Neutrality Thesis*: he defines law in terms of value-orientation instead of referring to a matter of social fact (1932, 255). One could say that, because law is defined in terms of the legal value of *Gerechtigkeit*, the identification of law by Radbruch's method does not need moral argument, so it is morally neutral. However, the reference to value in the definition of law makes it impossible to identify law on the basis of social fact alone. Law is that part of the cultural reality engaged in the effort to realize justice. To identify law one needs to consider the meaning of cultural reality; it is not enough to appeal simply to facts. Identification of law is not value-neutral, because the orientation towards justice has to be considered (1932, 264). Radbruch's very definition of law is therefore non-positivistic. What kind of non-positivist position does he hold?

We have already seen (in 3.4) that Radbruch's post-war writings are sometimes seen as a form of natural law theory. In that earlier section I dismissed the idea that Radbruch is a natural law theorist, because of two important features of Radbruch's idea that law which completely disregards the value of justice lacks a legal nature. First, the values involved are the values specific to law: they are emphatically not moral values. Radbruch distinguishes between different absolute values, of which only the good is a moral value. This makes his theory different from modern natural law theorists who do connect moral values directly to law. Second, Radbruch is concerned with a baseline in value-orientation: the question whether a law can be denied legal character is one of complete disregard of justice. Radbruch does not use his absolute values to criticize law except in this limiting case; his is a formal, not a substantive approach. In both respects his ideas differ from natural law's key idea that objective moral values are the critical measure for law. Radbruch recognizes the important influence of (political) morality on the content of law by way of the value of *Zweckmäßigkeit*, but this is also the component of the *Rechtsidee* that is determined relativistically. The value of the good, of which *Zweckmäßigkeit* is the legal translation, is subject to different interpretations. Precisely the moral component in law is denied objectivity. This relativism of Radbruch's is at odds with natural law's objectivist ethics. Neither does natural law theory admit of such a limited guiding role for values as proposed by Radbruch. Radbruch developed the test of "übergesetzliches Recht" to criticize the Nazi regime, but he limited such criticism to two instances in which a legal system does not deserve its name: when a system flagrantly disregards justice in the name of legal security, or when a system does not even aim at the realization of justice (1946, 89).[25] Natural law theory promises more than the limited criticism of Radbruch's twofold test, although it is doubtful whether it can accomplish much more than Radbruch's theory, due to the vague nature of its values.

Radbruch thus advances ideas that prevent characterization of his theory as positivism or as natural law theory. He defines law in terms of value-orientation, which makes the theory non-positivistic; but he is relativistic about the content of morality, which makes it different from natural law theory. The next question to ask, however, is whether Radbruch's theory answers the objections raised against positivism and natural law theory. With regard to legal positivism he does to a large extent. Because Radbruch sees law as value-oriented he provides a complete theory, both of the nature of law and of the nature of values. However, his relativism does not give enough support to develop standards of evaluation. Radbruch does not make an arbitrary distinction between legal and moral elements: his *Rechtsidee* contains both specifically legal and external moral values and he explicates the relations between these values. Compared to natural law theory, the advantages of Radbruch's theory are less clear-cut. Again, his account of the

[25] I will not again go into the ambiguity of justice in Radbruch's post-war work. I have drawn attention to the tension between justice as a formal and a substantive value in several instances, concluding that it is not clear which interpretation he favoured. If we could conclude definitively that Radbruch thought of justice as substantive, he would come closer to natural law theory than I have argued here.

*Rechtsidee* with its combination of legal and moral values is more precise than the more general account of objective moral values proposed by a natural lawyer like Finnis. His account of the nature of values, however, suffers from similar difficulties as that of natural law theory: Radbruch's view of absolute values as being *a priori* valid also relies on a kind of self-evidence that is just as problematic as that proposed by Finnis. I will not go into the other problems besetting his theory, discussed in Chapters 4 and 7, which give enough reason not to follow Radbruch's approach as a whole. The aspects of his theory that have repeatedly turned out to be valuable — the relations and conflicts between the values of the *Rechtsidee* — can also be used in a pragmatist legal theory.

*Selznick*

If we look at Selznick's theory in terms of the debate, it seems at first that he can be brought under the heading of natural law theory. What Selznick calls his naturalism has definite natural law leanings, which he has articulated in the article 'Sociology and Natural Law'. Selznick shares with natural law theory the belief in the importance of universal moral values, and the idea that these are inherently connected to human nature (1961, 102). In a sense, he is more of a natural law theorist than the other three anti-positivists discussed because unlike Dworkin, Fuller, and Radbruch, he gives a prominent role to human nature in his theory. But that is not the complete story. Selznick also gives a key role to Hartian positivism in the definition of law. For the identification of a legal system Selznick adopts Hart's idea that there must be a combination of primary and secondary rules (Selznick 1969, 5). Unlike Radbruch, who positions his theory as contrasting with positivism and natural law theory (1932, 240-251), Selznick is concerned to combine the insights of the two. We should explore the question how the positivist and naturalist elements combine.

Selznick's own explanation is that the combination is based on two features of his own theory: the distinction between weak definition and strong theory, and the focus on empirical instead of analytical connections (1992, 442). To the first claim I would add that the distinction between weak definition and strong theory is grounded in the perspective on law that Selznick uses: the sociologist's (moderately) external perspective. This he has in common with Hart. Because of that perspective, Selznick agrees on the need to identify a legal system by way of a fairly simple factual criterion such as the occurrence of a combination of primary and secondary rules. As part of his claim for a weak definition of law, Selznick can be said to advocate neutrality in the identification of a legal system. Unlike Hart, however, he combines this with a strong theory: a highly evaluative theory of legal systems thus identified. Selznick develops a (moral) value theory based on a human nature argument that finds part of its inspiration in natural law ideas, and uses it to evaluate strengths and weaknesses in existing law.

The affinity with natural law theory is found in the strong, evaluative, theory based on human nature. He averts the traditional criticism of natural law theory by denying a necessary connection between law and morals, trading it for a variable empirical connection. At this point, I would say, both his sociological background and his pragmatist philosophy moderate his natural law claims. Selznick is more interested in empirical proof for connections between law and moral values than in a conceptual argument that the two cannot logically be separated. Nevertheless, he does argue for an affinity between law and justice based on his general argument of value-oriented normative systems, without additional evidence. But the connection is no more than affinity: "There is inclination but not necessity" (1992, 444). Whether the promise of justice is fulfilled and in what circumstances it can be, needs to be examined. Selznick criticizes both legal positivism and natural law theory for not being sufficiently empirical (444).

Within Selznick's framework, the urge to incorporate both positivist and natural law elements is understandable: he tries to combine a sociological perspective with the recognition of value-orientation. However, the effort is not completely successful because Selznick also incorporates some of the problematic aspects of the theories. Most of these belong to natural law theory. As I have already argued in Chapter 7, Selznick's idea of moral universals is not quite convincing. That aspect of his theory is closest to natural law theory and it suffers from similar weaknesses: the lack of a convincing argument that certain values are universal, and the vagueness of such values as critical standards. Selznick avoids most of the problems of a positivist theory, mainly because he gives legal positivism a non-standard interpretation. Selznick in part characterizes the difference between positivism and natural law as an orientation towards different values: clarity, certainty and autonomy in the case of positivism, substantive justice in the case of natural law (1992, 437). But as I have tried to show in this chapter, positivism is not concerned with the value-orientation of law at all. In the discussion between Hart and Fuller, we saw that Hart interprets Fuller's principles not as value-laden but as formal criteria. He also rejects the idea that aspiration has a role to play in respect to these principles. These are indications that Hart interprets clarity and certainty as baseline criteria, not as aspirational values. If legal positivism is concerned with values it is so negatively, concerned to keep them at bay. Selznick reinterprets legal positivism to fit his own framework. Similarly, his acceptance of the neutral identification of law is limited: it only concerns the identification of legal systems, not of specific legal rules. Because of the limited role of positivism and the unsolved problems of natural law aspects, the reconciliation of positivism and natural law theory does not quite materialize.

This does not mean that Selznick's theory is not a valuable option. On the contrary. There are a number of ideas in his theory which make it a viable alternative to legal positivism and natural law theory. The most important one is his pragmatist account of values. Although his idea of moral universals resembles natural law theory, his theory of the nature of values is different from natural law theory because of its pragmatist basis. Selznick rejects absolute claims about value objectivity: the validity of values is provisional. Additionally, Selznick has an eye for the context of ideals that is lacking in natural law theory. His is a more dynamic view of values: Selznick's view leaves room for adaptation of values to changing circumstances, which in natural law's objectivist view is difficult. I should not, however, obscure the fact that Selznick shares the natural law's idea of a core of enduring values, and to the extent that he does, he is subject to the same criticism. But, as I have tried to show in the previous chapter, the pragmatist side of his theory escapes the criticism of vagueness and of unwarranted self-evidence. A key idea deriving from pragmatism is the notion of variability. This is one of the things Selznick shares with Fuller: they both focus on the degree to which law exhibits certain features. In Selznick's case, it is most notably the degree in realization of the ideal of legality, which is parallelled by Fuller's account of the aspirational aspect of the principles of legality.

The central shared insight of the anti-positivists Selznick, Radbruch, and Fuller, is the belief that attention to values in the context of law should primarily look at 'distinctively legal' ideals. They all distinguish specifically legal values from broader social or moral values, the differences lying in their views on the relations between the two types of values. This is the point at which their theories can be combined, as I have shown in section 7.3. If Selznick's idea of a master ideal is modified to allow more leading ideals of law, Radbruch's theory of the antinomies of law can be used to account for the relations between these legal ideals and other social ideals. Fuller's principles of legality can be seen as a concretization of specifically legal ideals of legality and justice.

The focus on relations between legal and social ideals is underpinned by yet another shared interest of Selznick and Fuller: the place of law in society. Neither views law in isolation; they relate law to societal purposes.[26] Selznick's sociological view of law answers the question: what does the law contribute to the functioning and flourishing of society? This creates an important difference between his view and traditional natural law theory: Selznick —and I think Fuller as well — takes conventional morality much more seriously than a natural law theory does. Law should not only be criticized from the standpoint of an objective critical morality, it can also be criticized from the standpoint of accepted social ideals. Deweyan legal pragmatism is committed to an experimental view of law's contribution to social goals: its view of law is instrumental in the sense that it is primarily interested in law's contribution to the good of society as a whole. It is not narrowly instrumental, meaning that it does not evaluate law only in terms of short-term goals and its efficiency in reaching those goals. But it does consider law as serving societal ideals, which means law's autonomy is not taken for granted but only warranted when it is needed to realize important values.

It is the pragmatist part of Selznick's theory which makes a novel contribution to the debate, more specifically it is Selznick's pragmatist value theory that creates an interesting alternative in the debate in legal philosophy. Selznick himself interprets the difference between legal positivism and natural law theory as a focus on different values (law and order values vs. moral values). I do not think that such an interpretation of the debate does justice to the different positions because it is in part the adequacy of the focus on values itself that is at issue: legal positivism also has the message that law's values are an element of law that is of minor importance. Other aspects of law, e.g. its rules, its authority, are seen as much more central. Anti-positivists are united in their rejection of that message: they believe that law's values merit at least similar attention as other aspects of law. Selznick has a special position because he gives such an extensive and inspiring account of the ideals of law in society.

[26] This is most obvious in Nonet & Selznick 1978, and Fuller's *The Principles of Social Order* (1981).

## 5. THE PROMISE OF A PRAGMATIST THEORY[27]

*Conclusions*

The greater part of this chapter has been devoted to an analysis and evaluation of the debate in contemporary Anglo-American legal theory between legal positivism and natural law theory. My focus in analysing that debate was on the relationship between law and morals, taking Hart's lead that a belief in the separation between law and morals is one of the marks defining legal positivism. Using a set of three different meanings of Hart's *Separation Thesis* to order the debate, I distinguished four main positions: exclusive legal positivism, inclusive legal positivism, anti-positivism, and natural law theory. In order to give a convincing account of the relationship between law and morals, these theories need to address the nature of law, of morality, and of the connection between the two. I will review the way these three aspects are dealt with.

Exclusive legal positivism first appears as a straightforward and clear descriptive theory of law, but it turns out to contain a number of problematic propositions. Exclusive legal positivism highlights the nature of law as an authoritative system of rules. The *Neutrality Thesis* is the key meaning of the separation between law and morals: identifying law is a matter of considering social facts, for instance by tracing a rule to an authoritative source. This would be a clear and simple test if it always worked. Unfortunately, as exclusive positivists acknowledge, it does not. To rescue the theory, an artificial separation is made between decisions based on law, that which is neutrally identified, and decisions based on morality, when the neutral test fails. If giving a good description of how law works would be the only concern, this move appears strange. However, the urge to rescue neutrality is understandable, once an account of morality is added to the theory. Exclusive positivism makes sense when one holds a subjectivist theory of morality: if moral judgment is essentially no more than a subjective preference, then it is vital to keep such judgments out of the legal domain to safeguard law's authority. And, if these judgments cannot be kept out completely, it is important to distinguish clearly between moral and legal judgments.

[27] This title echoes that of John Patrick Diggins: *The Promise of Pragmatism. Modernism and the Crisis of Knowledge and Authority* (1994). My approach is more optimistic than that of Diggins: his conclusion is that the promise of pragmatism has not been fulfilled. I agree that many who are labelled neo-pragmatists, e.g. Richard Rorty, do not contribute much to the project of the first generation of pragmatists, i.e. Dewey and James, but I am optimistic about what one *could* do with the theories of the original pragmatists.

Unfortunately, most exclusive positivists do not explicate their theory of morals, which makes their theories incomplete. Moreover, a subjectivist theory of morality is problematic, because it overlooks, first, the important role of shared moral values underlying both the legal system and the morality of the individual, and, second, the possibility that subjective influences are limited in law because legal officials are trained to adhere to the morality that comes with their role. Because the exclusive positivist view depends on this theory for its rationale, its plausibility is undermined as well.

Inclusive legal positivism makes an effort to incorporate criticism of the *Neutrality Thesis* by giving up that thesis and making the *Explicit Moral Content Thesis* its core. It turns out that this position is unstable because it tries to combine two inconsistent ideas. Inclusive positivism holds that moral argument is part of legal reasoning but only because existing legal systems have explicitly incorporated a reference to morality. Thus, the fact of the moral content of law is contingent, but once moral demands have been recognized they are inescapably involved in the identification of legal rules. The inconsistency in this position arises because the moral element in law opens up the legal system in a way that threatens the contingency of the moral element. Either contingency is taken seriously, which means using factual sources for the identification of legal rules. Or the moral element is taken seriously, which means acknowledging that identification of legal rules involves open-ended moral argument. Thus, inclusive legal positivism has to accept the *Neutrality Thesis* to remain positivist or to reject both that thesis and the *Explicit Moral Content Thesis* and become anti-positivist.

Anti-positivism rejects both the *Neutrality Thesis* and the *Explicit Moral Content Thesis*. The identification of law necessarily involves moral argument and moral demands are included in the legal system without being recognized explicitly by an authorized lawgiver. In natural law theory these features of anti-positivism are combined with an objectivist account of morality and a partial rejection of the *Moral Fallibility Thesis*. Natural law theory holds that certain moral values are objective and universal and that these moral values form the basis of any legal system. There is variation within natural law theory in the extent to which a failure to reflect moral values disqualifies a legal system as law, but there is a bottom line of flagrant immorality beneath which a system no longer deserves the name law. The focus of modern natural law theory, however, is on the justification of the universal moral values, and that is precisely where the theory encounters problems. Its method of justification, which is based on the self-evidence of ultimate values, is insufficient to provide a firm basis for a substantive theory of morality and law. The idea that anyone can acknowledge the validity of universal values does not hold up in the face of disagreement. To the extent that these values do command general support, their meaning is too vague to supply relevant standards to evaluate law.

Other anti-positivist theories fare better because they do not make such a strong claim on behalf of moral values. Unlike natural law theory starting from a theory of moral values, their starting point is with the values of the law. Anti-positivists recognize that legal values and principles are continuous with moral values, but combine this with recognition of the distinctively legal. Of anti-positivist theories the most compelling option is a non-positivist theory that brings together ideas of Selznick, Fuller, and Radbruch. To identify a legal system, a fairly straightforward institutional criterion such as Hart's suffices: a combination of primary rules of conduct and secondary rules of recognition, change, and adjudication. Specific legal provisions, however, cannot be identified in such a way. Depending on the case in hand, both traditional legal sources (e.g. statutes and case law) and principles and values, legal as well as moral, must be taken into account. Legal ideals have an important place in determining the specific legal character of a system. These ideals are gradually developed in the practice of law; they are complex because they consist of more specific values with links to other, non-legal values. These constituting values will often make conflicting demands so that full realization of the ideal is hard to reach. This picture of law makes it less easy to identify critical standards than it would appear in a natural law view. Both the ideals internal to the legal practice and ideals of broader social significance have to be reconstructed, which puts a serious responsibility on the person articulating that reconstructed ideal. Articulating and using such ideals is an inescapable part of a genuine fulfilment of the tasks belonging to a legal order.

*Non-Positivism and Pragmatism*

Two main ideas characterize the non-positivism that forms the main subject of this book: the recognition of distinctively legal ideals, and law's relative autonomy, the interaction between law and other social practices. In 7.4 these features were discussed as a result of an effort to combine the best of Selznick's and Radbruch's theories of law, and they were an illustration of what a pragmatist theory of values might yield. In the present chapter these two features indicated a way out of the deadlock of positions pro and contra the separation between law and morals. This can be done because of the shift in focus generated by a non-positivist theory: the issue of separation is set in the key of values. This enables one to distinguish between legal values and moral values: the separation between law and morals then softens to become a distinction between kinds of values. Law's distinctive ideals, such as justice and legality, belong intrinsically to law, whereas moral ideals have a more contingent relationship to law. Distinctively legal ideals are an important reason for the autonomy of law, but because they are dependent on other, moral ideals to gain full meaning, this autonomy is limited. As a consequence, the initial separation between legal and moral values turns out to be a bond: for a genuine understanding of a legal ideal we need to consider the moral values with which it is intertwined. So morality enters when values are called upon in interpretation, which constitutes a rejection of the *Neutrality Thesis*: to identify the law in such a case includes reference to moral values. Similarly, a non-positivist view rejects the *Explicit Moral Content Thesis*: because the boundary between law and morality is blurred, it is not possible to pinpoint when moral considerations enter the field of law. On the other hand, the *Moral Fallibility Thesis* must be accepted, for at least three reasons. Although law contains its own critical standards, the most important ones in the form of legal ideals, these are incompletely realized. Moreover, the articulation of these ideals is in the hands of the people who use them as critical standards; their judgment as to the quality of the law depends on their interpretation of the ideals as well. And finally, the bulk of substantive critical standards used to evaluate law are moral values, the social and political values law was designed to serve. It is an open question to what extent law really does serve them.

Although it may be clear what is non-positivist about the position advocated here, the pragmatist character of that position needs a more detailed account. There are two aspects which are primarily responsible for the pragmatism underlying this value theory of law: the provisional, experimental view of (legal) ideals and the view of law as a practice. Both aspects remain obscured in the context of the debate between positivism and natural law: there the focus is on law as a system of rules, principles and values — on a body of legal norms. For a pragmatist, this is not enough: law must also be regarded as a practical enterprise. To use the familiar sociological phrase: there is not only the law in the books, but also the law in action.[28] I have primarily regarded ideals as the leading values that can be found in a legal system. As such, ideals are on a par with legal rules and principles as part of positive law: the material with which people engaged in legal practice work.

[28] The phrase originates with Pound (1910). Another way to formulate the difference: law as a product versus law as a practice (Van der Burg 1999, 65). This is more precise than Pound's formulation because the difference does not attach to the written law only, unwritten norms are part of law as a product as well.

Once we make that practice the main object of attention, the role of norms and values in people's activities and the influence of people's activities on norms and values becomes a key issue. That is the core of a pragmatist view on ideals in law: the relationship between ideal and activity.

The same relationship is central to the pragmatist understanding of ideals as arising out of problem-solving experience. Thus, the shift in focus brings in that dimension of the pragmatist theory as well. I will not repeat the specifics of the pragmatist theory of values, but I will pay attention to the way it works in the context of law. Certain peculiarities of the practice of law determine the particular development of ideals: these peculiarities are related to, again, law's relative autonomy and the procedural nature of its central ideals. The tendency towards autonomy found in law finds expression in the need for coherence and the related conservatism. There is a need to make the body of norms into a coherent legal system without gaps and especially without contradictions. As a result, new ideas are interpreted in line with existing legal principles to form a coherent whole: cherished principles are not surrendered, they are slowly adjusted. That is the autonomous tendency, which is counteracted by the responsive tendency. Law is not isolated, it is about all kinds of other practices: when these generate new problems, the legal practice has to respond. Of the two, this is the preferred quality of law in a pragmatist view. Law is instrumental in solving concrete social problems, and because these problems change legal answers must adapt (Dewey 1924, 361).[29] Legal practice then appears as a way of coping with changing social situations and a change in positive law is one of the mechanisms to do this successfully. Gradually, the practice of law will incorporate the change in values that occur in the practices with which it interacts. For instance, Dutch law of tort expanded the rules of consumer protection in reaction to a greater concern for product safety.

This more or less direct incorporation of social values is subject to transformation in the light of law's own ideals. The practice of law tends to resist uses of positive law for purposes that conflict openly with legal ideals. A good example is the Dutch political decision, out of a need for more

[29] Because of the insistence that law interacts with other social practices, pragmatism can be regarded as an interactional theory of law. Fuller saw law as an interactional phenomenon: it arises out of interactions between people and it serves to order and facilitate such interaction (1981, 230) Especially in Dutch legal philosophy, interactionism is sometimes regarded as a third theory of law distinct from legal positivism and natural law theory (e.g. Franken 1990, 42; Witteveen 1996, 61-62). It is not quite clear which authors, except Fuller, are to be regarded as interactionists, but it can certainly be argued for certain Legal Realists, e.g. Karl Llewellyn.

efficiency, to abolish the right of appeal for refugees. The procedural ability at law to be recognized as a refugee was thus severely limited. The rule was challenged because it contradicted legal ideals of equality and a fair trial. Recently, it has been reversed: a bill passed by parliament in 2000 reintroduces the right to appeal.[30] Such an example shows that the procedural ideals of the law are powerful checks when responding to social problems. This is a feature of law that is to be applauded rather than deplored, even in an instrumentalist view such as pragmatism. Law can be viewed as providing the means to social ends in two ways.[31] First, it can be regarded as simply subservient to social ends; then law is seen as a mechanism to realize pre-given goals. Second, it can be seen as performing special social functions, for which law needs to be an autonomous practice with authority. It is the second role that is primary. The practice of law has a special task in realizing and shaping social values, which it performs by guarding its own ideals in the course of executing its functions. To return to my example: the right of appeal for refugees is not only a matter of fair procedure but also of equal concern and respect. Realization of legal ideals helps shape broader social ideals.

30 This is article 84 of the Vreemdelingenwet 2000 (Aliens Act 2000), which became effective April 1, 2001. The former rule (since 1995) was article 33e Vreemdelingenwet (Aliens Act); see Vermeulen (2000, 390) on the new law.

31 Compare Westerman 1999, who distinguishes routine activity from creative activity (as two extremes on a continuum). In routine activity means and ends are separated, while in creative activity there is a continuous interplay between means and ends. Rulemaking can be more routine or more creative (162).

# REFERENCES


Alexy 1985

Robert Alexy, 'Rechtsregeln und Rechtsprinzipien', *Archiv für Rechts- und Sozialphilosophie, Beiheft 25*, 1985, p. 13-29

Aristotle 1934

Aristotle, *The Nicomachean Ethics*, H. Rackham (ed.), Cambridge: Harvard University Press [orig. English ed. 1926, orig. Greek unknown]

Arrington 1989

Robert L. Arrington, *Rationalism, Realism, and Relativism: Perspectives in Contemporary Moral Epistemology*, Ithaca: Cornell University Press 1989

Baratta 1959

Alessandro Baratta, 'Relativismus und Naturrecht im Denken Gustav Radbruchs', *Archiv für Rechts- und Sozialphilosophie* (45) 1959, p. 505-537

Beauchamp 1991

Tom L. Beauchamp, *Philosophical Ethics: An Introduction to Moral Philosophy*, New York: McGraw-Hill 1991 [2nd ed., orig. 1982]

Beyleveld & Brownsword 1986

Deryck Beyleveld and Roger Brownsword, *Law as a Moral Judgment*, London: Sweet & Maxwell 1986

Bix 1996

Brian Bix, 'Natural Law Theory', in: Dennis Patterson (ed.), *A Companion to Philosophy of Law and Legal Theory*, Oxford: Blackwell 1996, p. 223-240

Black 1972

Donald J. Black, 'Book Review of: Philip Selznick (with Philippe Nonet and Howard M. Vollmer), *Law, Society and Industrial Justice*, New York 1969', *American Journal of Sociology* (78) 1972, p. 709-714

Blok & Vedder 1998

Peter Blok and Anton Vedder, 'Nut en nadeel van articulatie van waarden', in: Wibren van der Burg and Frans W.A. Brom (eds.), *Over idealen: Het belang van idealen in recht, moraal en politiek*, Deventer: Tjeenk Willink 1998, p. 189-198

Boisvert 1988

Raymond Boisvert, *Dewey's Metaphysics*, New York: Fordham University Press 1988

Bonsmann 1966

Paul Bonsmann, *Die Rechts- und Staatsphilosophie Gustav Radbruch's*, Bonn: H. Bouvier & Co. 1966

Bransen & Slors 1996

Jan Bransen and Marc Slors (eds.), *The Problematic Reality of Values*, Assen: Van Gorcum 1996

Brecht 1959

Arnold Brecht, *Political Theory: The Foundations of Twentieth-Century Political Thought*, Princeton: Princeton University Press 1959

Van den Brink 1998

Bert van den Brink, 'Idealen in conflict: Het bestaan van idealen en de verwachting van harmonie', in: Wibren van der Burg and Frans W.A. Brom (eds.), *Over idealen: Het belang*

*van idealen in recht, moraal en politiek*, Deventer: Tjeenk Willink 1998, p. 199-216
Van den Brink 2000
Bert van den Brink, *The Tragedy of Liberalism: An Alternative Defense of a Political Tradition*, Albany: State University of New York Press 2000
Van der Burg 1991
Wibren van der Burg, *Het democratisch perspectief: Een verkenning van de normatieve grondslagen van de democratie*, Arnhem: Gouda Quint 1991
Van der Burg 1997
Wibren van der Burg, 'The Importance of Ideals', *Journal of Value Inquiry* (31) 1997, p. 23-37
Van der Burg & Brom 1998
Wibren van der Burg and Frans W.A. Brom (eds.), *Over idealen: Het belang van idealen in recht, moraal en politiek*, Deventer: Tjeenk Willink 1998
Van der Burg & Van Willigenburg 1998
Wibren van der Burg and Theo van Willigenburg (eds.), *Reflective Equilibrium: Essays in Honour of Robert Heeger*, Dordrecht: Kluwer Academic 1998
Van der Burg 1999
Wibren van der Burg, 'Two Models of Law and Morality', *Associations* (3) 1999, p. 61-82
Cohen 1983
Marshall Cohen (ed.), *Ronald Dworkin and Contemporary Jurisprudence*, Totowa: Rowman & Allanheld 1983
Coleman 1982
Jules Coleman, 'Negative and Positive Positivism', in: Marshall Cohen (ed.), *Ronald Dworkin and Contemporary Jurisprudence*, Totowa: Rowman & Allanheld 1983, p. 28-48 [orig. article 1982]
Covell 1992
Charles Covell, *The Defence of Natural Law: A Study of the Ideas of Law and Justice in the Writings of Lon L. Fuller, Michael Oakeshott, F.A. Hayek, Ronald Dworkin & John Finnis*, Houndmills: Macmillan 1992
Daniels 1980
Norman Daniels, 'Reflective Equilibrium and Archimedean Points', in: *Justice and Justification: Reflective Equilibrium in Theory and Practice*, Cambridge: Cambridge University Press 1996, p. 47-65 [orig. article 1980]
Darwall 1998
Stephen Darwall, *Philosophical Ethics*, Boulder: Westview 1998
Descartes 1637
René Descartes, *Discours de la Méthode*, in: Charles Adam & Paul Tannery, *Oeuvres des Descartes, VI: Discours de la Méthode & Essais*, Paris: Librairie Philosophique J. Vrin 1973 [orig. 1637]
Devereux 1994
Daniel T. Devereux, 'Separation and Immanence in Plato's Theory of Forms', in: Gail Fine (ed.), *Plato 1: Metaphysics and Epistemology*, Oxford: Oxford University Press 1999, p. 192-214 [orig. 1994]
Dewey 1920
John Dewey, *Reconstruction in Philosophy*, in: Jo Ann Boydston (ed.), *The Middle Works, 1899-1924, Volume 12*, Carbondale and Edwardsville: Southern Illinois University Press 1988 [orig. 1920]

# REFERENCES

Dewey 1924
John Dewey, 'Logical Method and Law', in: Larry A. Hickman & Thomas M. Alexander (eds.), *The Essential Dewey, Volume I*, Bloomington: Indiana University Press 1998, p. 355-362 [orig. article 1924]

Dewey 1925
John Dewey, *Experience and Nature*, La Salle: Open Court 1989 [orig. 1925]

Dewey 1929
John Dewey, *The Quest for Certainty*, in: Jo Ann Boydston (ed.), *The Later Works, 1925-1953, Volume 4*, Carbondale and Edwardsville: Southern Illinois University Press 1984 [orig. 1929]

Dewey 1931
John Dewey, 'Context and Thought', in: Richard J. Bernstein (ed.), *On Experience, Nature and Freedom: Representative Selections*, New York: Liberal Arts Press 1960 [orig. article 1931]

Dewey 1939
John Dewey, 'Theory of Valuation', in: Jo Ann Boydston (ed.), *The Later Works, 1925-1953, Volume 13*, Carbondale and Edwardsville: Southern Illinois University Press 1988 [orig. 1939]

Diggins 1994
John Patrick Diggins, *The Promise of Pragmatism: Modernism and the Crisis of Knowledge and Authority*, Chicago: University of Chicago Press 1994

Dreier 1981
Ralf Dreier, *Recht-Moral-Ideologie: Studien zur Rechtstheorie*, Frankfurt am Main: Suhrkamp 1981

Dreier 1999
Ralf Dreier, 'Gustav Radbruchs rechtsphilosophische Parteienlehre', *Archiv für Rechts- und Sozialphilosophie* (85) 1999, p. 497-509

Dreier & Paulson 1999
Ralf Dreier and Stanley L. Paulson, 'Einführung in die Rechtsphilosophie Radbruchs', in: Dreier and Paulson (eds.), *Gustav Radbruch: Rechtsphilosophie* (Studienausgabe), Heidelberg: Müller 1999, p. 235-250

Dworkin 1978
Ronald Dworkin, *Taking Rights Seriously*, Cambridge: Harvard University Press 1978 [2nd ed., orig. 1977]

Dworkin 1985
Ronald Dworkin, *A Matter of Principle*, Cambridge: Harvard University Press 1985

Dworkin 1986
Ronald Dworkin, *Law's Empire*, Cambridge: Belknap 1986

Dworkin 1996
Ronald Dworkin, 'Objectivity and Truth: You'd Better Believe It', *Philosophy and Public Affairs* (25) 1996, p. 87-139

Edwards 1967
P. Edwards (ed.), *The Encyclopedia of Philosophy*, New York: MacMillan 1967

Emmet 1994
Dorothy Emmet, *The Role of the Unrealisable: A Study in Regulative Ideals*, New York: St. Martin's Press 1994

Finnis 1980
John Finnis, *Natural Law and Natural Rights*, Oxford: Clarendon Press 1980

## REFERENCES


Finnis 1992

John Finnis, 'Natural Law and Legal Reasoning', in: Robert P. George (ed.), *Natural Law Theory: Contemporary Essays*, Oxford: Clarendon Press 1992, p. 134-157

Franken 1990

H. Franken, *InLeiden tot de rechtswetenschap*, Arnhem: Gouda Quint 1990 [5th ed., orig. 1982]

Frankena 1939

W. K. Frankena, 'The Naturalistic Fallacy', in: Steven M. Cahn and Joram G. Haber (eds.), *Twentieth Century Ethical Theory*, Englewood Cliffs: Prentice-Hall 1995, p. 129-138 [orig. 1939]

Fuller 1958

Lon L. Fuller, 'Positivism and Fidelity to Law — A Reply to Professor Hart', *Harvard Law Review* (71) 1958, p. 630-672

Fuller 1969

Lon L. Fuller, *The Morality of Law*, New Haven: Yale University Press 1969 [2nd ed., orig. 1964]

Fuller 1981

Kenneth I. Winston (ed.), *The Principles of Social Order: Selected Essays of Lon L. Fuller*, Durham: Duke University Press 1981

Füßer 1996

Klaus Füßer, 'Farewell to "Legal Positivism": The Separation Thesis Unravelling', in: Robert P. George (ed.), *The Autonomy of Law: Essays on Legal Positivism*, Oxford: Clarendon Press 1996, p. 119-162

Gauthier 1986

David Gauthier, *Morals by Agreement*, Oxford: Clarendon Press 1986

George 1992

Robert P. George (ed.), *Natural Law Theory: Contemporary Essays*, Oxford: Clarendon Press 1992

George 1996

Robert P. George (ed.), *The Autonomy of Law: Essays on Legal Positivism*, Oxford: Clarendon Press 1996

Gert 1988

Bernard Gert, *Morality: A New Justification of the Moral Rules*, New York: Oxford University Press 1988 [revised edition of *The Moral Rules* 1966]

Hampshire 1949

Stuart Hampshire, 'Fallacies in Moral Philosophy', in: Steven M. Cahn and Joram G. Haber (eds.), *Twentieth Century Ethical Theory*, Englewood Cliffs: Prentice-Hall 1995, p. 162-173 [orig. article 1949]

Hare 1952

R. M. Hare, *The Language of Morals*, Oxford: Oxford University Press 1972 [orig. 1952]

Harré & Krausz 1996

Rom Harré and Michael Krausz, *Varieties of Relativism*, Oxford: Blackwell 1996

Harris 1996

John Harris, *Property and Justice*, Oxford: Clarendon Press 1996

Hart 1958

H. L. A. Hart, 'Positivism and the Separation of Law and Morals', in: *The Philosophy of Law*, Ronald Dworkin (ed.), Oxford: Oxford University Press 1977, p. 17-37 [orig. article 1958]

## REFERENCES


Hart 1965

H. L. A. Hart, 'Book Review of: Lon L. Fuller, *The Morality of Law*, New Haven 1964', *Harvard Law Review* (71) 1965, p. 1281-1296

Hart 1994

H. L. A. Hart, *The Concept of Law*, Oxford: Clarendon Press 1994 [2nd ed., orig. 1961]

Den Hartogh 1995

Govert A. den Hartogh, 'Social and Critical Morality: Or: How to Avoid 'Protestantism' in Moral Philosophy and Moral Education', *Societas Ethica Jahresbericht 1995*, p. 63-74

Hippel 1951

Fritz von Hippel, *Gustav Radbruch als rechtsphilosophischer Denker*, Heidelberg: Lambert Schneider 1951

Hoerster 1989

Norbert Hoerster, *Verteidigung des Rechtspositivismus*, Frankfurt am Main: Alfred Metzner 1989

Horwitz 1992

Morton J. Horwitz, *The Transformation of American Law 1870-1960: The Crisis of Legal Orthodoxy*, New York: Oxford University Press 1992

Inwood 1992

Michael Inwood, *A Hegel Dictionary*, Oxford: Blackwell 1992

Jaeger & Selznick 1964

Gertrude Jaeger and Philip Selznick, 'A Normative Theory of Culture', *American Sociological Review* (29) 1964, p. 653-669

Joas 1993

Hans Joas, *Pragmatism and Social Theory*, Chicago: University of Chicago Press 1993

Joas 1997

Hans Joas, *Die Entstehung der Werte*, Frankfurt am Main: Suhrkamp 1997

Kant 1785

Immanuel Kant, *Grundlegung zur Metaphysik der Sitten*, Karl Vorländer (ed.), Hamburg: Felix Meiner 1965 [orig. 1785]

Kaufmann 1987

Arthur Kaufmann, *Gustav Radbruch: Rechtsdenker, Philosoph, Sozialdemokrat*, München: Piper 1987

Kaufmann 1997

Arthur Kaufmann, *Rechtsphilosophie*, München: C. H. Beck 1997 [revised edition of *Grundprobleme der Rechtsphilosophie* 1994]

Kelsen 1934

Hans Kelsen, *Reine Rechtslehre: Einleitung in die rechtswissenschaftliche Problematik*, Aalen: Scientia 1994 [orig. 1934]

Kim 1966

Jisu Kim, *"Methodentrialismus" und "Natur der Sache" im Denken Gustav Radbruchs: Zugleich Quellenstudien zu ihren kultur-philosophischen Vorfragen bei Windelband, Rickert, und Lask*, dissertation Freiburg im Breisgau 1966

König 1999

Peter König, 'Gustav Radbruch, die materiale Wertethik und das Rechtsstaatsprinzip', in: Maria-Sibylla Lotter (ed.), *Normenbegründung und Normenentwicklung in Gesellschaft und Recht*, Baden-Baden: Nomos 1999

Korsgaard 1996

Christine Korsgaard, *Creating the Kingdom of Ends*, Cambridge: Cambridge University

Press 1996
Larmore 1992
Charles Larmore, 'The Limits of Aristotelian Ethics', in: John W. Chapman and William A. Galston (eds.), *Virtue: Nomos XXXIV*, New York: New York University Press 1992
Lask 1905
Emil Lask, 'Rechtsphilosophie', in: *Gesammelte Werke, Band 1*, Tübingen: Mohr 1923/1924, p. 275-331 [orig. article 1905]
Llewellyn 1940
Karl N. Llewellyn, 'The Normative, the Legal, and the Law-Jobs: The Problem of Juristic Method', *Yale Law Journal* (49) 1940, p. 1355-1400
Lyons 1982
David Lyons, 'Moral Aspects of Legal Theory', in: *Moral Aspects of Legal Theory: Essays on Law, Justice, and Political Responsibility*, Cambridge: Cambridge University Press 1993 [orig. article 1982]
MacCormick 1978
Neil MacCormick, *Legal Reasoning and Legal Theory*, Oxford: Clarendon Press 1978
MacCormick & Weinberger 1986
Neil MacCormick and Ota Weinberger, *An Institutional Theory of Law: New Approaches to Legal Positivism*, Dordrecht: Reidel, 1986
MacIntyre 1984
Alasdair MacIntyre, *After Virtue: A Study in Moral Theory*, Notre Dame: University of Notre Dame Press 1984 [2nd ed., orig. 1981]
Mackie 1977
J.L. Mackie, *Ethics: Inventing Right and Wrong*, London: Penguin 1990 [orig. 1977]
Maris 1988
C.W. Maris, 'Gelijkheid en recht filosofisch beschouwd', in: C.W. Maris (ed.), *Gelijkheid en recht*, Deventer: Van Loghum Slaterus 1988, p. 35-68
Mertens 1998
Thomas Mertens, 'Rechtspositivisme, nazisme en Radbruchs these van het wettelijk onrecht', in: Y. Buruma e.a. (eds.), *Recht door de eeuw : Opstellen ter gelegenheid van het 75-jarig bestaan van de Faculteit der Rechtsgeleerdheid van de Katholieke Universiteit Nijmegen*, Deventer : Kluwer 1998, p. 263-282
Miller 1976
David Miller, *Social Justice*, Oxford: Clarendon Press 1976
Moore 1992
Michael S. Moore, 'Law as a Functional Kind', in: Robert P. George (ed.), *Natural Law Theory: Contemporary Essays*, Oxford: Clarendon Press 1992, p. 188-242
Munzer 1990
Stephen Munzer, *A Theory of Property*, Cambridge: Cambridge University Press 1990
Nonet 1976
Philippe Nonet, 'For Jurisprudential Sociology', *Law and Society Review* (10) 1976, p. 525-545
Nonet & Selznick 1978
Philippe Nonet and Philip Selznick, *Law and Society in Transition: Toward Responsive Law*, New York: Harper & Row 1978
Nussbaum 1992
Martha Nussbaum, 'Human Functioning and Social Justice: In Defense of Aristotelian Essentialism', *Political Theory* 1992, p. 202-246

# REFERENCES


Oakeshott 1975
Michael Oakeshott, *On Human Conduct*, Oxford: Clarendon Press 1975

Ollig 1979
Hans-Ludwig Ollig, *Der Neukantianismus*, Stuttgart: Metzler 1979

Patterson 1996
Dennis Patterson (ed.), *A Companion to Philosophy of Law and Legal Theory*, Oxford: Blackwell 1996

Paulson 1994
Stanley L. Paulson, 'Lon L. Fuller, Gustav Radbruch, and the "Positivist" Theses', *Law and Philosophy* (13) 1994, p. 313-359

Paulson 1995
Stanley L. Paulson, 'Radbruch on Unjust Laws: Competing Earlier and Later Views?', *Oxford Journal of Legal Studies* (15) 1995, p. 489-500

Perry 1926
Ralph Barton Perry, *General Theory of Value: Its Meaning and Basic Principles Construed in Terms of Interest*, Cambridge: Harvard University Press 1967 [orig. 1926]

Postema 1986
Gerald Postema, *Bentham and the Common Law Tradition*, Oxford: Clarendon 1986

Pound 1910
Roscoe Pound, 'Law in Books and Law in Action', *American Law Review* (44) 1910, p. 12-36

Radbruch GRGA
Arthur Kaufmann (ed.), *Gustav Radbruch, Gesamtausgabe*, Heidelberg: Müller 1987-present (20 volumes planned)

Radbruch GRGA 1
Arthur Kaufmann (ed.), *GRGA Band 1: Rechtsphilosophie I*, Heidelberg: Müller 1987

Radbruch GRGA 2
Arthur Kaufmann (ed.), *GRGA Band 2: Rechtsphilosophie II*, Heidelberg: Müller 1993

Radbruch GRGA 3
Winfried Hassemer (ed.), *GRGA Band 3: Rechtsphilosophie III*, Heidelberg: Müller 1990

Radbruch GRGA 5
Hermann Klenner (ed.), *GRGA Band 5: Literatur- und Kunsthistorische Schriften*, Heidelberg: Müller 1997

Radbruch GRGA 6
Gerhard Haney (ed.), *GRGA Band 6: Feuerbach*, Heidelberg: Müller 1997

Radbruch GRGA 7
Monika Frommel (ed.), *GRGA Band 7: Strafrecht I*, Heidelberg: Müller 1995

Radbruch GRGA 9
Rudolf Wasserman (ed.), *GRGA Band 9: Strafrechtsreform*, Heidelberg: Müller 1992

Radbruch GRGA 15
Heinrich Scholler (ed.), *GRGA Band 15: Rechtsvergleichende Schriften*, Heidelberg: Müller 1999

Radbruch GRGA 16
Günter Spendel (ed.), *GRGA Band 16: Biografische Schriften*, Heidelberg: Müller 1988

Radbruch 1903
Gustav Radbruch, *Der Handlungsbegriff in seiner Bedeutung für das Strafrechtssystem*, in: GRGA 7, 1995, p. 75-167 [orig. dissertation 1903]

Radbruch 1914
Gustav Radbruch, *Grundzüge der Rechtsphilosophie*, in: GRGA 2, 1993, p. 9-204 [orig. 1914]
Radbruch 1922
Gustav Radbruch, *Entwurf eines allgemeinen deutschen Strafgesetzbuches*, in: GRGA 9, 1992, p. 47-160 [orig. 1922]
Radbruch 1923/24
Gustav Radbruch, 'Rechtsidee und Rechtsstoff. Eine Skizze', in: GRGA 2, 1993, p. 453-460 [orig. article 1923/24]
Radbruch 1924
Gustav Radbruch, 'Die Problematik der Rechtsidee', in: GRGA 2, 1993, p. 460-467 [orig. article 1924]
Radbruch 1932
Gustav Radbruch, *Rechtsphilosophie*, in: GRGA 2, 1993, p. 205-450 [orig. 1932]
Radbruch 1934
Gustav Radbruch, 'Der Relativismus in der Rechtsphilosophie', in: GRGA 3, 1993, p.17-22 [orig. article 1934]
Radbruch 1945
Gustav Radbruch, 'Fünf Minuten Rechtsphilosophie', in: GRGA 3, 1993, p. 78-79 [orig. article 1945]
Radbruch 1946
Gustav Radbruch, 'Gesetzliches Unrecht und übergesetzliches Recht', in: GRGA 3, 1993, p. 83-93 [orig. article 1946]
Radbruch 1948a
Gustav Radbruch, *Vorschule der Rechtsphilosophie*, in: GRGA 3, 1993, p. 121-227 [orig. 1948]
Radbruch 1948b
Gustav Radbruch, 'Die Natur der Sache als juristische Denkform', in: GRGA 3, 1993, p. 229-254 [orig. article 1948]
Radbruch 1951
Gustav Radbruch, *Der Innere Weg: Aufriß meines Lebens*, in: GRGA 16, 1988, p. 165-297 [orig. 1951]
Railton 1986
Peter Railton, 'Moral Realism', in: Steven M. Cahn and Joram G. Haber (eds.), *Twentieth Century Ethical Theory*, Englewood Cliffs: Prentice-Hall 1995, p. 673-700 [orig. article 1986]
Rawls 1971
John Rawls, *A Theory of Justice*, Cambridge: Harvard University Press 1971
Rawls 1993
John Rawls, *Political Liberalism*, New York: Columbia University Press 1993
Raz 1972
Joseph Raz, 'Legal Principles and the Limits of Law', in: Marshall Cohen (ed.), *Ronald Dworkin and Contemporary Jurisprudence*, Totowa: Rowman & Allanheld 1983, p. 73-87 [orig. article 1972]
Raz 1979
Joseph Raz, *The Authority of Law: Essays on Law and Morality*, Oxford: Clarendon Press 1979

Raz 1986
Joseph Raz, *The Morality of Freedom*, Oxford: Clarendon Press 1986
Reale 1990
Giovanni Reale, *A History of Ancient Philosophy, Part II: Plato and Aristotle* (translation: John R. Catan), Albany: State University of New York Press 1990
Rescher 1987
Nicholas Rescher, *Ethical Idealism: An Inquiry into the Nature and Function of Ideals*, Berkeley: University of California Press 1987
Rickert 1926
Heinrich Rickert, *Naturwissenschaft und Kulturwissenschaft*, Tübingen: Mohr 1926 [6/7th ed., orig. 1899]
Rorty 1980
Amélie Oksenberg Rorty (ed.), *Essays on Aristotle's Ethics*, Berkeley: University of California Press 1980
Rorty 1979
Richard Rorty, *Philosophy and the Mirror of Nature*, Oxford: Blackwell 1980 [orig. 1979]
Russell 1935
Bertrand Russell, 'Science and Ethics', in: James Rachels (ed.), *Ethical Theory*, Oxford: Oxford University Press 1998 [orig. 1935]
Sandel 1982
Michael Sandel, *Liberalism and the Limits of Justice*, Cambridge: Cambridge University Press 1982
Santayana 1905
George Santayana, *The Life of Reason, Volume Two: Reason in Society*, New York: Dover Publications 1980 [orig. 1905]
Schuyt 1983
C. J. M. Schuyt, *Tussen macht en moraal: Over de plaats van het recht in de verzorgingsstaat en democratie*, Alphen aan den Rijn: Samsom 1983
Searle 1964
John Searle, 'How to Derive "Ought" from "Is"', in: Steven M. Cahn and Joram G. Haber (eds.), *Twentieth Century Ethical Theory*, Englewood Cliffs: Prentice-Hall 1995, p. 408-417 [orig. 1964]
Seidel 1999
Knut Seidel, *Rechtsphilosophische Aspekte der 'Mauerschützen'-Prozesse*, Berlin: Duncker & Humblot 1999
Selznick 1949
Philip Selznick, *TVA and the Grass Roots: A Study in the Sociology of Formal Organization*, New York: Harper Torchbooks 1966 [orig. 1949]
Selznick 1957
Philip Selznick, *Leadership in Administration: A Sociological Interpretation*, Berkeley: University of California Press 1984 [orig. 1957]
Selznick 1959
Philip Selznick, 'The Sociology of Law', in: *Sociology Today*, Robert K. Merton, Leonard Broom and Leonard S. Cottrell, Jr. (eds.), New York: Basic Books 1959, p. 115-127
Selznick 1960
Philip Selznick, *The Organizational Weapon*, Glencoe: Free Press 1960 [2nd ed., orig. 1952]
Selznick 1961
Philip Selznick, 'Sociology and Natural Law', *Natural Law Forum* (6) 1961, p. 84-108

Selznick 1968
Philip Selznick, 'The Sociology of Law', in: *International Encyclopedia of the Social Sciences, Volume 9*, New York: Macmillan and Free Press 1968, p. 50-59
Selznick 1969
Philip Selznick (with Philippe Nonet and Howard M. Vollmer), *Law, Society, and Industrial Justice*, New York: Russell Sage Foundation 1969
Selznick 1970
Philip Selznick, 'Book Review of: Lon L. Fuller, *Anatomy of the Law*, New York 1968', *Harvard Law Review* (83) 1970, p. 1474-1480
Selznick 1973
Philip Selznick, 'Commentary and Debate: Rejoinder to Donald J. Black', *American Journal of Sociology* (78) 1973, p. 1266-1269
Selznick 1976
Philip Selznick, 'The Ethos of American Law', in: Irving Kristol and Paul Weaver (eds.), *The Americans: 1976*, Lexington: Lexington Books 1976, p. 211-236
Selznick 1987
Philip Selznick, 'The Idea of a Communitarian Morality', *California Law Review* (75) 1987, p. 445-463
Selznick 1989
Philip Selznick, 'Dworkin's Unfinished Task', *California Law Review* (77) 1989, p. 505-513
Selznick 1992
Philip Selznick, *The Moral Commonwealth: Social Theory and the Promise of Community*, Berkeley: University of California Press 1992
Selznick 1995
Philip Selznick, 'Kommunitaristischer Liberalismus', *Der Staat: Zeitschrift für Staatslehre, öffentliches Recht und Verfassungsgeschichte* (34) 1995, p. 487-502
Selznick 1998
Philip Selznick, 'Legal Cultures and the Rule of Law', in: Martin Krygier & Adam Czarnota (eds.), *The Rule of Law after Communism: Problems and Prospects in East-Central Europe*, Aldershot: Dartmouth 1998, p. 21-38
Seung 1993
T. K. Seung, *Intuition and Construction: The Foundation of Normative Theory*, New Haven: Yale University Press 1993
Shiner 1992
Roger Shiner, *Norm and Nature: The Movements of Legal Thought*, Oxford: Clarendon Press 1992
Shuman 1963
Samuel I. Shuman, *Legal Positivism: Its Scope and Limitations*, Detroit: Wayne State University Press 1963
Soper 1977
E. Philip Soper, 'Legal Theory and the Obligation of a Judge: The Hart/Dworkin Dispute', Marshall Cohen (ed.), *Ronald Dworkin and Contemporary Jurisprudence*, Totowa: Rowman & Allanheld 1983, p. 3-27 [orig. article 1977]
Stevenson 1963
Charles L. Stevenson, *Facts and Values: Studies in Ethical Analysis*, Westport: Greenwood Press 1963

Tamanaha 1997
Brian Z. Tamanaha, *Realistic Socio-Legal Theory: Pragmatism and a Social Theory of Law*, Oxford: Clarendon Press 1997
Teubner 1983
Gunther Teubner, 'Substantive and Reflexive Elements in Modern Law', *Law and Society Review* (17) 1983, p. 239-285
Tjong 1967
Zong Uk Tjong, *Der Weg des rechtsphilosophischen Relativismus bei Gustav Radbruch*, Bonn: Ludwig Röhrscheid 1967
Urmson 1958
J.O. Urmson, 'Saints and Heroes', in: A. I. Melden (ed.), *Essays in Moral Philosophy*, Seattle: University of Washington Press 1958, p. 198-216
Vedder 1998
Anton Vedder, 'Waarden en het web van zin en betekenis', in: Wibren van der Burg and Frans W.A. Brom (eds.), *Over idealen: Het belang van idealen in recht, moraal en politiek*, Deventer: Tjeenk Willink 1998, p. 39-54
Vermeulen 2000
B.P. Vermeulen, 'De procedures in de Vreemdelingenwet 2000', *Ars Aequi* (49) 2000, p. 384-391
Vulpius 1995
Carola Vulpius, *Gustav Radbruch in Oxford: Zur Aufarbeitung eines Kapitels länderübergreifender Rechtsphilosophie*, Heidelberg : Müller 1995
Van Wijk/Konijnenbelt 1997
H.D. van Wijk, W. Konijnenbelt, R.M. van Male, *Hoofdstukken van administratief recht*, 's-Gravenhage: Vuga 1997 [10th ed.]
Waldron 1988
Jeremy Waldron, *The Right to Private Property*, Oxford: Clarendon Press 1988
Waldron 1992
Jeremy Waldron, 'The Irrelevance of Moral Objectivity', in: *Law and Disagreement*, Oxford: Clarendon Press 1999, p. 164-187 [orig. article 1992]
Walker 1978
Ralph C. S. Walker, *Kant: The Arguments of the Philosophers*, London: Routledge & Kegan Paul 1978
Waluchow 1994
W.J. Waluchow, *Inclusive Legal Positivism*, Oxford: Clarendon Press 1994
Ward 1992
Ian Ward, 'Radbruch's "Rechtsphilosophie": Law, Morality, and Form', *Archiv für Rechts- und Sozialphilosophie* (78) 1992, p. 332-354
Weinreb 1987
Lloyd L. Weinreb, *Natural Law and Justice*, Cambridge: Harvard University Press 1987
Westerman 1997
Pauline Westerman, *The Disintegration of Natural Law Theory: Aquinas to Finnis*, Leiden: Brill 1997
Westerman 1999
Pauline Westerman, 'Means and Ends', in: Willem J. Witteveen and Wibren van der Burg, *Rediscovering Fuller: Essays on Implicit Law and Institutional Design*, Amsterdam: Amsterdam University Press 1999, p. 145-168

## REFERENCES


Wiener 1973
Philip P. Wiener (ed.), *Dictionary of the History of Ideas: Studies of Selected Pivotal Ideas*, New York: Charles Scribner's Sons 1973

Wilk 1950
Kurt Wilk (translator), *The Legal Philosophies of Lask, Radbruch, and Dabin*, Cambridge: Harvard University Press 1950

Windelband 1903
Wilhelm Windelband, 'Was ist Philosophie?', in: Wilhelm Windelband, *Präludien*, Tübingen: Mohr 1903, p. 1-57 [2nd ed., orig. 1883]

Witteveen 1996
Willem Witteveen, *De geordende wereld van het recht*, Amsterdam: Amsterdam University Press 1996

Witteveen & Van der Burg 1999
Willem J. Witteveen and Wibren van der Burg, *Rediscovering Fuller: Essays on Implicit Law and Institutional Design*, Amsterdam: Amsterdam University Press 1999

Wolf 1959
Erik Wolf, 'Umbruch oder Entwicklung in Gustav Radbruchs Rechtsphilosophie?', *Archiv für Rechts- und Sozialphilosophie* (45) 1959, p. 481-503

Von Wright 1963
Georg Henrik von Wright, *The Varieties of Goodness*, London: Routledge & Kegan Paul 1972 [orig. 1963]

# INDEX

# Law and Philosophy Library

1. E. Bulygin, J.-L. Gardies and I. Niiniluoto (eds.): *Man, Law and Modern Forms of Life.* With an Introduction by M.D. Bayles. 1985 ISBN 90-277-1869-5
2. W. Sadurski: *Giving Desert Its Due.* Social Justice and Legal Theory. 1985 ISBN 90-277-1941-1
3. N. MacCormick and O. Weinberger: *An Institutional Theory of Law.* New Approaches to Legal Positivism. 1986 ISBN 90-277-2079-7
4. A. Aarnio: *The Rational as Reasonable.* A Treatise on Legal Justification. 1987 ISBN 90-277-2276-5
5. M.D. Bayles: *Principles of Law.* A Normative Analysis. 1987 ISBN 90-277-2412-1; Pb: 90-277-2413-X
6. A. Soeteman: *Logic in Law.* Remarks on Logic and Rationality in Normative Reasoning, Especially in Law. 1989 ISBN 0-7923-0042-4
7. C.T. Sistare: *Responsibility and Criminal Liability.* 1989 ISBN 0-7923-0396-2
8. A. Peczenik: *On Law and Reason.* 1989 ISBN 0-7923-0444-6
9. W. Sadurski: *Moral Pluralism and Legal Neutrality.* 1990 ISBN 0-7923-0565-5
10. M.D. Bayles: *Procedural Justice.* Allocating to Individuals. 1990 ISBN 0-7923-0567-1
11. P. Nerhot (ed.): *Law, Interpretation and Reality.* Essays in Epistemology, Hermeneutics and Jurisprudence. 1990 ISBN 0-7923-0593-0
12. A.W. Norrie: *Law, Ideology and Punishment.* Retrieval and Critique of the Liberal Ideal of Criminal Justice. 1991 ISBN 0-7923-1013-6
13. P. Nerhot (ed.): *Legal Knowledge and Analogy.* Fragments of Legal Epistemology, Hermeneutics and Linguistics. 1991 ISBN 0-7923-1065-9
14. O. Weinberger: *Law, Institution and Legal Politics.* Fundamental Problems of Legal Theory and Social Philosophy. 1991 ISBN 0-7923-1143-4
15. J. Wróblewski: *The Judicial Application of Law.* Edited by Z. Bańkowski and N. MacCormick. 1992 ISBN 0-7923-1569-3
16. T. Wilhelmsson: *Critical Studies in Private Law.* A Treatise on Need-Rational Principles in Modern Law. 1992 ISBN 0-7923-1659-2
17. M.D. Bayles: *Hart's Legal Philosophy.* An Examination. 1992 ISBN 0-7923-1981-8
18. D.W.P. Ruiter: *Institutional Legal Facts.* Legal Powers and their Effects. 1993 ISBN 0-7923-2441-2
19. J. Schonsheck: *On Criminalization.* An Essay in the Philosophy of the Criminal Law. 1994 ISBN 0-7923-2663-6
20. R.P. Malloy and J. Evensky (eds.): *Adam Smith and the Philosophy of Law and Economics.* 1994 ISBN 0-7923-2796-9
21. Z. Bańkowski, I. White and U. Hahn (eds.): *Informatics and the Foundations of Legal Reasoning.* 1995 ISBN 0-7923-3455-8
22. E. Lagerspetz: *The Opposite Mirrors.* An Essay on the Conventionalist Theory of Institutions. 1995 ISBN 0-7923-3325-X

# Law and Philosophy Library

23. M. van Hees: *Rights and Decisions.* Formal Models of Law and Liberalism. 1995 ISBN 0-7923-3754-9
24. B. Anderson: *"Discovery" in Legal Decision-Making.* 1996 ISBN 0-7923-3981-9
25. S. Urbina: *Reason, Democracy, Society.* A Study on the Basis of Legal Thinking. 1996 ISBN 0-7923-4262-3
26. E. Attwooll: *The Tapestry of the Law.* Scotland, Legal Culture and Legal Theory. 1997 ISBN 0-7923-4310-7
27. J.C. Hage: *Reasoning with Rules.* An Essay on Legal Reasoning and Its Underlying Logic. 1997 ISBN 0-7923-4325-5
28. R.A. Hillman: *The Richness of Contract Law.* An Analysis and Critique of Contemporary Theories of Contract Law. 1997 ISBN 0-7923-4336-0; 0-7923-5063-4 (Pb)
29. C. Wellman: *An Approach to Rights.* Studies in the Philosophy of Law and Morals. 1997 ISBN 0-7923-4467-7
30. B. van Roermund: *Law, Narrative and Reality.* An Essay in Intercepting Politics. 1997 ISBN 0-7923-4621-1
31. I. Ward: *Kantianism, Postmodernism and Critical Legal Thought.* 1997 ISBN 0-7923-4745-5
32. H. Prakken: *Logical Tools for Modelling Legal Argument.* A Study of Defeasible Reasoning in Law. 1997 ISBN 0-7923-4776-5
33. T. May: *Autonomy, Authority and Moral Responsibility.* 1998 ISBN 0-7923-4851-6
34. M. Atienza and J.R. Manero: *A Theory of Legal Sentences.* 1998 ISBN 0-7923-4856-7
35. E.A. Christodoulidis: *Law and Reflexive Politics.* 1998 ISBN 0-7923-4954-7
36. L.M.M. Royakkers: *Extending Deontic Logic for the Formalisation of Legal Rules.* 1998 ISBN 0-7923-4982-2
37. J.J. Moreso: *Legal Indeterminacy and Constitutional Interpretation.* 1998 ISBN 0-7923-5156-8
38. W. Sadurski: *Freedom of Speech and Its Limits.* 1999 ISBN 0-7923-5523-7
39. J. Wolenski (ed.): *Kazimierz Opalek Selected Papers in Legal Philosophy.* 1999 ISBN 0-7923-5732-9
40. H.P. Visser 't Hooft: *Justice to Future Generations and the Environment.* 1999 ISBN 0-7923-5756-6
41. L.J. Wintgens (ed.): *The Law in Philosophical Perspectives.* My Philosophy of Law. 1999 ISBN 0-7923-5796-5
42. A.R. Lodder: *DiaLaw.* On Legal Justification and Dialogical Models of Argumentation. 1999 ISBN 0-7923-5830-9
43. C. Redondo: *Reasons for Action and the Law.* 1999 ISBN 0-7923-5912-7
44. M. Friedman, L. May, K. Parsons and J. Stiff (eds.): *Rights and Reason.* Essays in Honor of Carl Wellman. 2000 ISBN 0-7923-6198-9

# Law and Philosophy Library

45. G.C. Christie: *The Notion of an Ideal Audience in Legal Argument.* 2000 ISBN 0-7923-6283-7
46. R.S. Summers: *Essays in Legal Theory.* 2000 ISBN 0-7923-6367-1
47. M. van Hees: *Legal Reductionism and Freedom.* 2000 ISBN 0-7923-6491-0
48. R. Gargarella: *The Scepter of Reason.* Public Discussion and Political Radicalism in the Origins of Constitutionalism. 2000 ISBN 0-7923-6508-9
49. M. Iglesias Vila: *Facing Judicial Discretion.* Legal Knowledge and Right Answers Revisited. 2001 ISBN 0-7923-6778-2
50. M. Kiikeri: *Comparative Legal Reasoning and European Law.* 2001 ISBN 0-7923-6884-3
51. A.J. Menéndez: *Justifying Taxes.* Some Elements for a General Theory of Democratic Tax Law. 2001 ISBN 0-7923-7052-X
52. W.E. Conklin: *The Invisible Origins of Legal Positivism.* A Re-Reading of a Tradition. 2001 ISBN 0-7923-7101-1
53. Z. Bańkowski: *Living Lawfully.* Love in Law and Law in Love. 2001 ISBN 0-7923-7180-1
54. A.N. Shytov: *Conscience and Love in Making Judicial Decisions.* 2001 ISBN 1-4020-0168-1
55. D.W.P. Ruiter: *Legal Institutions.* 2001 ISBN 1-4020-0186-X

*Volumes 1–55 were published by Kluwer Academic Publishers.*

56. G. den Hartogh: *Mutual Expectations.* A Conventionalist Theory of Law. 2002 ISBN 90-411-1796-2
57. W.L. Robison (ed.): *The Legal Essays of Michael Bayles.* 2002 ISBN 90-411-1835-7
58. U. Bindreiter: *Why Grundnorm?* A Treatise on the Implications of Kelsen's Doctrine. 2002 ISBN 90-411-1867-5
59. S. Urbina: *Legal Method and the Rule of Law.* 2002 ISBN 90-411-1870-5
60. M. Baurmann: *The Market of Virtue.* Morality and Commitment in a Liberal Society. 2002 ISBN 90-411-1874-8
61. G. Zanetti: *Political Friendship and the Good Life.* Two Liberal Arguments against Perfectionism. 2002 ISBN 90-411-1881-0
62. W. Sadurski (ed.): *Constitutional Justice, East and West.* 2002 ISBN 90-411-1883-7
63. S. Taekema: *The Concept of Ideals in Legal Theory.* 2003 ISBN 90-411-1971-X

KLUWER LAW INTERNATIONAL – THE HAGUE / LONDON / NEW YORK